ENDORSEM

LAST WORDS OF CHRIST

If you are one who values the powerful duality of God's Word as both truth and literature, *Last Words of Christ* was written for you. Wallace Clausen does a masterful job of unpacking the theological implications of Christ's final words, seven in all, which encapsulate Jesus' final thoughts during his inexorable march towards death and victory. In doing so, Clausen brings to life the most magnificent story of Scripture, illuminating the marvelous majesty of the cross.

Rob Seims
Associate Regional Director
South Puget Sound Region Young Life

In his enlightening book, *Last Words of Christ: A Call to Understanding*, Clausen presents a wide-ranging perspective on God's salvation plan as viewed through the lens of Christ's spoken words on the cross. The scope of this exploration is immense and well-researched, opening with the creation narrative in Genesis and continuing through the New Testament, supported by input from a wide range of Christian thinkers. Seldom has the age-old struggle of good vs. evil, light against darkness been so evident as when these crucifixion statements are seen as a cohesive summation of God's saving work overcoming evil in the world, rather than the disjointed, dying utterances of the Son of God on the cross. It is a biblical tour de force and I was both blessed and educated, as will all be who read this important book.

Tim Teusink, M.D., M.A. (Bioethics)
SIM – France Quartier les Mians

Wallace Clausen offers a stimulating look at Christ's Seven Last Words that is rich with theological meaning and contextual insight. His work is careful, well-researched, and the theory he offers in uniting these iconic words is completely plausible. I read it with fascination and found his conclusions to be inspirational.

Dr. Keith Carpenter,
Senior Pastor, Kent Covenant Church.
M.Div., and D.Min, Fuller Seminary

Clausen raises a fascinating question for us to consider: were Jesus' final utterances from the cross only responses to his horrific predicament, or might he also have been offering an intentional, final evaluation—a "capstone"—to his rapidly-fleeting life? With a high regard for Scripture as God-breathed, Clausen at the same time reminds us to read it also as literature, affirming that the authors of the gospels selected the stories—and their words—to convey deeper, symbolic meaning as well.

(Mr.) Lynn C. Conver, M.A.
(Linguistics, University of Oregon)
Linguist/Translator and Editor
Wycliffe Bible Translators and SIL International

LAST WORDS
OF CHRIST

A CALL TO
UNDERSTANDING

Genesis to Revelation –
a new look into His final thoughts

WALLACE R. CLAUSEN

Deep River
B O O K S

DEDICATION

To Tyler & Blake; Lucas & Chloe –
the next generation of kingdom citizens.

May the tools in this book
equip you to read, interpret,
and construct biblical meaning.

CONTENTS

Interlude

PART II: The Cross in Darkness

Narrative Findings and Reflections

PREFACE

P oetically, Israel's ancient prophet Isaiah proclaims: "See, my servant will act wisely; he will (1) be raised (2) and lifted up (3) and highly exalted" (52:13; numbers added).

Isaiah is foretelling the climax event of the one referred to as "the servant." Christians identify him as Jesus. More so, this prophetic passage ends with a stunning revelation: "For he bore the sin of many, and made intercession for the transgressors" (53:12).

Why Isaiah's words are astonishing is not because they are written hundreds of years in advance of the crucifixion; rather, it is his vision that the servant will make intercession. Christ, from the cross, completes this foretold act: "Father, forgive them, for they do not know what they are doing."

This picture of Calvary speaks to the wisdom of God's servant. In Isaiah's threefold portrait, the servant accomplishes what no other human has: He will rise from the dead and be lifted up to a position of glory and exaltation.

That statement shocks the mind: Of the billions who have lived, only the servant has escaped death. What did he know? What did Christ say from the cross that informs life journeys today?

In *Last Words of Christ*, I employ several textual features to aid investigation into Jesus' last thoughts. Among them is the customary use of the term *words* to represent the servant's last seven statements. When encountering his last words, I boldface them, for example, the **First**

Word, which is equivalent to writing the Lord's initial utterance from the cross quoted above.

Throughout this book, specialized language appears, such as ***messiah***. On a word's first appearance it is boldfaced and italicized, signaling placement in a glossary at the end of the book.

Isaiah's prophetic descriptions further reveal that Scripture is comprised not only of literal language (the surface level meaning of a word), but often contains symbolic language. I refer to this dual structure—literal and symbolic—as viewing lenses that are explained more fully in the Introduction. At times, the terms *literal* and *real-time* are used interchangeably. These terms refer to biblical content describing events as they occurred or were reported in biblical history. On the other hand, the symbolic lens, often referred to as *figurative* or *metaphoric*, considers content found in the reoccurring patterns of Scripture. This leads to ***theology*** and *biblical theology,* nomenclature used to promote outcomes of these lenses. Yet, biblical theology can be hard to define.[1] In *Last Words of Christ*, when referring to it, I do so informally and without precision common to theologians.

To inform readers of chapter objectives and content, I use the phrases **In this chapter** or **The purpose of this chapter.** Similarly, each chapter concludes with summary remarks. To speed chapters along, rather than incorporating lengthy quotations from Scripture, I use *story retells*. Retells are adaptations of biblical passages and often lay the foundation for a chapter's content. They are identified by indented blocks of text and labeled.

Finally, this book is divided into two parts, each consisting of several sections. Section tabs, located at the start of such sequences, provide brief overviews of coming chapters. An interlude separates the book's two major parts while a findings and reflection chapter draws attention to the work's conclusion.

ACKNOWLEDGMENTS

This project is a compilation of collegial effort. Dave B, Jeff L, and Dave P read the first draft, one that by far wasn't ready for public eyes. Their thoughtful remarks aided in the book's second draft. Dr. Keith C read still another, offering hopeful comment and encouragement. Spanning all revisions was the tireless critiquing and reading by my mentor, Keith J. Without Keith's constant support and guidance this book would have remained an unpublished manuscript. Much is owed to my friend whom I met as a result of a home Bible study nearly fifty years ago. (Indeed, how mysterious is the timing and ways of the Holy Spirit!) To Dr. Frank Spina, professor of Old Testament at Seattle Pacific University, whose illuminating class on the **Pentateuch** gave seed to it all. Furthermore, gratitude is owed to the authors of the many works I consulted in preparation (see bibliography). Three, Dr. T. Desmond Alexander, Dr. Jeremy R. Treat, and Dr. Stephen G. Dempster particularly aided understanding of the Garden of Eden, the role of humanity as priest or servant-kings, and the ensuing storyline flowing throughout the Old Testament (Hebrew Bible). Also, to the professionals at Deep River Books: to Tamara B, senior editor, for project oversight and coordination; to Amit D, for technical typesetting in this graphics-heavy work; and to Andy C, who discovered this manuscript on *The Writer's Edge*, much is owed, as is to Joe Bailen, Contajus Designs, for the striking image of Christ on the book's cover. As always seems the case of writers, I am indebted to the craftsmanship of my editor, Michael Degan, whose knowledge and skill proved so beneficial. More so, are the many educators—teachers, specialists, and para-educators—who worked tirelessly training and implementing our school's literacy initiative, noteworthy the school's literacy coaches. Such collegial undertaking propelled my understanding of literature, eventually enabling my grasp of interpretive tools which proved so essential in constructing meaning of Christ's last words. Finally, but not least, to my wife Karlen, who over the four years this was written and rewritten, while maintaining faith that drafting would someday end, yet surely must have wondered, *What is he doing?* And now, dear, we know the answer to that unspoken question.

Part I

THE CROSS IN LIGHT

When first read, the Bible appears to be a divided book. For example, there is an Old Testament and a New Testament; a division of people—Hebrew and non-Hebrew (or Jew and Gentile); and a division of salvation (by law or by grace). As readers come to the New Testament, they understand that the crucifixion is the center of this divide. What's more, implanted in the middle of the crucifixion is an imaged-based division. This is described in Mark's Gospel by the strange statement, "At the sixth hour darkness came over the whole land until the ninth hour." That darkness comes at the midpoint of the crucifixion. Visually this separates the crucifixion into halves: a time of daylight and a period when darkness covers the land.

Mark's statement, therefore, effectively divides Christ's last words by these two referents. After all, he spoke half his statements in the light of day; the other half he spoke during darkness.

The importance of this separation into light and darkness is profoundly important to the question, "What do the last words of Jesus mean?" Organizationally, this book is similarly segmented into two parts, with the first half examining Christ's morning statements and the latter part his sayings in darkness.

Part I contains three sections. The first considers the language style of the Bible. Viewed from two lenses—literal and symbolic—this section illustrates how literary style contributes to the text's inspired story.

Section II begins the development of Christ's words as narrative statements by concentrating on his primary mission: the offering of forgiveness. This is immediately heard in the first utterance. Further, it comes within context of covenant and community. Summarily, the first three words take aim at a forgiven people who are blessed as they come to dwell in God's kingdom.

Section III looks more closely at these themes. Four chapters discuss the rise of Christ's kingdom and new covenant. A fifth chapter ends this section by focusing on the coming Holy Spirit.

We can never lose sight
of the mystery of the Cross,
or repudiate it as a symbol.

Thomas P. Rausch, S.J.

Section I

LANGUAGE

Section I considers the Bible's use of literary language and how meaning is affected, particularly when heard through Jesus' final words. The Introduction and Prelude broaden understanding of how symbolic language often embodies figurative communication. Jesus' first miracle, in which he changes water into wine, demonstrates the interconnected relationship between literal and symbolic text. Section I concludes with a historical recall of Christ's final words. Using this as background, a reader is prepared for the narrative story behind the final seven statements.

Introduction

SCRIPTURE AS SYMBOLIC COMMUNICATION

After three grueling years of public ministry, years when many proclaim Jesus the Messiah, yet also years when he is demonized, his life comes down to six final hours. From the cross he makes seven statements. These will be his "last words." Of them we wonder, Are they spoken as a capstone to his life and mission, or are they just seven, separately held final thoughts?

This question is important because few authors ask it. Surveying crucifixion literature for the laity, two categories are commonly encountered. One is books adapted from collections of Lenten sermons. The other is inspirational or meditational musings. The latter is almost always treated topically. That is, each of the last statements drives toward some inspirational point or life application. While they are authentically motivating, too often their aim splinters what Jesus says into small, unrelated fragments. On the other hand, sermons tend to marry a mixture of strong preaching inclined toward humility and awe at how a great God suffers in bringing salvation. Still, their content seldom speaks to a cohesive whole. Partly this is due to a tradition of interpreting each final statement by itself, as if each word were a tree and only by looking at each tree might his life be seen. Yet, that intended forest-like view is blocked, ironically, by those separately held trees.

These generalizations return me to the question at hand. Are we to comprehend Jesus' final words as separate fragments, or rather do they speak to a collective whole? Shouldn't we expect to find in his last words a testimony to what he came to accomplish? If we believe that his life did not just happen, did not just evolve in some haphazard way, then shouldn't we expect his final statements to be a continuation, even a crystallization, of that remarkable life and message?

Is it possible that, in our rush to write and talk about *each word*, we have somehow failed to comprehend their consolidated meaning? In *How God Became King*, N. T. Wright concludes the church has misunderstood the basic intent of Jesus' mission. He asserts believers have misread the gospel message with an overemphasis on *cross* largely to the neglect of *crown*.[2] Could it also be that Christ's last words, so long analyzed on the strength of each statement, are not heard for the message they proclaim? Should we not listen to those anguished words and hear in them the fullness of Christ, the triumph of his message and mission? The pursuit of that question guides this book.

This book began at the conclusion of a life group, my church's name for small groups that meet in homes to study the Bible. At that time our pastor had decided to use Randy Frazee's curriculum *The Story* to focus both pulpit ministry and life-group studies into a cohesive, year-long conversation as we journeyed through the Bible.[3] By late spring we arrived at the crucifixion, and I found myself wondering about those final words, initially their sequence. (That was necessary since they are spread over the four gospels and there is no actual "list." However, by comparing one account to another, a chronology of some accuracy can be compiled.)

While I independently ordered those statements, my small group's yearlong study concluded. But by then I was smitten. I kept coming back to them. As I did, I was struck by a single verse that Mark wrote, but also found in Matthew and Luke. That verse proved pivotal in launching this project: "When the sixth hour had come, darkness fell over the whole land until the ninth hour" (15:33 NASB).

As a visual learner, I converted Mark's verse to graphic form. This resulted in a drawing of a half-shaded box, light on top and dark on bottom. Into it I inserted Mark's text:

> And when the sixth hour had come,
> darkness fell over the whole land until the ninth hour.

Immediately I saw within Mark's verse a contrast, where the morning period (light of day) sat opposite the afternoon (darkness). Viewed this way, the text reveals Scripture's dominant image: light and darkness. Mark's literal statement, therefore, holds veiled within it symbolic meaning in which the cross holds the biblical interplay between the forces of good (light) and evil (darkness). It is fitting, indeed, that the cross—the battleground of and for mankind—should be bathed in this twilight picture.

In my mind's eye, I could also see a second image filled with Jesus' final statements. After all, he spoke half his words during morning light, while the other half he called out in afternoon's gloom. These illustrations reveal how the Bible presents through two lenses: a literal lens that describes historical events, and a second, figurative or symbolic lens that anticipates a coming future.

In that sense the Bible is like a camera: it employs lenses to capture the story being told. At times these lenses reveal the story of actual events, or events as they are reported to have happened. But there is also a surprisingly large piece of content that alludes to a broader story, one that is hidden, as it were, behind a veil. This type of veiled story is particularly prevalent in the Old Testament. For example, we read in Exodus of the ancient tabernacle and its construction. Of it God speaks to Moses, commanding worship based on a representational system of sacrifices. Significantly, that system—with the tabernacle, furnishings and festival days—was to be made "like the pattern I will show you" (Ex. 25:9) that is based on a copy of the heavenly things themselves (see

Heb. 9:23, Col. 2:16-17). In this way the literal command to construct a tabernacle informs a veiled intent.

When reading the crucifixion story, it is important to use both viewing lenses. Yet even as a photographer composes his piece by selecting lenses, the crucial element is filtering light. In this book the filter I use is one that captures God's story holistically. In this way the Bible is viewed as more than just a collection of books separated one from another. More properly, these story collections may be thought of as roads where all eventually merge on to one super freeway. This eventual coming together produces a main thoroughfare, one that travels the landscape of Scripture. Bible scholars often term this super freeway the **meta-story** or **meta-narrative**. Ultimately, the seven last words of Christ, when heard through this narrative, disclose God's project of redemption and restoration.

Such a view returns me to the Introduction's opening thought. When Jesus speaks his final words, in that real-time moment, only those present at Calvary authentically hear him. And as they do, they listen to each word spoken one at a time, spread out over those six terrible hours. But is this true for hearers today? The truth is, we cannot hear his words authentically just as they were spoken; we were not there. But we can hear them biblically when we read them narratively, hearing them in the overall story of Scripture. This means we hear them as life echoes, their sounds ringing triumphantly at the end of his arduous journey.

This quest to hear Christ authentically leaves today's believer with choices. One is to read his utterances as seven, separately held statements, thereby trying to duplicate the experience of those historically present at Golgotha (which is an impossible task). Or we can approach them as they are presented, which is through the literary pages of inspired text. It is on this latter choice that this book—and its story of the crucifixion—is framed.

The next chapter, the Prelude, demonstrates how the literal lens and its symbolic counterpart affect biblical meaning. Its purpose is to clarify and illustrate the importance of reading Scripture through both lenses.

If only one sightline is used, the reader is left with an impoverished comprehension of what the Bible is revealing. But by viewing Scripture through both lenses, a robust understanding of biblical content emerges. This merging of lenses produces a bifocal optic. Through that magnification the richness of the cross story is acutely seen, which is not unlike the effect of the temple curtain being torn apart on Jesus' death, exposing the holy of holies for all to see. These two lenses, then, when read together, unveil the meaning of Jesus' words on the cross.

Prelude

WEDDING WINE

1. The Biblical Text

A hallmark of Jesus' teaching is his frequent and remarkable use of metaphor, in which words take on meaning apart from literal description. For example, he likens the blessed to being "poor in spirit" or to those who "hunger and thirst." His disciples are the "salt of the earth" or a "light-lamp" to the world. He compares Solomon's lavish garments to "garden clothing" of meadow flowers, or the carefree life of birds to contrast how kingdom citizens are to cease from fretting about earthly treasures. More so, he is master of the parable, describing the kingdom of God as a vineyard, a wedding feast, and a realm where laborers toil in equity and grace.

In these literary associations, Jesus is carrying on a long-standing tradition in which God's prophets spoke through story drama. Drama whose theater produced sound bites and stunning visual images conveying God's commentary to an apostate nation. Such as Hosea's marriage to a prostitute, or Jeremiah's visit to a potter's house where a clay vessel is ruined, or Ezekiel's warning when he packs belongings as if going on a long journey (into exile).

It is significant, then, as readers come to Scripture, that believers embrace both (a) its literal language as well as (b) its symbolic arm. Unfortunately, this crossover from literal to implied meaning (symbolic language) is often lost when a strict rendering of the literal text is a reader's primary goal. Throughout this book, this tension about how a believer is to read the Bible will be constantly in view.[4]

Such tension between literal language and symbolic meaning is demonstrated in John's Gospel where the story of Jesus' first miraculous sign is told. It takes place in Cana of Galilee. The story retell below, adapted from John's Gospel, illustrates how literal language often holds symbolic meaning, similar to how prophets used story drama to communicate God's message to ancient Israel.

> The wedding was long anticipated. For a small, tucked away town it would be the event of the year. Many were invited, some traveling as far as Nazareth. Both villagers and herdsmen attended; rich and not so rich, those who followed the customs of ancient Israel and those who kept their distance. But in the course of several days, the joy of the wedding overshadowed such distinctions. It was turning out as hoped: a grand occasion in sleepy Cana, until a crisis arose. Suddenly all was at risk: the wine had run out!
>
> At this point Mary enters the story. Aware of the impending crisis, she turns to her son, "They have no more wine." Jesus replies, "Dear women, why do you involve me? My time has not yet come." Mary ignores this attempt to deflect her request by saying to a group of servants, "Do whatever he tells you." At this point Jesus seems to change his mind about not getting involved and commands some servants to fill six nearby ceremonial jugs with water. The servants comply, and then Jesus issues a most singular command: "Now draw some out and take it to the master of the banquet."
>
> The narrative shifts to the master, or headwaiter (NASB), who, on receiving the water now turned into wine, sips it in astonishment. Immediately he calls for the bridegroom. "Everyone brings out the choice wine first and then the

cheaper wine after the guests have had too much to drink; but you have saved the best till now." Here John ends this short story, noting it was the Lord's first miraculous sign, and because of it the disciples put their faith in him.

The point of this story retell is to find in the literal text a symbolic communication. This is uncovered by following the story's dialogue to see how it advances John's Gospel. While Mary clearly tells Jesus, "They have no more wine," narratively John is informing the Jewish people (and likely the Greek world as well) that they do not have Christ. That is, they do not have the "wine" which is God's son. Similarly, Mary commands the servants, "Do whatever he tells you." In this way the text points to the importance of listening to and obeying Christ. This may be heard later in John's Gospel when Jesus says, "If you love me, you will obey what I command." And then there is the headwaiter's comment, "but you have saved the best till now." This is likely an allusion to how Christ saw himself as the last in a long line of prophets—many of whom were killed (see Mt. 21:33-38, 23:37-38). As a result, John's wedding dialogue points toward a coming future.

In this story images are also part of John's foreshadowing communication. This is understood through the six ceremonial jugs, containers used to hold purification waters. However, in John's telling these vessels signal a change from water as a means of ritual cleansing. Ironically, these containers will soon be replaced by the very essence of the "water-wine" they now hold. In that sense, what Jesus says at the Last Supper helps a reader understand that John is relating this wedding story to Jesus' blood. We hear this wine-blood connection as Jesus declares in the Upper Room, "This cup (of wine) is the new covenant in my blood" (Luke 22:20).

Read this way, John's opening story draws attention to his Gospel's ending. John sums up the wedding story's miraculous sign of changing water into wine by stating that the disciples "put their faith in Jesus." This language of a "sign" foreshadows the end goal of John's Gospel:

"Jesus did many other miraculous signs . . . but these are written that you may believe that Jesus is the . . . Son of God, and that . . . you may have life in his name" (Jn. 20:30).

The Cana wedding, therefore, indicates that John was writing symbolically. That is, John selected events and words to draw a representational picture of a coming future, one that would culminate on the cross. Read this way, the wedding story is not that much different than John's portrayal of Christ at another site—that in Samaria, where Jesus held a conversation with a woman at a well (see Jn. 4:1-26). There, symbolic language is used as Jesus likens himself to well water, which, if drunk, wells up to eternal life.

These two examples, the wedding story featuring wine and the well story featuring water, demonstrate the importance of how symbolic expression often is an agent connecting one story to another. Viewed this way, the language of Cana finds significance when it is linked to the Last Supper, where Jesus commands, holding a cup of wine, "Do this in remembrance of me." Crucial to this linkup is how the wine of the Last Supper is an allusion to the wine-blood of the cross. In this way, the Cana wedding story links three seemingly separate biblical events: It joins not only the Cana wedding to the Last Supper, but most importantly the cross. Our take-away: when John describes the Cana wedding, he holds in mind the crucifixion. He is writing symbolically. He is using a literal event to look ahead to a coming theological moment. More so, coming at the start of John's Gospel, Cana provides readers an invaluable key to interpret its message: It is written in symbolic language.

Symmetry is another literary feature that frequently connects one story to another. Biblical symmetry is:

* an association between two or more texts or images (separated by a "boundary");

* that can be compared for similarities or contrasted for differences.[5]

Scriptural Illustration of Symmetry

Genesis	John's Gospel
In the *beginning*, God created the heavens and the earth.	In the *beginning* was the Word, and the Word was with God, and Word was God.
God saw that the *light* was good, and he separated the light from the *darkness*	The *light* shines in the darkness, but the *darkness* has not understood it.
Now the serpent *was more crafty* than any of the wild animals...	The Word became flesh ... full of grace and *truth*.

When these opening verses in Genesis and John are placed side by side, important comparisons are revealed. The above table draws attention to: (1) beginning, (2) light, and (3) darkness–while (4) providing a contrast between deception (crafty) and truth.

Displaying these passages side by side allows their striking images to be emphasized. This comparison can be "colored" where Genesis = darkness/black, and John = light/white. This visual enhancement suggests a theological tone in which Genesis prefigures a shadowy "darkness" that emerges out of the Garden of Eden (see Gen. 3:14), but in contrast a hopeful prospect of a new beginning is found in John's biography of Jesus. Seen this way, a symmetrical comparison and contrast is established. More so, the Bible's theological message is revealed more clearly once the literal wording is stripped away.

The importance of this illustration is to observe how the Bible, as literature, uses symmetry to connect one passage to another.[6] Such comparisons reveal biblical truths. Truths that are discovered in the Bible's symbolic language rather than solely a literal reading. In this way the Bible's use of literal and figurative reading lenses rises to the surface.

In short, by placing passages "side by side," we can make important comparisons that develop vital theological ideas. How this translates to Jesus' last words will be seen as this "story" of the crucifixion goes forward.

In this chapter, the case for (1) reading the Bible not so much literally but symbolically is presented. That Scripture contains literary devices does not negate its overriding nature: The Bible is inspired by the Holy Spirit. Nevertheless, the Spirit's inspiration occurs within a literary environment. This understanding gives rise to (2) reading the Bible from a dual viewpoint. In this book that perspective is referred to as a dual, or bifocal, lens. There is a literal lens, and there is a symbolic lens. The importance of using (3) literary tools such as dialogue, images, and symmetry to construct biblical meaning is an important reading strategy for the laity. This discussion on the literary characteristic of the Bible paves the way for understanding the cross-content of this book. More so, it offers the careful reader of Scripture an important framework for understanding the biblical message in general.

2. Dual Lenses

The above section illustrates the importance of reading the Bible from a two-lens view. The Cana wedding issues a call for such a focus, where the literal lens (the actual words of Scripture) needs to be combined with its figurative counterpart (the symbolic lens) to produce a robust understanding of the text. Yet, an important caveat is to hold the cross in view. By this means, the dialogue and images of John's wedding story are brought into sharp clarity. In other words, the biblical intent of John's symbolic language is to reveal the cross.

The question of whether to consider the Bible literally or symbolically is particularly germane when a reader comes to the crucifixion. It is there that Jesus is down to his last breath. Savaged by soldiers, this badly beaten man has not the strength to drag his cross up to Calvary's heights, nor sufficient energy to think straight. He is so near death by the time the Romans puncture his body with spikes that maintaining existence is barely possible. Worn and battered, he must conserve his breath, clinging desperately to life. He has but six hours to live; hours filled with excruciating pain and suffering.

From his vantage high above the landscape, as Christ looks down upon the Roman troops and out to the mocking crowd, what will he say? How important are the words he chooses to speak? That is a question the cross asks. Does Jesus carefully select his final words, or is what he says merely disgruntled, incoherent ramblings of a man who is practically out of his mind with pain? It is nearly impossible to speak well, more so to think clearly, even to mouth words when acute pain infuses the body. That is Jesus' quandary. Not just what to say, but how to say it economically given the thin thread of life still seeping through him.

He carefully selects seven statements—most are found in the ancient repository of Israel's scrolls. This fact indicates Jesus has predetermined what he will say prior to the crucifixion's ordeal. But it must be asked, will his utterances make sense when heard from the cross? Are his statements coherently strung together? He begins with a plea for forgiveness, not for himself, but for his earthly brothers and sisters. We also hear a cry of thirst, more than understandable given his extreme dehydration. But then there is also that awful statement which has been described as **dereliction** of duty ("why have you forsaken me?"). It begins to sound like the product of a confused mind, given his insistence that he and the Father are one, while at the same time stammering words that speak of betrayal to his God.

Viewed literally his seven statements lack cohesion. Given the context of suffering, cohesion hardly seems important, even possible. Will he find the strength, will he manage the pain, and will he be able to marshal his last energies to speak one final proclamation? Or does he just say words? Speaking whatever comes to mind, kind of a rattling machine gun spitting out seeds which he has "cherry picked" from Old Testament verses? He glances about, seeing Mary and John, watching the two thieves next to him, even the soldiers below. Does the descending darkness covering the land dim his desire for God? Does he find in those who came out to watch prompts for his statements, such as the soldiers and their need for forgiveness? Or, does he rise above pain and torture to control his last words, and in doing so speak one final, united message, a testimony where all seven statements combine to powerfully define his mission?

The task of *Last Words of Christ* is to place the Messiah's cross-thoughts into a biblical context rather than just a historical setting. This book challenges the conventional tradition of interpreting his last remarks as though they are seven separate and therefore disjointed statements. These words, since they are sourced in the Bible, are no longer viewed as "historic" words. They are biblical words, statements best understood when they are read and interpreted as scriptural communication rather than historical records. They are not just words uttered on a cruel cross in some distant time and place. They are words known today because they reside in the sacred *cannon* of Scripture. As such, they are best understood when read as Scripture, not history. They are theological thoughts.

3. Tools of Literature

Returning to the Cana wedding account, it is clear that John wrote symbolically. He has followed Jesus for three years, absorbing the Lord's use of language and speaking style, so it is not surprising that the pupil would narrate by approximating the Master's speech. John's writing is filled with nuance. But not only is John's. Scripture is emblazoned with exquisite, story style communication. This style is found in the opening books of the Bible; it is also prominent in describing ancient Israel's history, and further it underlies the nation's rich poetic and wisdom traditions.

In this book we will examine the Bible's symbolic style to construct meaning for Christ's cross words. We will follow the history of ancient Israel up to Christ, at times even forging ahead into a coming future to understand the epic meaning behind his last words. And in doing so, we will discover that Jesus' last words have everything to do with the biblical story's first words.

The crucifixion is a story told in literary terms, based on biblical history but informed through many genres. In this vast collection, we will encounter story plot and conflict, climax and resolution. We will read metaphorically but authentically, seeking to tie the cross' old, old story to the Bible's beginning story, and to its many stories in-between. In doing so we will connect a myriad of dots, seemingly fragmentary bits found in an oft confusing and disjointed Old Testament. But as we do, we will come to see how they form into a kind of breadcrumb trail, whose complex path eventually converges at the cross. This long story, with its many dots, will become for us a meta-story. An overriding story whose arc, "from the beginning," takes direct aim the cross.

If the biblical text is formed of symbolic communication, then how is it to be understood? That is a question Jesus' disciples asked: "Explain to us the parable . . ." (Mt. 13:36).[7] It is also the question that under-scores this book.

If you ever had a teacher who taught literature, you must thank her. Likely without realizing it, she was teaching more than just how to read great novels. Your teacher, it turns out, was instructing and preparing you nearly as well as a seminary student being taught to exegete a verse or a passage. That is because the Bible, while it is inspired Holy Ghost text, is also text that comes to its readers in a literary format.

In this book those same tools you were taught in high school, or middle school, perhaps even elementary school, are also the same tools used to interpret the story of the cross. That is because the Bible, at a core level, is quality literature. Its interpretation is foundationally formed when it is read in such a manner.

In the Cana wedding we discovered that dialogue pointed to John's use of foreshadowing. But that was only one feature of many literary resources. In *Last Words of Christ*, focus is also on:

- Key words
- Images
- Numbers

- Repetition
- Metaphor
- Symmetry

Most importantly, these features are used within a biblical context. In that way the literal language of Scripture will be seen to stage the Bible's symbolic aim. Combined, literal words and literary language give rise to the story behind the crucifixion and Christ's seven last words.

In the next chapter, emphasis shifts from literary discussion to Christ's actual statements spoken from the cross. That leads to an overview of all seven words. Surprisingly, this is unusual for a book on his last words. Mainly, authors begin by examining the first word, and when done, proceed to the next statement, following chronologically each of the seven thoughts as though they have little or no connection to one another. Often, they seem more intent on searching out "life applications" than on unearthing theological truths. In the coming chapters we will reverse that trend as we gather at the cross to listen not so much to what he says but rather to hear what he means.

Chapter 1

WORD LIST

More than a miracle of the moment, in John's view it was a *three-year* miracle. Translation: Cana was an everlasting miracle, one that would see no end of days. In that way it was different from other countless "everyday" miracles the Messiah would command. Yes, he healed many, restored sight, gave legs to the lame, and health to the infirmed. But those miracles, though deeply important to individuals, nevertheless were not sustaining. Cana, however, was not only the first, it was of eternal importance. Cana spoke directly to the cross. It drew a connection to Jesus' last discourse in the Upper Room and the brutal killing field of Golgotha. More so, by foreshadowing the **Holy Eucharist** it gave light to the coming new covenant of God's in-breaking kingdom.

Had the Apostle Paul been able to read John's Gospel, he could have identified with it. While Paul is noted at times for his scorching rhetoric, such as his letters to the Corinthians, he was also skilled in using figurative language. Chapter 4 of Galatians is a showpiece. For example, in discussing Abraham and God's promised favor, Paul spoke of Abraham's two sons, the one born to Hagar and the one born to Sarah, saying: "His son by the slave woman was born in the ordinary way; but the son by the free women was born as the result of a promise. These things may be taken *figuratively*, for the women represented two covenants" (Gal. 4:23–24, emphasis added).

Much like a multifaceted diamond, symbolic language refracts light differently depending on the medium through which it passes. For example, when a person sees an object beneath the surface of water, the refraction of light causes an apparent change in its appearance. Similarly, refractive powers of symbolism, often expressed in the text through metaphor, enhance meaning. We found in the Cana wedding that water became more than wine; it became a symbolic prefiguration, anticipating the coming blood of the cross.

Through the realness of water turned into wine, Jesus' first miracle announces the conclusion of his ministry. Our takeaway is to notice how real-time events point toward future happenings by means of the Bible's dual focus. Having introduced the literal and symbolic lenses, **in this chapter** I take up Jesus' seven last statements. Initially, (1) a listing of those statements as they occur in the four gospels will be displayed. That will lead to a chronological sequence. Then (2) they will be reviewed in their historic context. The purpose is to gain knowledge of what Jesus said. The significance of this ordering will be seen in the next chapter when those statements are treated within Mark's strange depiction of darkness falling upon the land.

1. Sequencing Final Words

From the cross, Jesus speaks seven statements, today commonly referred to as his last words. In search of those tortured utterances, the scriptural record is consulted. Starting with Matthew and progressing through the other gospels, the cry of his real-time voice is heard once again.

TABLE 1-1:   The Seven Statements Found in the Gospels

Statements	Citations
"Eli, Eli lema sabachthani?"	Matthew 27:46; also, Mark 15:34
"Father, forgive them, for they do not know what they are doing."	Luke 23:34

"Truly, I tell you, today you will be with me in Paradise."	Luke 23:43
"Father, into your hands I commit my spirit!"	Luke 23:46
"Dear woman, here is your son," and to the disciple, *"Here is your mother."*	John 19:26-27
"I am thirsty."	John 19:28
"It is finished."	John 19:30

No Gospel records all seven. There is no explicit written record of the order in which they were spoken. A solution may be determined with some degree of accuracy by comparing one account to another. Most who seek such an ordering agree in the placement of the first five statements. Of the last two, I prefer John's "finished" to Luke's "committing."

TABLE 1-2:   Sequencing the Final Words from the Cross

Word Order	Statement Content
1st Word	*Prayer for forgiveness*
2nd Word	*Paradise promise*
3rd Word	*Speaks to Mary and John*
4th Word	*Statement of abandonment*
5th Word	*Declares his thirst*
6th Word	*Cry of completion*
7th Word	*Prayer of committing his spirit*

These seven crucifixion statements are retold below. Of them, much has been written; movies have been made and artists have rendered. The actual texts themselves, however, are dry, almost sterile. As Fleming Rutledge says, "What we need to reflect upon today is the striking fact that the Four Evangelists tell us nothing at all about Christ's physical suffering."[1] Or, as other writers indicate, they are void of emotional content. But isn't that to our advantage? We want to come to them fresh, to hear him, and construct our own frame of reference. More so, we leave off our foreknowledge to provide a clean slate to build anew his final moment of passion, the hour of the cup. Let us now hear him. Listen as he speaks, sometimes faintly, other times in a loud voice, even at times in a shattering cry.[2] Let us take hold of these words and listen to him before we wrestle and contort them, trying to grasp their meaning.

2. The Literal Lens: Historic Words

The First Statement

How long he hangs there before he first speaks is uncertain, but the words spoken prior to darkness occur sometime between the third to the sixth hour, that is 9 a.m. to noon. He still feels the torment of pain, the searing ache coming from spikes piercing hands and feet. Breathing is nearly impossible as the weight of his upper body sinks onto his diaphragm. Blood still flows, though more slowly, draining raw wounds, now somewhat clotted and pinched-off by bruising and swelling. Looking down from the cross, a squad of Romans are nearby. A mallet is flung carelessly to the ground; unused spikes lay as litter. As he did during the wilderness temptation, Jesus meditates on Israel's ancient psalms while his eyes fix on the soldiers' activity.[3]

They divide my garments among them and
cast lots for my garment.

(Ps. 22:18)

Farther away are mockers. The rabble is present to watch how this man dies. Tongues flow freely; they fear not this miracle worker now. They rebuke him with taunts reminiscent of prophetic writings, such as Psalm 22:6–8:

> *But I am a worm and not a man,*
> *scorned by everyone and despised by the people.*
> *All who see me mock me;*
> *they hurl insults, shaking their heads:*
> *"He trusts in the LORD," they say,*
> *"let the LORD rescue him.*
> *Let him deliver him,*
> *since he delights in him."*

These words of prophecy are confirmed in real-time, as Matthew writes in 27:35-44:

> *When they had crucified him, they divided up his clothes by casting lots. And sitting down, they kept watch over him there. Above his head they placed the written charge against him: THIS IS JESUS, THE KING OF THE JEWS.*
>
> *Two rebels were crucified with him, one on his right and one on his left. Those who passed by hurled insults at him, shaking their heads and saying, "You who are going to destroy the temple and build it in three days, save yourself! Come down from the cross, if you are the Son of God!" In the same way the chief priests, the teachers of the law and the elders mocked him. "He saved others," they said, "but he can't save himself! He's the king of Israel! Let him come down now from the cross, and we will believe in him. He trusts in God. Let God rescue him now if he wants him, for he said, 'I am the Son of God.'"*

Similarly, in the courts of the religious leaders and before Pilate just hours prior, he endured such jeers and debasements, intermixed with blows and beating and floggings. How easy it would have been to summon a legion of angels! To have ended "his hour" then and there. To prevail over the so-called mighty by showing who he truly is.[4] Once again the mockers berate him, railing and decrying his temple-building statement, no matter how badly they misconstrue it. Soon though, soon he will indeed raise up the temple of his body, and that in three days! But to give way to temptation and come down from the cross or to call forth an angel troop would be to fail the mission for which he now endures. And so somehow, in the midst of this havoc and commotion, he summons the grace to pray:

"Father, forgive them, for they do not know what they are doing."

(Luke 23:34)

The Second Statement

What was it that caused one of the thieves to stop mocking? Was it the sign atop the cross? Or was it the manner Jesus responded to insults? After all, who prays for their crucifiers? The two thieves didn't; but one did notice. In the tumult of angry voices, he found himself drawn toward this badly beaten man, hanging there between himself and the other bandit. Sufficiently torn inside, he speaks to his brother criminal:

> *"Don't you fear God,"* he said, *"since you are under the same sentence? We are punished justly, for we are getting what our deeds deserve. But this man has done nothing wrong."*

> Then he said, *"Jesus, remember me when you come into your kingdom."* Jesus answered him, **"Truly I tell you, today you will be with me in paradise."** (Luke 23:40–43)

The Third Statement

With those words the mocking begins to subside. The morning lengthens and noon approaches. Nearly three hours have passed. The three crucified ones have gone still, saving what little energy remains, each with his own thoughts. Suddenly Jesus stirs. He lifts his head and scans the crowd. His gaze settles on his mother; compassion binds his heart. His ministry has taken him away from home much of the time. Sadness emanates from his gaze. Standing next to Mary is her sister, and also Mary of Magdala, and nearby is John. John was there at the beginning when his mother urged him to do something about the wine shortage. Filled with love, Jesus speaks for the third and final time that morning:

"Woman, here is your son," and to the disciple,
"Here is your mother."

(John 19:26–27)

The Fourth Statement

Jesus grows quiet again. The afternoon arrives, and the day wanes. The three crucified ones are wracked with pain. Intermittently, groans can be heard. The sky has darkened; an unearthly dark descends over the whole land as far as anyone can see, but seeing is difficult in darkness. The hour Jesus has relentlessly marched toward these past three years has arrived. Yet, in spite of his weakened condition, he raises his voice in a mournful, shattering pitch and says:

"Eloi, Eloi lema sabachthani?"
(which means *"My God, my God, why have
you forsaken me?"*)

(Mark 15:34)

The Fifth Statement

Strange words from this Son of God. Not everyone hears clearly. What did he say? Some think he is calling for Elijah. A rolling sensation courses through the crowd. Elijah? Could it be? People stand transfixed, uncertain what will happen. They do not have long to wait. His voice scratchy, he announces faintly:

"I am thirsty."

(John 19:28)

Quickly there is movement as two men rush to grab a stick, forcing a sponge sopped in wine-vinegar onto it. It is hoisted high; he loosely gums it.

The Sixth Statement

There is silence again. Then suddenly he cries out in a surprisingly loud shout:

"It is finished."

(John 19:30)

The Seventh Statement

No one moves. Eyes strain to register what they are seeing. Faces contort, tears stream from reddened eyes, noses run. The crowd clutches one another straining to witness the end. As the Messiah expires, he proclaims a final statement, in a jagged yet somehow regal voice:

"Father, into your hands I commit my spirit."

(Luke 23:46)

The crucifixion is over. The ministry started at Cana by an astounding miracle has now closed; blood drips down to a dry earth . . . like spilled wine.

Conclusion

In this chapter, the passion of the crucifixion is revealed. Although Scripture provides descriptions of the cross, including the trial, the narratives remain quiet concerning the extent of that suffering. It is almost as if the gospel writers are loath to admit the unutterable shame that is the cross. The shame the Lord bares for mankind.

Section Conclusion

In this chapter, *the literal lens* depicted the historic words of Christ on the cross. By contrast, the Introduction and Prelude described *the symbolic,* or *figurative lens*. This was seen through the literary features of *key words* and *images*. By this means, Scripture's *literal words* anticipated, through their symbolic meaning, a coming future. Further, the Bible's *symbolic language* demonstrated, through the imagery of water turned into wine, a foreshadowing of his death on the cross. By such means we previewed the literary construction of the Bible containing both literal and symbolic statements.

In the coming section these two aspects will blend with other literary elements—including use of word repetition, number meaning, and metaphor—to comprehend the Bible's story construction. We will see the significance of this in chapter 2, in which Mark's statement of darkness falling on the land is cast as a biblical image. The purpose, therefore, of Section I was to familiarize readers with the Bible's second lens, the viewfinder that focuses and gives clarity to the Bible's overall narrative story.

The remainder of this book, while often consulting the historicity of the period from the Last Supper to the crucifixion, will not again place sole emphasis on those six horrific hours. Instead, the crucifixion will serve as a kind of table on which to display the narrative language of the cross and what it discloses. In the coming two chapters, the first three utterances will be examined more for what they proclaim than what was done to Jesus. Yet humanity ought not ever forget that brutal 'hour' as he lay spiked to those rough beams.

As noted earlier, this examination into Jesus' seven last statements will be guided by Mark's strange statement of darkness occupying the land. Viewed visually, the result groups those words into two separate divisions. One occurs during the period of light; the other after darkness has fallen. The effect is transforming. No longer are his words heard as seven, separate statements. Instead, they are formed into two conversations. Section II takes up those words spoken in light.

Chronology

CHRIST'S SEVEN LAST WORDS

Order	Statements in Light	Citations (RSV)[1]
First Word	*"Father, forgive them; for they know not what they do."*	Luke 23:34
Second Word	*"Truly, I say to you, today you will be with me in Paradise."*	Luke 23:43
Third Word	*"Woman, behold, your son!"* Then he said to the disciple, *"Behold, your mother!"*	John 19:26–27
Order	**Statements in Darkness**	**Citations**
Fourth Word	*"Eli, Eli, lama sabach-tha'ni?"* that is, *"My God, my God, why hast thou forsaken me?"*	Matthew 27:46; also Mark 15:34
Fifth Word	*"I thirst."*	John 19:28
Sixth Word	*"It is finished."*	John 19:30
Seventh Word	*"Father, into thy hands I commit my spirit!"*	Luke 23:46

Section II

FORGIVEN

Section II examines Christ's first three words, those spoken in light, through symbolic and representational language. Concentrating on the first three utterances, they announce not only forgiveness but the advent of a new community. It is in anticipation of this community that Jesus, from the cross, addresses his final message.

Chapter 2

FORGIVE THEM

A brief story-retell adapted from the passion narratives opens this chapter.

The real-time cross experience leaves his followers nearly paralyzed with grief and uncertainty. Perhaps some—as they watched and waited and silently prayed—hoped for a last-minute reprieve, a last-minute miracle. Momentarily a glint of optimism broke the pall; some thought the Master cried out for Elijah. Was that it? Could there yet be a miracle? If only Elijah would come. But he didn't. Why? The hurt and disbelief that He was dead—it just couldn't be—it was impossible. This man, the Son of Man, was too good, too righteous for this kind of end. Only a week ago multitudes flocked as he rode into Jerusalem on a donkey. The people ran and shouted, tossing fronds his way. Singing praises. Oh, the glory of it!

But now evening approaches. The thieves' legs have been broken; the soldiers come upon Christ, yet all know he is dead. Even so, a spear is thrust into his side and retracted. Blood and bodily liquids flow out. He is dead. Why hurt him more? His spirit given up, his body is emptied of its marvelous life.

Then it was Joseph, a well-to-do disciple from Arimathea, who went to Pilate and asked for the body. Surprisingly, Pilate did not protest. He seemed glad to be done with it, all of it. And so Joseph took the body of the Lord, wrapped it in clean linen, and put it in his own tomb. A large stone closed off the entrance; the day, indeed the past three years, sealed shut. The hour of the cross over.

Having examined Christ's last words from the framework of history in the preceding chapter, the purpose of the remainder of this book is to discover their narrative meaning. From the cross Jesus speaks seven statements. His first is most important. All others are hinged to this one intercessory prayer. Jesus, becoming man, yet also remaining God, makes a simple plea for his earthly friends:

Father, forgive them, for they do not know what they are doing.

This is the most literal of his last words. Little symbolism resides here; no metaphoric language needs interpretation. *Father—forgive—them. They just don't realize what they are doing. They don't understand the nature of your truth or your ways. They need to be forgiven.*

There is but one question that needs examination: Who? On whose behalf does the Messiah ask these eternal words? Before that question is considered, however, it is prudent to place all of his sayings into a narrative setting. His words are not spoken without context, so before the question of who can be examined, it is wise to establish this biblical framework.

The idea that a passage can support more than literal meaning is based on a pattern of usage common to the Bible. For example, Genesis contains the story of Joseph and his captivity in Egypt, where he rose to a position of authority second only to Pharaoh. Of the moment Joseph divulges his identify to his brothers, the text records:

I am your brother Joseph, the one you sold into Egypt! And now, do not be distressed and do not be angry with your- selves for selling me here, because it was to save lives that God sent me ahead of you. . . . But God sent me ahead of you to

preserve for you a remnant on earth and to save your lives by
a great deliverance. (Gen. 45:4–7)

In this manner, the text speaks literally. But the words of Joseph
contain an allusion to not only saving the lives of his family but to a
far larger "remnant" who will be "preserved." These words call to mind
a coming community that is still four hundred years into the future.
And yet, these words may also be even more forward looking than that,
sighting all the way to Christ. This look forward is seen in the fullness
of Joseph's story, which contains symbols of a future savior. For this reason, many Bible scholars seize on Joseph as a symbolic *type* of Christ.[1]
This example serves to illustrate how biblical text may say one thing but
have another in mind. That "another in mind" is what, in Section I, was
referred to as symbolic language, which we now examine.

Image and the Cross

A dominant image that fills the written Word of God is *light and darkness*. This image occurs so often it can be seen as a pattern. It first occurs
in the creation story and is expressed as part of the literal account:

And God said, "Let there be *light*," and there was light. God
saw that the light was good, and he separated the light from
the *darkness*." (Gen. 1:3–4, emphasis added)

Veiled as it is within creation language, this pattern is not always
recognized. Yet its symmetry is quite pronounced and can be found
throughout Scripture in the contrasting images of light and darkness.
This may be seen in Mark's Gospel where the cross is set both in the
light of day as well as the afternoon's darkness:

> And when the sixth hour had come,
> darkness fell over the whole land until the ninth hour.

A great deal of debate has occurred over Mark's sudden appearance of darkness over the land. That is, was it actual or did Mark use

it as a metaphorical comment expressing God's wrath as His son lay on the cross? The point taken here is not to engage in that debate but to recognize, through its inclusion in the biblical text, its significance to the crucifixion story. In its strangeness it is evocative; for the careful reader of Scripture it cannot be ignored. It is not only part of the literal text, but it draws the reader back to "the very beginning," to the initial use of this pattern, or *motif,* where light is separated from darkness (see Gen. 1:3).

Given the singular importance of light and darkness as a biblical image, I elect to visually apply it to the cross. By this means, Mark's description splits the six-hour chronology of the cross into two three-hour segments. Table 2-1 shows Christ's **First** through **Third Words** *separated* from his **Fourth** through **Seventh.** In this way the biblical image of light and darkness, in mirror-like manner, reflects Genesis' intent to separate light from darkness. This act functions as a metaphorical hinge, swinging Christ's words into two time periods: those (a) spoken in the morning, and (b) those in the afternoon. The result is a theological doorway giving entrance into the meaning of the cross. This doorway consolidates Jesus' statements into two, unified blocks of content.

This image (see Table 2-1, next page) transforms the cross account from historical to narrative; it also organizes the remainder of this book. Guided in this way the current chapter and those following examine his words from this twofold time consolidation. This permits his last words to be perceived as falling into two distinct conversations: one in the morning (period of light), with the other in the afternoon (period of darkness). This image-based model progressively transforms Jesus' literal but isolated seven utterances into two, jointly held conversations. In this way Jesus' words gain traction far beyond historic but fragmented meanings.

In this chapter, therefore, I show how Mark's statement of darkness affects the theological meaning of Jesus' three utterances made in the morning time of light. Beginning with the **First Word** a discussion

Table 2-1:   Division of Light and Darkness—Separating Christ's Last Words (RSV)

Period	Time	Statements	Statements	Statements
Light (morning conversation)	3rd through 6th hours	Father, forgive them; for they know not what they do.	Truly, I say to you, today you will be with me in Paradise.	Woman, behold your son! Behold, your mother!
At the sixth hour darkness came over the whole land until the ninth hour. (Mk. 15:33)				
Darkness (afternoon conversation)	**6th through 9th hours**	Eli, Eli, la'ma sabach-tha'ni? (My God, my God, why hast thou forsaken me?)	I thirst.	It is finished. —————— Father, into thy hands I commit my spirit!

is framed by the question, (1) Who are the forgiven? Next, I examine (2) humanity's response to that forgiveness (heard in his **Second Word**), and then (3) conclude with the emergence of a forgiven community (the **Third Word**).

1. Who Are the Forgiven?

During the morning period of light, which is from the third to the sixth hour, Jesus makes three statements. The first is to offer forgiveness through an intercessory prayer: a request that the Father "forgive them." Paramount is to discern "them." A review of the gospels offers several audiences in the immediate locale. At the foot of the cross Roman soldiers squat and cast lots; they have just crucified Jesus and are prime *them* contenders. To his right and left are criminals, men in desperate need of forgiveness. They are joined by those who linger in the area, mockers come out to witness the show and hurl insults. Numbered also among them is the religious hierarchy, chief priests, and scribes. Together they comprise a vast crowd of "them."

In the trial held that morning the remainder of the religious leaders are found. Here are council members, men whose dignity might have forbidden their transport to Golgotha, along with Roman officials such as Pilate, who pronounced the sentence of death. And then there is King Herod; he was in Jerusalem during Passover and saw Jesus early that same morning. Or them could be the rabble cobbled together by the religious leaders to press Pilate into a decision that favored releasing Barabbas. All were part of the narrative context that day, and all stand well in need of God's forgiveness.

But what of the Lord's followers who were there, some lurking in the shadow of darkness? Such as the disciples who accompanied him to the garden, subsequently fleeing on his arrest. Or, for example, the non-descript young man who fled naked (see Mk. 14:51–52). Then there is Peter, the one Christ identifies as the building block of his coming church, yet he was also the one for whom a cock crowed. With each revelation comes another audience, the context widening from the immediate scene at the cross, spreading out geographically and eventually through time so that forgiveness encompasses all whom Jesus met and ministered to during his three years. Linked by ministry, it is appropriate to conclude that anyone Jesus encountered, whether in real time, in the future, or in the past, is included in his intercessory prayer. John's Gospel nicely summarizes "them" in 3:16 as "whoever believes," and so the answer to the Lord's forgiveness is an inclusive all, spanning geography, time, and all races and classes of people.

2. Humanity's Response

It is at this point that biblical theology enters the discussion: The Roman soldiers may be co-opted as representatives of Rome's government. They become, symbolically, figures of man's governmental reign. They deserve this interpretation since Rome, in the days of Christ, was the apex of humanity's governmental and political power. Rome ruled. Its direct power as well as its influence extended north into Europe and east through the Mediterranean Basin. In this context the Roman presence stages the rule of man against the reign of God, represented by Christ.[2]

As previously noted in the review of the seven statements in chapter 1, Jesus turns to the criminals and says to one, "Truly I tell you, today you will be with me in Paradise" (Luke 23:43). While this remark was specific to one criminal, what is occurring is an integration of Christ's three separate statements into one unified message. First, Christ prays for forgiveness for the inclusive all. In doing so, he freely offers God's forgiveness. All categories of people are included; none are omitted. But an offer tendered is not the same as an offer accepted. For mankind's reply to Jesus' offer, his second statement must be sought. The two criminals, those men pronounced guilty for their wrongdoings, or theologically for theirs sins, represent all people. To that end Scripture declares, "all have sinned and fall short of the glory of God" (Rom. 3:23).

The second statement reveals the human response to Jesus' prayer. It is one thing for Jesus to offer forgiveness, it is another for mankind to accept. God's gift requires a desire on the part of mankind to want to be forgiven. This is a repeated theme in the **Hebrew Bible**, in which the people of Israel, over and over, turned their backs on God, rejecting his desire that they turn away from idolatry (see Jg. 10:6, Ezek. 14:6, Zech. 1:1–6). Couched, then, in Jesus' second statement lies a question: Who will accept this offer of forgiveness?

Returning to the flanking criminals, as representational mankind, Luke records a split response:

> One of the criminals who hung there hurled insults. "Aren't you the Messiah? Save yourself and us!" But the other criminal rebuked him. "Don't you fear God," he said, "since you are under the same sentence? We are punished justly, for we

are getting what our deeds deserve. But this man has done nothing wrong." Then he said, "Jesus, remember me when you come into your kingdom." Jesus answered, "Truly I tell you, today you will be with me in paradise." (23:39–43)

In this second conversation we hear not only God's willingness to forgive all, but we find in it a varied response. Not all elect to receive forgiveness. There are those who stay the course of the unrepentant. They stand off to the side and continue to hurl insults at God's mercy, while others engage in the spirit of Jesus' overall discourse, such as Matthew describes in the Sermon on the Mount:

Blessed are the poor in spirit;

For theirs is the kingdom of heaven. (5:3)

3. Coming into View: A Forgiven Community

In the first two statements, therefore, is found a conversation bound up in forgiveness. Is this by accident? Or is the third utterance that morning also tied to this theme? At first glance it seems not as Jesus hands off the care and well-being of his mother to John. This action, however, is seen through the literal lens. Stepping back and changing lenses, a different image comes into focus. Understood that way the third statement adds to the richness of the cross conversation.

This is found in the story retell below based on the passion narratives (italicized text is the **Third Word** quoted from the Bible).

Jesus has been silent for some time. He last spoke with the offer of paradise. Perhaps an hour, maybe longer has passed without further utterance. The feistiness of the morning as the unruly mocked Jesus has subsided. The fun of making sport is passed; the tempo and tenor of angry, traumatizing words has slowed to a trickle. Stillness settles in. Those watching Jesus see movement as he shifts his head. He seeks out his mother, gazing at her, sensing and feeling with his amazing ability to not only know another's hurt but to empathetically feel and live it. Mary, perhaps feeling his eyes on her, looks up. They hold each other tight. Jesus speaks a short refrain as remarkable for its message as its brevity.

"Woman, here is your son."

And to the disciple [John], *"Here is your mother."*

Heard in real time, this is not unexpected. These are words, after all, of a son who is dying and feels concern for his mother. It is not the words that are remarkable, therefore, but how they message his kingdom that must be grasped. We need to hear them in context with the first two forgiveness statements. Then we can understand their significance as part of the morning's light-filled, all-embracing conversation without being caught up in the real-time pathos of a son's love for his mother.

Mary and John now enter the conversation, but in the narrative text they are perceived, as were the thieves and Romans, representationally.[3] They might be outsiders to the religious establishment, but as forgiven people they are insiders to God.[4] They are not like those who need to hear God's forgiveness, nor are they as the criminals where one turns to God but the other rejects that offer. No, Mary and John long ago settled their articles of faith. As such, they are now citizens of Christ's coming kingdom.

In saying "behold your mother" and "behold your son," *Jesus is instructing his kingdom how to act as forgiven citizens.* Mary and John represent not so much man's need for forgiveness as they present reasons why God forgives. Forgiven citizens of the kingdom are expected to act in the manner now symbolically on display, as Mary, the new mother, and John, the new son, embrace each other.[5]

Fleming Rutledge writes along these lines:

The saying is not about being nice to your mother. It is about the new community that comes into being through the power of Jesus. . . . When the Christian community is working the way it is supposed to, people are brought together who have absolutely nothing in common, who may have diametrically different views on things, who may even actively dislike each other. The Christian community, when it is not grieving the Holy Spirit, comes into being without regard to differences. . . . In giving his mother to the disciple, he is causing a new relationship to come into existence that did not exist before. The disciple and the woman are not individual people here. They are symbolic: they represent the way that family ties are transcended in the church by the ties of the Spirit.[6]

Summary

Mark's statement concerning darkness not only splits the cross statements into two divisions (see Table 2-1) but acts to shepherd Jesus' three morning utterances into one continuous conversation that expands into a discourse on forgiveness. In the next chapter, this discourse continues by rethinking forgiveness with an implication for living in the new community.

Chapter 3

A COMMUNITY WITHOUT CONDEMNATION

Mark is in a rush. He has not the time or patience of John to eloquently open his Gospel with a sublime prologue; or a Matthew or a Luke who tenderly write the story of Jesus' birth. Mark immediately begins with the forerunner John the Baptist. In this way Mark recalls Israel's ancient past, reminding readers that before the Messiah's coming there will be a heralding voice. Further, Mark associates Jesus with the land of Galilee. In this way he doubles down on ancient traditions that claim when the Messiah comes he will walk among the people who dwell in a land of darkness (see Is. 9:1–2). Moreover, Mark notes, "Jesus came from Nazareth in Galilee" and "Jesus went into Galilee," as well as describing his Capernaum ministry. Of Christ's tour throughout Galilean towns, Mark makes known its importance the first time he quotes Jesus: "The *kingdom of God* has come near. *Repent* and *believe* the good news!" (1:15, emphasis added).

In this way Mark ties together the Elijah-figure John the Baptist, (see Mk. 9:11–13), the land of darkness (Galilee), and Christ's initial kingdom proclamations (repent and believe). Mark locates Jesus' early ministry as one in which he invades the land around the Sea of Galilee. This land of darkness was part of historic Israel's fracture when rebellion swept through, splitting apart a once united kingdom. If there were ever a time in Israel's history and ever a place where the Jewish nation needed the welcoming illumination of God, it is here in this northern province, this Galilee of the Gentiles.

Jesus too seems in a hurry to begin his mission. Thus, Mark writes: "Without delay he called them, and they left their father Zebedee in the boat with the hired man and followed him" (1:20). This reference to the "father Zebedee" clearly identifies "them" as the brothers John and James. Mark next locates Jesus in Capernaum where he teaches "with authority" (1:27), and through miracles verifies his credentials. Such enactments draw people to him. Wherever he travels there is a buzz: village folk throng wayside stops, seashores are overrun, and houses are mobbed as the countryside clamors to hear this new voice of authority, to see this One who proclaims God's forgiveness.

Story retell below is based on Mark 2:1–12.

> Mark records of the conclusion of Jesus' circuit through the Capernaum countryside: "A few days later, when Jesus again entered Capernaum, the people heard that he had come home." Quickly they rush a house he is visiting, filling it full. Frustrated by being unable to gain entrance, four men who carry a paralytic sit dejectedly outside. Suddenly a plan is conceived; they ascend to rooftop bearing their friend. Pulling apart its earthen construction, entry is forced as they lower the paralyzed man. Mark states: "When Jesus saw their faith, he said to the paralytic, 'Son, your sins are forgiven.'"

> Were the men disappointed by this response? After all, Jesus had not performed the hoped-for miracle. Instead, almost unbelievably, he addresses the infirmed man's sin—forgiving him—if that is even possible. Whatever these four men think Mark doesn't disclose. Instead, he writes of the teachers of the law, noting their indignation at the blaspheming words Jesus dares to utter. They contest him thinking, "Who can forgive sins but God alone?"

Which, of course, is exactly the reason Jesus withholds physical healing. He immediately challenges their assumption he has no authority to forgive. "But that you may know that the Son of Man has authority on earth to forgive sins … I tell you," and now he speaks directly to the paralytic, "get up, take your mat and go home." The crowd is amazed. Not only have they witnessed the hoped-for miracle, they are provided a preview of the coming clash between temple leaders and Christ.

In this chapter, the above story serves as partial background for a threefold examination of forgiveness, repentance, and kingdom—all with an eye toward the coming new community. The question, Is repentance a necessary prerequisite for forgiveness? gives aim to this discussion. I begin by (1) considering the relationship between Jesus' **First Word** on the cross—forgiveness—and repentance. Following is (2) the development of forgiveness and the in-breaking kingdom; and then (3) the blending of kingdom, belief, and repentance completes this examination.

1. Forgiveness without Repentance?

From the previous chapter, we must recall the presence of the two thieves alongside Jesus on the cross. In that discussion they came to be seen not only as individuals but as representatives of humanity. One rejected Christ's offer of forgiveness; the other accepted it. Yet, it must be asked, Was repentance visible in the thief who turned to Jesus? It was this thief who said, "Don't you fear God?" concluding by comparison the rightfulness of their being crucified as they were getting what their life deeds deserve. But of Jesus he said, "This man has done nothing wrong."

The thief's confession of wrongdoing is more reflective of a factual statement than a repentant cry of godly sorrow. This is the point of contention: Can forgiveness be granted without repentance? In some

Christian circles, repentance is prerequisite to forgiveness. Certainly it was expected in ancient Judaism.

How then can we comprehend a forgiveness that seems not joined to repentance? And yet, according to Scripture, Jesus did grant forgiveness without evidence of repentance. With Luke's account of the paralytic in mind, L. Gregory Jones builds this case:

> Even so, the forgiveness that Jesus proclaimed and enacted was controversial, primarily because he seemed to diverge from Israel's understandings and practices in crucial ways. For example, he both claimed divine authority to forgive sins and offered forgiveness without necessarily presuming prior repentance.[1]

As recalled from the story retell above, the four men who lowered the paralytic before Jesus sought only the man's healing. Of the man himself, no voice is given. We only hear Jesus who says, "Son, your sins are forgiven." It is at this point that the entrance into the story by the teachers of the law is crucial. They regard forgiveness without prior repentance to be a thing of blasphemy. It is most certainly not the practice of their ancient ways. Which is precisely the point of the healing, to validate not only that Jesus as the Son of Man has the power to heal, but that he has the authority to forgive. And apparently, the authority to forgive even before being requested. Indeed! What kind of forgiveness is this?

Here forgiveness is dissociated from the forms of the Levitical priesthood. This is a forgiveness in which no offering is required, where no animal is brought for the priest to conduct rites and make **atonement**. This forgiveness literally rocks the religious world of the teachers of the law. This is a radical forgiveness; an unheard of forgiveness. However, as verified by Jesus' miracle of healing, it is a forgiveness from God.

This is not the only time Jesus brings forgiveness to one who has not repented. In chapter 8 of John's Gospel is the story of a woman taken in adultery and brought before him in the temple courts. Those charging her aim to trap Jesus into forgiving her iniquity and thus violating the ancient law requiring stoning. Aware of this, Jesus bends down and writes with his finger on the ground. Those present watch and observe; gradually they begin departing, leaving at last only Jesus and the woman. To her Jesus asks a sole question: "Woman, where are they? Has no one condemned you?" To her reply Jesus responds, "Then neither do I."

There is much in this brief account. It associates the presence of God through the figuration of John's wording: "But Jesus bent down and started to write on the ground *with his finger*" (8:6, emphasis added). N.T. Wright reminds his readers of the singular importance of that image by referring to Luke's Gospel where Jesus is accused of deriving his miraculous powers from the devil, but not God. "By Beelzebub, the prince of demons, he is driving out demons." To this Jesus counters, "But if I drive out demons by the finger of God, then the kingdom of God has come to you" (Lk. 11:14-20). Of that phrase, "by the finger of God," Wright suggests those who watch Jesus would be drawn back to the "powerful works which Moses did at Pharaoh's court."[2] Exodus records: "The magicians said to Pharaoh, 'This is the finger of God'" (8:19). This reference is the source, then, of Moses' might in causing the plagues that come upon Egypt.

Further development of "the finger of God" occurs when Moses is given a second set of the stone tablets (the first being smashed on the ground in outrage to the golden calf).[3] This leads to God again giving Moses commandments that have been written by his own hand (see Ex. 34:1). This connection to Israel's ancient past, when God used his finger to write, Jesus now replicates. In this way Christ uses his finger to bridge the gap between stoning a woman for violating the seventh commandment and Jesus' authority to forgive such sins. In this case the mercy of God predominates and communicates the desire to forgive rather than condemn. This is John's intent in 8:6 as he describes how Jesus "bent down and started to write on the ground with his finger."[4] Through this use of symbolic language the message of forgiveness without condemnation is seen to clearly resonate among the woman's accusers, who depart without casting stones.

John's story refines what it means to forgive. "Has no one condemned you? Then neither do I." We understand that Jesus not only forgives as God, but as God neither does he condemn. Thus, forgiveness without repentance is accomplished and taught in the "living parable" of the woman caught in adultery.[5] Examples as these serve L. Gregory Jones' conclusion: "In one sense repentance prepares us to receive God's grace, but in another, more profound sense we discover through our repentance that God's grace has already found us."[6]

Here is another mystery of cross forgiveness: Can it be granted to those who reject it, such as those at the cross who mocked his offer? So, we find at the cross forgiveness is offered freely and without reservation. It is offered to all humanity *even before it is sought*. It is offered this way to demonstrate the free gift of grace, given entirely of God's love, which cannot be earned, deserved, or bought. If repentance is a prerequisite, it becomes a kind of required work, and thus it negates the fullness of grace.

From the cross Jesus offers forgiveness for all. It is offered even before all seek it. The paralytic in Luke did not seek forgiveness; it was granted and thereby lends itself a sign of Jesus' authority to forgive. The adulterous woman did not seek forgiveness, but she happily received Jesus' forgiveness and the emotional security of not being condemned. His was not a halfway offer—granting forgiveness but still clinging to condemnation. His forgiveness is a perfect mirror of grace, unmerited, unachievable, yet fully granted. In this manner we may reconcile divergent views of forgiveness to include confession and repentance.

2. Forgiveness and the Kingdom

Forgiveness may be likened to a key used to enter the kingdom. No one comes in without being forgiven. That is why the conversation with the thief is so fundamental. Yet in the **Third Word** Jesus seems to be pointing out that the forgiven must be transformed; they must become people who embody empathy, care, and love. In other words, kingdom citizens must be willing to forgive even as they have been forgiven, and then transform their state of forgiveness by sharing, embracing, and extending to others the emotional security that flows out of forgiveness. Here is Jesus' gracious offer that withholds condemnation, a truth imparted in the Lord's Prayer: "Forgive us the wrong we have done, as we have forgiven those who have wronged us" (Mt. 6:12 REB).

In this kind of difference making, forgiveness unlocks the doors of hurt and emotional bondage present in the lives of others. It extends God's forgiveness by turning its axis outward. At Calvary, this outward turning is revealed through the progressive transition from an inward reception, as seen on the part of the thief, to "another-person orientation" viewed in the embrace-response by Mary and John. This "another-person" embrace widens forgiveness from a constricted, ego-centric attitude of "I have been forgiven" to a maturing, life-based response of emotional security for all.

This is illustrated in Mark's Gospel in the story captioned the "Rich Young Man" (10:17-22). In that story a wealthy young man approaches Jesus. He asks, "What must I do to inherit eternal life?" What is interesting is Christ's response. He does not, as might be expected, enjoin the man to "repent" of his sinful life style and receive him (Jesus) into his heart. No, rather the Lord looks lovingly at the man and points to what he lacks: "Go, sell everything you have and give to the poor, and you will have treasure in heaven. Then come, follow me."

In this exchange, repentance is not immediately visible. Rather the cost—expressed as a spiritual metaphor—which requires the wealthy man to become "poor" in material goods, eludes the young man's desire to gain eternal life. Therefore, the "poverty" Jesus requires is becoming dependent on God rather than one's own self-sufficiency. It is a poverty the young man is unwilling to acquire.

Repentance, therefore, is seen in Jesus' instruction to the man to become poor. Had the young man been willing to acknowledge his spiritual poverty, that act of repentance would have guided him into a life of discipleship ("Then come, follow me," 10:21). Thus, we find that the young man remains outside of Christ's forgiveness because his heart is unwilling to repent of its self-sufficiency. Like the thief on the cross who rejected Christ's forgiveness, so too does this wealthy (self-sufficient) young man fail to receive forgiveness. Repentance, therefore, acts to remove blockages, issues that seal off one's heart to forgiveness.

Applying these teachings to the **Third Word**, we find Mary and John, individually and collectively, in a state of brokenness.[7] Their spiritual poverty is not so much caused by sin as by true grief, though to place sin into the setting might not be unrealistic, particularly in the case of John. After all, he was in the garden and fled with the rest of the disciples. Peter gets all the "credit" as the one who forsakes the Lord, but John's footsteps closely echo the roster's crow (see Mk. 14:27–31b).

Mary's brokenness is more apt to be exactly what it is: a mother's love exhausted at the sight of her son being crucified, but perhaps plagued by doubts of how this could happen to the One whose birth and life were so clearly marked by God. Both individuals, then, experience brokenness; both require emotional relief that avails from an empathic embrace, the kind where communion is best communicated through silence. Therefore, in Mary's and John's private "guilt" they each find a new resolve and a new release by a different kind of forgiveness, a cross-based forgiveness that is embracing, accepting, and loving toward all—a forgiveness without condemnation or guilt.

The kind of communion Mary and John now experience is the kind of communion that the cross, and the cross background of the Upper Room, presents. This sense of oneness that Jesus has pointed Mary and John toward is the kind of real-life, authentic emotional security he came to provide as Healer. At the meal table of the Upper Room, Jesus insists that he and his father are one. The oneness of the Trinitarian God is fundamental for the oneness of individual well-being, and the basis of wellness for the entire human community, and beyond, including, as Jones correctly states, a communion "with the whole Creation."[8]

Mary and John figuratively express the kind of communion that existed in the garden prior to the fall. In that period of man's history, oneness was a constant experience. It existed in relationship between the Creator and his image bearers. The essence of God's forgiveness is found in the cross conversation during the period of light. Such forgiveness may be understood through (a) God's reception of the once-banished-but-now-being-restored mankind; (b) a healing provision for individuals and societal groups resulting in the removal of guilt; and (c) God's embracing of humanity and all creation without condemnation.

These conclusions place a narrative framework around the work of the cross, specifically the morning conversation. Once we see Mary and John as representational citizens of the kingdom, we come face to face with the need for like actions. In context with the cross' period of light, the Messiah's words declare first the need to be forgiven so that we might enter into communion with this Trinitarian God. As instruments of His grace, we are called to love and forgive others, and so live out the second part of Jesus' reply when questioned as to the greatest commandment, which is to love others in the communities in which they dwell. In this way forgiven humanity is expected to resolve competing interests and find a collective and harmonious way toward the destiny God foreordained before the foundation of the world was laid.

3. Discipleship: Repentance and Forgiveness

At the outset of the Messiah's public ministry is the presence of John the Baptist. Mark quotes the prophet Isaiah: "I will send my messenger ahead of you, who will prepare your way—a voice of one calling in the wilderness, 'Prepare the way for the Lord'" (1:2–3).

John comes challenging the Jewish people, whose traditions teach they are the 'called of God.' That is, they are the people of Abraham's covenant. Their ancestors formed the nation of Israel. A nation, however, that was unable to keep God's commands, and in the end was sent not only into Babylonia captivity but lost their political nationhood as well. Once ruled by their own kings, in the time of Christ they are a subject people under Roman rule. John's call for repentance is to pivot the nation back to the God of Abraham, Isaac, and Jacob; back to a covenant people.

Jesus begins his ministry, significantly, with the words: "The time has come. . . . The kingdom of God is near. Repent and believe the good news!" (Mk. 1:15). Here, repentance is directly tied to the good news that God is bringing. It alerts the Jewish people that a new kind of kingdom is arriving. The people are cajoled by John to get ready to live in that kingdom by (a) repenting of how they are living and their unfaithful ways and (b) believing the good news that Jesus is announcing. In this way, repentance is directly tied to preparing them to live in that now in-breaking kingdom. [9]

This background contextualizes our discussion of forgiveness and the forgiven, of grace and discipleship, of kingdom community and new life. Viewed this way, repentance is found in the heart response of the now broken but accepted/accepting community that received the Lord's good news. Repentance is revealed in the community's embrace of one another. It is there, in that acceptance without condemnation, where the fruit of John's preparatory message blossoms (see Mt. 3:6–8). By looking closer at the cross, particularly the sequence and response found in the **First** and **Second Words**, an informed understanding of repentance and grace under God's in-breaking community may be gained.

In the **First Word** Jesus forgives all. God's forgiveness awaits not mankind's repentance. It is the first step back in a sequence that Adam's race is to follow. In the **Second Word** comes the thief's response. As the thief seeks God's offer through Christ's gift of forgiveness, his action prefigures mankind. His request reflects the requisite attitudes of repentance, which are described in the Sermon on the Mount. The sermon's compilation of Christ's teachings is alternately referred to as the Magna Charta of the Kingdom, or the Manifesto of the King. [10] Christ's teaching sermon to his disciples begins with the Beatitudes. [11] Of the eight, the first four depict a repentant heart. [12]

Table 3-1: Beatitudes of a Repentant Heart

Beatitude	Repentant Attitude
Poor in spirit	Impoverished, Without (God)
Mourn	Broken, Grieve
Meek	Humble, Submissive
Hunger and thirst	Famished, Depleted

So then, where sits repentance in this discussion of forgiveness, grace, and kingdom community? By paying close attention to what Jesus taught his disciples—repent, believe, and the kingdom—we find how these three interrelated instructions message his good news. Repentance acknowledges one's poverty, of a life without God (first beatitude—spiritual poverty). It informs God of one's desire to turn away from the present course of life and turn back to the state of the Edenic garden prior to mankind's fall. Repentance clears the mind and soul of disbelief. Its mournful tears wash away the cloud of confusing ideas that have so long served to separate from God's ways and God's thoughts (second beatitude—mourn). Further, it embraces God's kingdom as the supreme realm, and God's kingship as the supreme king over life. Repentance submits all authority to the Creator-God (third beatitude—meek). Finally, through repentance's intense desire to find Him, God makes himself known. In this way the fourth beatitude (hunger) closes the loop of this "repentance sequence."

Beginning as an individual response to God's forgiveness, repentance leads to a corporate fellowship as its end point. This is the desired heart response of the now-broken but accepted/accepting community that embraces the Lord's good news. Repentance is revealed in the community's worship of God and esteem for one another. It is there, in a fractured and fragmented community, where humanity takes up the cross and discovers … God, who is dwelling in his kingdom. It is in that realm that humanity, already recipients of forgiveness and called by grace, is enabled through the beatitudes of repentant hearts to chart lives characteristic of Christ's kingdom.

SUMMARY

Forgiveness is the first proclamation of the King's kingdom, unlocking entrance into a forgiveness-filled environment in which disciples are expected to act like Mary and John, beholding each other in love, not competing against or rejecting one another or thrashing around in anger and pent-up emotion as did the mockers that morning. They are not to let divisiveness split them into contesting, separate segments. Rather, as citizens of God's community, believers are expected to do the works of light while it is yet day. Soon will come a time of darkness when none can work (see Jn. 9:4).

Christ makes three statements from the cross in the period of light. Each has a distinct audience: the first is a prayer to his Father, the second a conversation with one of the condemned thieves, and the third directed at his mother and John. While each statement can be understood in isolation, it is also true that the three, from a narrative framework, form a cohesive, integrated message. What began as three separate statements has progressively come to be viewed as one united proclamation. In this way forgiveness finds those who accept it, and acceptance leads to a (repentant) community of disciples who are embraced by God and who embrace each other.

From the figurative lens of images and symbols, these three separate utterances are transformed into one coherent, cross sermon that forms the foundation of Jesus Christ's announcement at the start of his public ministry: "The time has come, the kingdom of God is near. Repent and believe the good news!" (Mk. 1:15).

Out of the cross, out of forgiveness, out of repentance in response to grace comes this new community; it is one that exists fundamentally as a forgiven and forgiving nation. Jones writes: "Moreover, the goal of repentance, as with grace, is to lead people into community."[13]

Conclusion: From Words to Conversations to Themes

Theme conclusions, developed from the words spoken in light, are displayed in Table 3-2.

Table 3-2:   Theme Proclamations from the Period of Light

Hours on the cross	First Word & Theme Element	Second Word & Theme Element	Third Word & Theme Element
3	*"Father, forgive them; for they know not what they do."*	*"Truly, I say to you, today you shall be with me in Paradise."*	*"Woman, behold your son!"* *"Behold, your mother!"*
	Forgiven/Forgiving >>>	*Accepted/Accepting >>>*	*Embraced/ Embracing >>>*

SECTION CONCLUSION

In the light of Jesus' three morning words, he speaks not in isolated, separatist thoughts. Keynoted by forgiveness, his words address more than an individual's need to be forgiven. His words, as the Embodiment of the Logos (see Jn. 1:1), are the wisdom of God for living. They break down barriers and divisions, leading to a maturing realization of what constitutes salvation. The Apostle Paul writes:

> But now in Christ Jesus you who once were far away have been brought near through the blood of Christ. For he himself is our peace, who has made the two one and has destroyed the barrier, the dividing wall of hostility. . . . His purpose was to create in himself one new humanity out of the two. . . . For through him we both have access to the Father by one Spirit. (Eph. 2:13–18)

Jesus' narrative from the cross addresses most boldly what God expresses through His own nature: Trinitarian Unity. God's **Third-Word** community is a united kingdom, symbolized in the Eucharistic bread, the manna come down from heaven in incarnational form. Those who gather at his meal table do so not just as saved individuals; rather—linked hand in hand, as were Mary and John—they are united into the saved community of God's kingdom. The twelve disciples are a *figural* community, drawn out of Israel's own past twelve-tribe nation. In Mary's and John's embracement is the fulfillment of God's intended unification of the human race.

In Section III, Jesus continues his kingdom discourse from the cross through announcements from two most usual heralds. Organizationally, content is built on the **Second Word**, which Jesus has not spoken alone. Of his seven statements, it is only the second where the reader hears an audible and interactive conversation—between Jesus and the thief occupying the cross to next to him. This singularity causes the careful Bible reader to pause and ask, Why are the words of a thief permitted alongside the words of the Messiah? Further, the reader must go on to ask, What is the message behind the second statement?

Section III

KINGDOM

From the period of light Jesus issues three statements. They reveal the framework of his gospel: A restored people, now forgiven, emerging out of darkness. Section III expands this as the cross speaks to two aspects of this forming community. Revealed through keywords by the lost but now redeemed thief, disclosure is made. Those words are *thy kingdom* and *remember me*. Section III, therefore, is the biblical story of Christ's kingdom and his covenant people.

Organizationally, this section devotes two chapters to kingdom and two to covenant, alternating each. Historical background is first developed before a more extensive look is presented in the follow-on chapters. The last chapter, on the rule and role of the Holy Spirit, concludes this section on kingdom and covenant.

Chapter 4

KINGDOM ECHOES

Echoes are reflected sound waves contacting distant objects. In a metaphorical sense, the biblical narrative is filled with echoes. The term *echo* is one that Stephen Dempster makes frequent use. For example, in citing Moses' birth story and the ark in which he was hidden, Dempster writes: "Moses' salvation from the water *echoes* backwards and forwards in the text; backward to the salvation of humanity from the judgement of the flood by Noah (Gen. 6–8), and forwards to the Israelite's future escape from the waters of the Red Sea."[1] Echoes assume symmetrical proportions in the theology of T. Desmond Alexander. He writes of the New Jerusalem: "The symmetrical dimensions of the New Jerusalem are most unusual for a city. . . . Undoubtedly, in John's vision the New Jerusalem is portrayed as a temple-city."[2] In this manner an echo might be found emanating between historic Jerusalem and the coming New Jerusalem. Frank Spina writes of the prostitute Rahab, designating her "as a representative of the entire Canaanite population."[3]

Understood through these literary elements, whether echo, symmetry, or representational character, there is an uncontested "voice" in Scripture that propels the immediate narrative along an intended trajectory. This "story voice" is phrased in Deuteronomy as "Hear O Israel." Some Bible versions have a note at Deuteronomy 6:4–9: "In Jewish tradition these verses are known as the Shema, from the first word in the Hebrew ('shema'), which means 'hear.'"

The above illustrates an overwhelming presence of a "metaphorical sound" heard in Scripture. Progressing from a literal and actual command to "Hear (shema) O Israel," such "hearing" includes the softer sounds discerned in literary echoes. Thus, we find Dempster writing, or Alexander, or Spina, all capturing an audible linguistic tone that ranges backward and forward in the Bible. It is this sound, this imperative command to shema, to hear, which provides the basis for the theological underpinnings found in the dialogue contained in the **Second Word.** That word's key thought, "remember me," calls the reader to hear (shema) a scriptural conversation implanted by the Holy Spirit.

> The thief: "Jesus, *remember me* when you come into your *kingdom.*"
>
> Jesus: "I tell you the truth, today you will *be with me* in *paradise.*"

"Remember me" becomes a navigational echo by which today's reader may hear the backward and forward reflection of scriptural sound. The thief's conversation is used to identify two major biblical strands: There is a *Kingdom* strand that Christ is bringing to Earth; and there is a *new covenant* strand. These are featured in the short story retell below.

> The criminals alongside Jesus had been mocking him earlier in the morning but had gone silent under the crucifixion's tortuous pain. Now they were at it again, only this time one relented, and in a moment of remorse turned on the other criminal, challenging him with an understanding that Jesus had done nothing wrong. He did not, unlike themselves, deserve to die. With that rebuke, he suddenly turns to the Messiah and says, "Jesus, remember me when you come into your kingdom."

This request forms a duet with Christ's reply, occurring as parallel phrases. This is observed in the following table.

Table 4-1: Parallel Echoes from the Cross

Thief	remember me	into your kingdom
Parallel Echo		
Jesus	be with me	in paradise

These phrases from the **Second Word** form an analogy in which "remember me" is likened to "be with me," as is "kingdom" to "paradise." **The purpose of** this chapter is to clarify this kingdom analogy. A brief review of ancient Israel's governance leads to the conclusion that Christ's in-breaking reign cannot be equated to Israel's ancient kingdom rule. The significance of this conclusion will be seen as the cross story goes forward in coming chapters.

Whose Kingdom?

Biblical echoes have historical referents, sound chambers emitting symbolic language. In the tradition of ancient Israel, the thief's request is couched in the great hope of the nation: its kingdom land. As the thief nears his death, he grasps hold of Israel's long held desire for security by turning the conversation to kingdom. But whose kingdom does Jesus bring when he refers to paradise? Kingdom is the subject of John Bright's work in a short but comprehensive review of ancient Israel. Bright writes, "The kingdom of Israel is not the Kingdom of God!"[4]

The Bible is filled with the history of ancient Israel and its trending toward and away from kingdom rule. This long story begins in the book of Samuel.

In the historical period known as Judges, the people call for subject rule by a king. They are dismayed, apparently, by the conduct of Samuel's sons. These same sons, worse now, are appointed heirs apparent to replace the aging Samuel in his role as leader-judge over the scattered tribal state of Israel. Using the sons' conduct as pretext, the people make their case before Samuel: "You are old, and your sons do not walk in your ways; now appoint a king to lead us, such as the other nations have." On hearing this, Samuel takes counsel from the LORD: "Listen to all that the people are saying to you; it is not you they have rejected as their king, but me.[5] As they have done from the day I brought them up out of Egypt until this day, forsaking me and serving other gods, so they are doing to you."

At first glance the text reports this as political rebellion—"It is not you they have rejected as king"—yet continuing the passage is tagged spiritual—"but me." The people are not so vested in their desire to have a king over them as they are in seeking their own rule, their own way. Of this Graham A. Cole writes, "But Israel was not content with God's kingship and sought to be like the nations around her even though the Torah warned of such kings and their aggrandizing ways (cf. Deut. 17:14-17 and 1 Sam. 8:1-9)."[6] From a biblical perspective, Israel has been in revolt and rebellion ever since they ousted Samuel's sons (indeed, as the text says, even from their days of liberation coming out of Egypt).

Fast forwarding through Israel's history we come to its consequential ending. It results first in the breakup of the nation into two separate political entities, a northern kingdom set in Samaria, known as Israel, and a southern one in Jerusalem called Judah. Both kingdoms will fall to invaders; first Israel to the Assyrians and then Judah to the Babylonians. The defeats were devastating. As John Bright writes, "The house of Judah fell never to rise again." He describes this "national catastrophe" as a "crisis in theology," in which Israel must "adjust, it must reinterpret itself, or perish."[7]

We understand by this, though Israel was once a kingdom and though Israel was God's chosen nation, Israel was never the kingdom of God. Israel's self-enactment of kingdom status can never be confused with God's enactment of kingdom. Of the former, Israel is just one in a long series of failed kingdoms throughout history. Yet there is a connection between Israel and her kingdom and between God and his. This understanding may be gained from Bright. "God's kingdom, far from being identified with the visible nation Israel, includes only those in Israel who obey him as his servants (Is. 65:13-15), while at the same time it reaches out to include those from all nations who acknowledge him and turn to him. . . . God holds the issues of history; he is a God whose kingdom comes. . . . The Kingdom of God is not man's creation, but God's."[8]

This is not to be confused with David's rule or his role in typology.[9] Graham A. Cole finds that it is only David in whom the Spirit of God finds a meaningful king: "Significantly, no other kings paraded before us in the OT Scriptures are said to be Spirit-enabled to lead and deliver God's people. Not even a reforming king like Josiah is an exception. . . . The rule of God is no longer direct as at Sinai; rather, a designated (anointed) agent will be the vehicle for the divine rule over his people, and ultimately the nations and the cosmos."[10]

The clarifying point is that God's kingdom is a future kingdom, one that cannot be affirmed in Israel's past. It can only be located within Jesus' ministry, of which it is found in abundance.

"The kingdom of God is near. Repent and believe the good news." The kingdom comes, and that Jesus brings it is central to understanding the biblical meta-story. It is Jesus who ushers in God's kingdom, and while he does so throughout the course of his life's work, it falls to the cross where it is established.[11] Of this work Jeremy Treat writes: "The kingdom of God is established on earth by the atoning death of Christ on the cross."[12] In *How God Became King*, N.T. Wright sees kingship as the overriding texture of the biblical story, culminating in

Jesus' crucifixion and resurrection as "the kingdom-bringing event. . . . It therefore announces that God has indeed become king on earth as in heaven."[13]

Summary

Through the life of the Messiah and as an outcome of his cross work comes God's new community. Of its formation, God in his forbearance leaves its proclamation to a thief.[14] This community is the long-awaited kingdom of God. The kingdom of ancient Israel was not that kingdom.

This review was presented to provide historical background for chapter 6 in which kingdom and king are set within the crucifixion narrative. But first an examination of the thief's other key phrase, "remember me," will establish historical footage for covenant.

Chapter 5

COVENANT ECHOES

Table 5-1: Key Word— "Remember me"

Speaker	Location / (Reference)	Statement
Jesus	Upper Room (Lk. 22:19)	This is my body given for you; do this in *remembrance of me.*
Thief	Cross (Lk. 23:42)	Jesus, *remember me* when you come into your kingdom
Jesus	Cross (Lk. 23:43)	Truly I tell you, today you will be with me in paradise.

In the **Second Word**, when Jesus tells the thief he will see him in paradise, the thief's preceding statement is arresting. It should give the careful reader of Scripture pause because it is the only time we hear another voice alongside the Lord's. In the previous chapter, consideration was given to the thief's use of *kingdom*. But also found in his brief request is another key word, *remember*. On the literal surface, his request is an urgent plea from a desperate man not to be forgotten. When examined narratively, however, "remember" echoes an entirely different view. Out of it comes (a) remembrance of a new covenant, and, (b) through that covenant, the remembrance of a promised royal seed who will be a blessing to all the earth.

When the thief speaks of remembrance, narratively he connects to Christ's new covenant. This can be seen in the table above in which his word "remember" finds a parallel to Jesus' use of it at the Last Supper. Tying these two utterances together is the cross. It is at the cross where the thief speaks. Jesus' refrain, given in the Upper Room, holds the cross in anticipation. By linking the thief's "remembrance" to the Last Supper, *the reader encounters a narrative pivot*. One direction goes forward to the cross, where the new covenant is consummated through Jesus' shed blood; the other returns to the past, where covenant history, which points forward to the cross, resides. In this way the command to remember forms a loop consolidating cross and covenant history.

But what is a biblical covenant? Covenant, after all, is not a word that forms part of our daily conversation. Other than certain prescribed legal situations, for most people covenant remains a strange word. **In this chapter** (1) the biblical meaning of covenant is taken up, followed by (2) the purpose of covenant as revealed in the Bible, before (3) concluding with its unmistakable value. This background will later serve when covenant is treated under the rule of the Holy Spirit.

1. Biblical Meaning of Covenant

The Oxford online dictionary defines covenant as "an agreement," for example, from a legal context: "a contract drawn up by deed." It is also, "a clause in a contract." It further distinguishes context, noting of theology: "the covenant between God and Israel in the Old Testament."[1]

William Barclay takes up covenant in his commentary on Hebrews, reminding us that a covenant ordinarily is an agreement between two parties and remains valid as long as both parties adhere to it. A covenant is a legal document, or agreement, rescindable at the failure of one party to keep it. This normal understanding of covenant, however, is not the case with God's covenants: "But God and man do not meet on equal terms. In the biblical sense of a covenant, the whole approach comes from God. Man cannot bargain with God; he cannot argue about the terms of the covenant; he can only accept or reject the offer that God makes."[2]

Sara Koenig writes similarly but expansively:

> People in the ancient world believed that if they did something for the gods, those gods would then do something for them. God, however, changes the equation from a transaction into an unmerited gift. This is a covenant—a relational document between two parties. Different synonyms such as "agreement" or "contract" capture some of what happens in a covenant, but don't quite cover the nuances of the word. Covenants can be conditional, as in the Mosaic covenant, or unconditional, as is this covenant God makes with David."[3]

Barclay likens it to a will: "The supreme example of such an agreement is a will. The conditions of a will are not made on equal terms. They are made entirely by one person, the testator, and the other party cannot alter them but can only accept or refuse the inheritance offered."[4]

Connecting this to the book of Hebrews we read:

> Now where there is a testament it is necessary for the death of the testator to be established; for a testament takes effect only when a death has occurred: it has no force while the testator is still alive. Even the former covenant itself was not inaugurated without blood, for when Moses had told the assembled people all the commandments as set forth in the law, he took the blood of calves, with water, scarlet wool, and marjoram, and sprinkled the law book itself and all the people, saying, "This is the blood of the covenant which God commanded you to keep." (9:16-20 REB)

2. Purpose of Covenant

Pulling these definitions and examples together we find that covenant informs the conditions God establishes to restore the human race. The biblical story reports that humanity has fallen from an original state of intimate union with the Creator. That special status was severed but not destroyed in the garden fall. Once cast as members of God's garden community, Adam's race finds itself banned to an outer world of darkness. Therefore, the central question the Bible asks is one of community: How will humanity return as members of God's family? The answer is found in God's covenants. Observed over time, his many covenants and numerous laws expressed in the Hebrew Bible exhibit a trend line, informing through legal conditions what it will take to reunite with God. However, the answer is not comforting. What it takes is beyond humanity's ability to deliver. That is the uncompromising message coming out of the Great Flood.

In the scriptural narrative leading up to the flood are found condemnatory charges: mankind is guilty of gross and wicked misconduct. It is an evil so horrible it has pained God to the point of near despair (see Gen. 6:6). Left solely to humanity's own devices, there is no solution. Seemingly the only course open is for God to "wipe from the face of the earth the human race," hence completing the promised death sentence (see Gen. 2:17). In other words, due to humanity's infliction of violence, in particular violence that leads to murder, man finds no way of regaining entrance into the garden of peace. Man cannot undue his sentencing. The untold acts of murder and humanity's disposition toward harm and hurt force a coming day of reckoning. The story reveals, once exile from the garden has occurred, that man's behavior has not progressed; indeed, it has worsened. Whereas Cain slew one there is need for Lamech to avenge himself "seventy plus seven times."[5] So staged, the garden's promised "death sentence" looms. It arrives in the form of a watery death.

However, found within that carnage is a God who "remembers" his own promise, a promise of a coming redeemer who will crush the serpent's head.[6] Narratively, Noah fills this role as a supporting actor. Noah is described as "a righteous man, blameless among the people of his time, and he walked with God" (Gen. 6:9). Noah, as a type of the coming Messiah, is man's lifeline; he is the first major figure in God's plan to renew the human race. That God holds this distinction in mind for Noah is revealed in the contrast of the two lines that form out of Adam and Eve. There is a line of "darkness," denoted through Cain. However, when we come to Noah we find he is the tenth generation (i.e., Adam to Noah equals ten generations). As the tenth generation from Adam, Scripture is signaling the start of a new thing.

After the flood, when Noah leaves the ark, God initiates this new thing by first blessing him and his family. This blessing includes reinstatement of the original garden commission: "Be fruitful and increase in number and fill the earth" (9:1). This blessing occurs within the biblical context of covenant:

> I now establish my covenant with you and with your descents after you and with every living creature that was with you. . . . This is the sign of the covenant. . . . I have set my rainbow in the clouds, and it will be the sign of the covenant between me and the earth. . . . Whenever the rainbow appears in the clouds, I will see it and remember the everlasting covenant between God and all living creatures of every kind on the earth. (9:9–17)

This is the first time Scripture speaks of covenant. Importantly, it is an everlasting covenant. Not only is this a covenant of promise ("remembrance;" see text), it is unmerited. This charter is based on God's provisioning and not mankind's ability to save himself from the watery death of the flood. This is understood by Scripture's description of the ark's construction. It is made of three floors: "lower, middle and upper decks" (6:16). Here is symbolic representation; the three decks figuratively reveal the Trinitarian God. The single ark speaks of His unity (see Deut. 6:4). Thus, Noah and his family are saved within the protective sphere of God. They are saved from the destructive waters that would "prevail" over them. Yet in the end, death was halted when the waters peaked and began to "subside." In this way the biblical story alludes to a coming redeemer, a Noah figure, who will protect and prevail until the forces of evil are drained (see 2 Pet. 2:4–10, 3:5–9). This work of judgment and rescue that Peter addresses, recalling the ark, is based on the cross work of the Messiah and in the promised blessings described in the last chapter of Peter's second *epistle* (3:10–18). Further, it is seen in the symbolism described by Paul when he writes of baptism (see Ro. 6:1–5).

Abram's Covenant of Blessing

As devastating as the deluge was, evil remained. It will take more than an ark and a watery grave to reverse course. It will take another covenant to illumine how God is moving in the course of human history. If story importance can be gauged by story length, then Noah's story is the dominant one after man leaves the garden. In length it comprises four chapters (6 to 9). But it pales when placed next to Abraham's life, which spans the next dozen (12 to 24). The story of Abraham is a story of covenant relationship. It is first encountered at the outset of chapter 12 when God "calls" Abram. In that calling is a promise that later becomes a covenant (see Gen. 15 and 17). Therefore, the three events of chapters 12, 15, and 17 may be referred to as God's covenant promise to Abraham and, through him, to mankind.

The promise to Abraham differs from the one given after the flood, which broadly includes all life and the earth itself. Now covenant focuses specifically on mankind. Importantly, it holds three aspects. They are God's promises to provide descendants, land, and blessings. All three are primary to achieving God's special project to restore and redeem Adam's race.

Covenant to Abram

Genesis 12 records:

> I will make you into a great nation
>
> and I will *bless* you;
>
> I will make your name great,
>
> and you will be a *blessing.*
>
> I will *bless* those who *bless* you,
>
> and whoever curses you I will curse;
>
> And all peoples on earth
>
> will be *blessed* through you. (12:2–3, emphasis added)

The features found in this covenant promise are significant. Of Abram's line, it will form into a future "great nation."[7] Abraham prophetically portends the renewing of God's community. More so, God's blessings will follow this line. In particular, out of this lineage will come one by whom all peoples on Earth will be blessed. Thomas Schreiner reminds readers of this, linking Abraham to a coming kingly line: "Blessings for the world would come from a royal figure."[8]

A third element of Abraham's promise is found in God's call. That call contains land and so he commands, go "to the land I will show you" (12:1). When the story advances to the fifteenth chapter, and again in the seventeenth, land forms an essential part of this now formed three-fold covenant: "to give you this land to take possession of it" (15:7). This is reaffirmed in the seventeenth chapter when God promises: "The whole land of Canaan, where you now reside as a foreigner, I will give as an everlasting possession to you and your descendants" (17:8). Further, in this covenant is a promise, spoken of Sarah, that "kings . . . will come from her" (17:16).

God's call to Abraham is not an isolated event in the long story of Old Testament history. It is intimately connected to the narrative that God is unfolding, a story that directly ties Eden, the fall, and the separation of two lines; hence it joins the flood, Noah's covenant, and now Abraham's covenant.[9] Seen holistically, all these events anticipate God's lavish gift of reunification with his image bearers. In Abraham's call and covenant promises is the act of the human race's redemption. It is echoed in Jesus' response to the thief's remembrance cry when the Lord says, "Today you will be with me in paradise."

This is God's answer to the question of how he will reacquire the race that was stolen out of the garden by the serpent. God responds by promising, through the legal might of his word, what he will do. Covenants, therefore, are not only God's promises, they are his guarantee. They are his word. As demonstrated in the flood story, the end result is one solely provided by God. Mankind stands condemned; indeed, humanity is powerless to overcome wrongdoing. But through the ark God figuratively navigates the hold darkness and death have on humanity. In Christ's new covenant promise, the crisis is fully rectified. As Schreiner summarizes: "The promises of land, seed, and universal blessing were covenant promises."[10]

3. Priceless Value of New Covenant

This talk of covenants is more than mysticism. It is also more than legal technicalities. The importance—indeed the absolute necessity of the new covenant—rises to the level of an imperative. The flood demonstrates this need: man cannot save himself from (the watery) death.

As for the new covenant's meaning: priceless. In economic terms, the covenant brought by the Messiah exceeds all the capital in the world. Jesus rhetorically asks, "For what will it profit a man if he gains the whole world and forfeits his soul?" (Mt. 16:26 NASB). The writer of Hebrews was correct to liken it to a will. As a will, it goes into effect on the death of the testator. Thus the phrase, "This cup is the new covenant given for you in my blood, which is poured out for you," signals the coming death of Jesus. Through this means, that is the cross, the will is activated. The terms of the will, what it offers and bequests, cannot be put aside. The will is a document of riches to those who are listed as heirs, treasures stored up in heaven. First, it permits entrance into the now come kingdom, and second, on an heir's death, entrance into paradise. Further, this covenant is guaranteed. The surety being God's own word. There can be no greater assurance than that (see Jer. 33:19–22). God puts his entire honor, his entire being as pledge. For God to fail to honor the conditions of this new covenant would be for God to cease being God. The new covenant is the greatest offer in man's history. And it is free. Its only requirement is to be claimed by its heirs.

Summary

The crucifixion defines and implements the new covenant. By it, God demonstrates his love for humanity. Since only God can navigate the watery death, the new covenant is a priceless inheritance.

Narratively the story of the flood shows mankind on the verge of being swept away. But the ark shows God's outreached hand of unmerited favor. Through the representational figures of Noah and his family, a man who is "blameless and walks with God," is the symbolic foreshadowing of a mighty savior and his community. It is this One, the story later reveals, who comes forth out of God's covenant to Abraham; it is this One who holds the title King. This is the royal figure who, on the cross, is able to withstand the prevailing and previously foreshadowed flood of death. Through cross and covenant, therefore, as with ark and Noah, God holds forth the instrument of blessing to all who enter within the favor of his covenant relationship. The **Second Word**, therefore, echoes condemned mankind's plea to be remembered. God answers back through covenants. He says, through the voice of his son, "Do this in remembrance of me."

In the next chapter we return to kingdom. However, this time kingdom is informed not by the thief but by the two major persons at Christ's trial. On one hand is Pilate, the prosecutor; across from him stands Jesus, the defendant. Yet, in a role reversal, it is Jesus who commands the trial, and through his defense he makes known to Pilate what the governor doesn't understand: the nature and purpose of God's kingdom.

Chapter 6

OF KINGDOM COME

In the preceding chapters, kingdom and covenant were disclosed in the cross conversation. This chapter resumes examination of kingdom, but from a different herald. No longer will the thief's voice be heard; now the informant shifts to the highest Roman official in the region: Pilate. This makes for a confrontation between the "man from Rome" and the "man from above" as the two are brought center stage during the crucifixion trial. Our listening purpose is to understand how charges and trial statements reveal the coming kingdom from above. **In this chapter** two questions act as guide: (1) What is the *nature* of the *Third Word's* coming kingdom? and (2) What is its *purpose*? The crucifixion trial, convened by Pilate at the duress of the Jewish leadership, reveals two aspects of its nature: (a) it is an invisible kingdom, and (b) it is a kingdom of truth. Both exceed Pilate's comprehension.

1. The Nature of the Coming Kingdom

Vicariously we sit in Pilate's courtroom listening as he questions Jesus. We are alert for key phrases about the nature of the kingdom. Once identified, we will expand understanding of kingdom and then proceed to its purpose. The story retell below is adapted from the trial narratives in John 18 and 19 (RSV).

The Trial: Pilate and Jesus

After the temple guards take Jesus captive in the garden of Gethsemane, he is brought before the chief priests and the Sanhedrin and subjected to an all-night grilling, a mixture of extreme insults and physical abuse. In the early morning hours, he is transferred to Roman authority and comes before the governor.

Pilate is not impressed by local Jewish quarrels over laws and customs. He immediately challenges the reason for such an intrusion: "What accusation do you bring against this man?" Affronted, the chief priests and teachers of the law respond they would not waste the governor's time if the man Jesus were not a criminal. Prepared for the governor's rebuke, the Jews seek to circumvent Pilate's effort to rid his office of responsibility for this trial. Their tactic forces the issue to a level Pilate cannot easily dismiss. He asks Jesus, "Are you the King of the Jews?" Jesus deflects this question back on Pilate: "Do you say this of your own accord, or did others say it to you about me?"

Pilate is incensed that a commoner would dare challenge his authority. He retorts angrily, "Am I a Jew? Your own nation and the chief priests have handed you over to me. What have you done?" Jesus ignores Pilate's question.[1] Assuming command of the trial he speaks to the issue of royal governance: "My kingship is not of this world; if it were of this world, my servants would fight." Pilate infers from this the kingship of Christ. Still, he is taken aback by the thought. He rhetorically asks: "So you are a king?" This line of questioning is dangerous for Pilate. He cannot permit a king who might rival the emperor of Rome. If Pilate finds Jesus to be a king he will have no choice but to condemn him to death, which he is reluctant to do.

Jesus continues to hold Pilate accountable: "You say that I am a king. For this I was born, and for this I have come into the world, to bear witness to the truth." Astounded by the almost mystical turn the trial takes, Pilate is left to mutter, "What is truth?" Yet he is relieved; Jesus poses no threat to Rome. After all, what threat is a mystic maniac whose kingdom is of another world? Clearly the man is just another in a sordid and very long line of Jewish crackpots. Most wax fervent against Roman authority and are easily dispatched. Crucifixion for such lot is almost too good. Not so with this itinerant rabbi. His other-world talk poses no threat. Turing to the Jews he proclaims, "I find no crime in him."

The Jews are enraged. They mean to have Jesus crucified, and they press their demand on Pilate. Pilate offers a prisoner release hoping to gain their appeasement. But this strategy fails. Pilate then hands Jesus over to his soldiers who mercilessly brutalize and mock him. Savaged, Pilate figures the man can now be returned to the Jews, leaving himself clear of any complaints the chief priests might bring against him. But it will not do. On seeing Jesus clad in purple and wearing a crown of thorns, the chief priests and other leading men storm: "Crucify him, crucify him!" Pilate is backed into a legal corner as the Jews continue their rant: "We have a law, and by that law he ought to die, because he claimed to be the Son of God." Visibly shaken, Pilate retreats into the palace to once again inquire of Jesus from whence he hails. Finding him unresponsive Pilate threatens, "Do you not know that I have power to release you or crucify you?" Unfazed, Jesus speaks directly: "You would have no power over me unless it had been given you from above."

Pilate is desperate to release Jesus, but a gathering crowd in the outside courtyard increases pressure to heed the religious leaders' position. Loud shouts threaten Pilate's resolve: "If you release this man, you are not Caesar's friend." Shaken by this reference to Rome, Pilate brings Jesus before the throng. John notes in his Gospel a cryptic reference: "It was about the sixth hour."[2] Pilate announces, "Here is your King." But the crowd is after blood. Pilate questions: "Shall I crucify your King?" The chief priests, sensing they have Pilate cornered, retort: "We have no king but Caesar." Pilate is checkmated; Jesus' fate is sealed, and the trial comes to an end.[3]

1-A. Kingdom Nature: 'From Another World'

In retelling the crucifixion trial, two key phrases arise: (a) *My kingship is not of this world,*" and (b) *"What is truth?"* A review of dialogue between Pilate and Jesus bears an unmistakable fact: Jesus is a king whose kingdom is "from another world" (Jn. 18:36). That much is certain. It is also unexpected. It is not what the worshipping, welcoming crowd thought as Jesus thronged his way to Jerusalem just a week prior. Contained in those adulations were the hopes of the past, the hopes of David's kingship and kingdom being reborn (see Mt. 21:5, 9). Many are sure Jesus is the long sought "Prophet" (Jn. 1:25). But in front of those celebrants, Jesus does not declare what he now states to a Roman governor: "My kingdom is not of this world" (18:36). How puzzled is Pilate. What kind of kingdom is this?

Kingdoms have three things in common: land, a ruler, and people over whom reign is established. Jesus earmarks all three within the spiritual context of his reply: His kingdom's realm is "not of this world." By saying this, Jesus points back to the beginning, to a garden where God has a kingdom. The Garden of Eden is a prototype; it may be seen as a microcosm of God's coming kingdom on Earth. T. Desmond Alexander describes Adam and Eve as likely being priests whose charge was to extend the boundaries of Eden throughout the "garden planet" earth. He likens this outward spreading by the First Couple as a "blueprint for the created world."[4]

Eden, as the locus of God's kingdom on Earth, is perceived to fulfill the three kingdom requirements: It contains land (the garden), it has a ruler (God), and it has subjects (Adam and Eve) over whom God reigns. But within his province he intends to make them his servants, or priest-kings, over his creation. Yet something has gone very wrong. The kingdom comes under assault, the devil attacks through a henchman (the snake), and the kingdom subjects are carried away. In the defeat of Adam and Eve, God's kingdom is left in ruins. Cole notes, "Ruptures now exist between God and humanity, humans and humans, humans and the environment."[5]

Adam and Eve, then, were to have been the subject rulers of the Edenic kingdom, serving in the absence of God. They were to have served God in the garden and, eventually, to have advanced this micro kingdom far beyond its limited boundaries, expanding it throughout planet Earth. Now, however, put outside the garden they face the "other world." Not the other world of which Christ speaks, but the other world that has become the captive world of Satan, a captive place in which they must dwell. It soon becomes a world of violence, where rule is by the strongest and reign supported by terror, attributes of the devil. Over time, evil kingdoms arise; Rome is one.

But the kingdom of Christ is not like that other world, the world that has emerged outside of Eden's gates. The kingdom of God comes in gentleness and meekness. Its king comes riding on a foal of a donkey. Here is a king whose creed consists of blessings and beatitudes, favoring those of spiritual poverty—for to such belong "the kingdom of heaven." It is a kingdom where citizens mourn and are comforted, where the meek inherit the earth, and those who hunger and thirst do so not so much for food as for the manna of kingdom truth. This is a kingdom whose citizenship rests on a new birth of the spirit. Here is an invisible kingdom, a kingdom of the Spirit of God. Thus, Jesus can say to a woman sitting at a well in Samaria, whom he encounters also at the sixth hour: "Yet a time is coming and has now come when the true worshipers will worship the Father in the Spirit and in truth, for they are the kind of worshipers the Father seeks" (Jn. 4:23). In that Samarian statement, as in his declaration to Pilate, and as "in the beginning" is a reoccurring echo: The kingdom of God is one of spirit and truth.

This kingdom from another world is not what Pilate expects when the Jews bring Jesus before him. Nor is it a kingdom that many expect in the vast crowds that have come to hear and see Jesus. Surprisingly, it is not a kingdom where "their" messiah would reign in the power and might of a David and therefore truly bring in the "kingdom of Israel." This kingdom is not a replay of ancient lore, nor is it a powerhouse to contest and defeat Rome. It is a strange kingdom; it is a kingdom not of this world.

This kingdom is not ruled by Rome, or occupied by those on the left or right, nor is it commanded by centrists. It is not possessed by one country; it is not American, European, or Asian. It is a kingdom whose base are citizens of the cross, those who are the forgiven and the forgiving; having themselves been forgiven and forgiven and forgiven (see Mt. 18:21–22).

1-B. Kingdom Nature: A Kingdom of Truth

> Pilate rhetorically concludes, "You are a king, then!" This is followed by Jesus' affirmation: "You are right in saying I am a king." Confused, Pilate retorts: "What is truth?" He asks because Jesus not only affirms kingship but states his kingdom is a kingdom of truth (see Jn. 18:37–38).

A "kingdom of truth" is the second great descriptor revealed in the conversation between Jesus and Pilate. Here stands Pilate, at the trial of Jesus, yet it is Jesus who uses the trial to make known that there is a far greater kingdom than Rome's. A far greater emperor than Caesar now stands before Pilate. He tells Pilate the kingdom of God is both invisible and a kingdom of truth.

All through the Jesus' ministry he uses a refrain that rings with this reality. John captures it in his Gospel as he writes, "I tell you the truth" quoting Christ in his conversation with Nicodemus. Or in chapter 8, speaking of Abraham's descendants, and then again in chapter 10 when Jesus likens himself to a shepherd does John employs this phrase. Matthew places "I tell you the truth" in the parable of the fig tree (see Mt. 21:21). Jesus uses the contrasting phrase, "You have heard ... but I tell you" several times in the Sermon on the Mount, implying what he now speaks is the truth (see 5:18–28). More to the point, Jesus uses it in reference to himself, stating, "I am the way and the truth and the life." The kingdom Jesus acknowledges to Pilate is a kingdom of spirit and truth. It is a kingdom that "does not come visibly." Rather, it is a kingdom "within you" (see Lk. 17:20–21).

Of the King who rules over this kingdom, John describes as the "only Son, who came from the Father, full of grace and truth." The kingdom Jesus ushers in is a kingdom that reflects his glory and personage. It is also a kingdom that finds an unholy kingdom abiding on Earth, that which was co-opted by Satan and his forces of evil.[6] Jesus himself describes that evil kingdom when he speaks of Satan as the "father of lies"—in direct opposition to his kingdom of truth.

Confronted by Pilate, Jesus pits his coming and now in-breaking kingdom against the representational kingdom of evil: Rome. This context is made known as Jesus declares his kingdom to be a kingdom of truth. Pilate has no reply. He can only ask, "What is truth?" Rome, as representational of humanity's governments, knows not nor understands such a statement. Rome understands a government of destruction; it is familiar with lies and intrigue, with rebellion and political assassinations. But rule by truth is as foreign a concept to Rome and Pilate as is the thought that a kingdom could be "of another world."

This cross conversation with Pilate is similar to one Jesus held with a group of Pharisees (see Jn. 8:31-59). In that exchange Jesus declares that he is not, as are the Pharisees, from below; that is, from Earth. Jesus is from above, that is, heaven. Jesus declares that his subjects, his disciples, are free because they embrace truth. They are not like those who are held captive by untruth. Those who reject God's truth belong to Satan, the "father of lies," and are enlisted in his kingdom as his subjects. [7]

As a result of the crucifixion hearing we find Pilate, contrary to all expectations, is the one on trial. By extension, Rome and evil are held accountable to the Court of Truth. Further, this Roman governor ironically finds himself in the strange position where, as we saw with the thief, he holds a conversation that ends up leading to theological revelation. In Pilate's case, it discloses the kingship of Christ and the nature of his kingdom. That kingdom is from another world, yet, through the symbols present, it appears to be one that is now invading the world of man and the realm of evil.

2. The Purpose of the Kingdom

Having examined the nature of the kingdom we turn to its purpose. To do this it is necessary to contextualize kingdom by going back to "the beginning." The importance of seeing Christ's kingdom as one of truth, thus light, is that it stands in direct contrast to Satan's false realm, which is darkness. When the devil caused a split in Eden's proto-kingdom by his victory over Adam and Eve, he achieved a break-away rebellion. In co-opting the realm of God, he subjugated Earth's inhabitants to his rule and ways. Since then God's forces have been striking blows on the gates of that principality, but it is only by means of the cross that the gates of darkness fall. Using the metaphor of captivity and liberation, this battle transpires within the redemptive/restorative biblical narrative. Old Testament scholars are apt to see in the exodus a type of the coming battle for redemptive liberation that occurs on the cross. By this means the cross is foreshadowed through Israel's escape from Pharaoh, the "king of Egypt." This allusion leads to the *new exodus*. Here Jeremy Treat is helpful, writing of Canaan's land:

> The place of land in the kingdom of God is clearly evident in
> the pattern of redemption set forth in the exodus. . . . God
> as king might deliver his people again through a *new* exodus,

resulting not only in a new land but in a new heavens and new earth.[8]

Bright also takes up the theme of a new exodus. He draws a foreshadowing parallel between Moses and Christ, between old and new covenants, and between escape from Egyptian bondage into liberation from sin and death:

> If redemption is to be a new exodus, must there not be a new Moses to lead it? If it is to involve a new Covenant, does it not need a new Moses to give it? Partly, however, the hope seems to have been nurtured by the prophecy in Deut. 18:15-19, where a prophet "like" Moses is promised. In any case, there was abroad in the time of Jesus a lively hope for "the prophet" (e.g., John 1:21, 25), whose coming would signal the redemption of his people.[9]

In this big picture of biblical theology, Israel's history provides a foreshadowing glance at the coming redemption God provides. The actual enslavement of the patriarchal tribes by the pharaohs is analogous to the captivity of mankind at the hands of the devil. In the Passover event and subsequent escape and liberation into a land of promise is found the foreshadowing 'exodus' of those redeemed by Christ. This "second exodus" is the New Exodus. Therefore, it is on the cross where life, held captive by death, wins its release from the curse of the garden judgment (see Gen. 3:14–19). From the cross comes a reverberating echo: Exodus and New Exodus. This is depicted in Table 6-1. In this way exodus may be understood to form an analogy:

Passover is to Exodus

as

Cross is to New Exodus.

Table 6-1:   Exodus and New Exodus

Exodus Escape from Bondage	New Exodus: Release from Captivity
"Select the animals ... slaughter the Passover lamb ... dip it into the blood ... put some on the top and on both sides of the doorframe." (Ex. 12:21-22)	"Look the Lamb of God, who takes away the sin of the world!" (Jn. 1:29)
"At midnight the LORD struck down all the firstborn in Egypt, ... to the firstborn of the prisoner, who was in the dungeon, and the firstborn of all the livestock." (Ex. 12:29)	"At noon, darkness came over the whole land ... With a loud cry, Jesus breathed his last." (Mk. 15:33–37)
"After 430 years, to the very day, all the LORD'S divisions left Egypt." (Ex. 12:41)	"When he ascended on High, He led captive a host of captives." (Eph. 4:8 NASB)

The purpose of the coming and now in-breaking kingdom of God is discovered in this foreshadowing act of Exodus and the symmetrical end game of Christ's new exodus. By it the Messianic King restores man to his original role as God's servant-rulers and provides for his redemption. In this way the last command of the Messiah King—"Go into all the world and make disciples"—may be likened to the garden task, "Be fruitful and multiply." While be fruitful and multiply is understood within a biological context, there is a theological overtone that takes precedence. The command to multiply is ultimately the king's directive to push outward from the garden into the "other world garden" of Earth. It is in this outward pushing that Jesus' final command, namely the Great Commission, may be found: "Therefore go and make disciples of all nations, baptizing them in the name of the Father and of the Son and of the Holy Spirit" (Mt. 28:19).

In the Great Commission, therefore, is heard the garden echo of the "great dominion command" (see Gen. 1:26–28). Mankind, according to Stephen Dempster, "being made in the image of God signifies humans exercising dominion as God's vicegerents of creation."[10] In other words, humanity visibly represents and serves the invisible God of creation. Again Dempster:

> Humanity is uniquely related to both God and the created order. Furthermore, these terms are relational and referential: humans are referential creatures; their being automatically signifies God. Since they are like God, they are best suited for a unique relationship to God, and this means that they also have a unique relation to their natural environment.[11]

Restored mankind, through the authority of the resurrected Christ, is to take the Great Commission throughout the garden planet making His name known. This fulfills the foreshadowing of the First Couple's charge "to be fruitful and multiply."

Jesus' command is further enhanced when the language of image is placed alongside it. Mathew records, "Then the eleven disciples went to Galilee, the mountain where Jesus had told them to go" (Mt. 28:16). Galilee is a key word that locates and anchors Jesus' ministry as one to the world, not just to the Jews. This connection is seen when Jesus is a young child and God dispatches an angel to visit Joseph in a dream. Joseph is commanded to take Mary and the child Jesus and "withdrew to the district of Galilee" (2:22). This he did and thus Jesus comes to live in Nazareth. That location is central to the great biblical motif of light and darkness that is painted by the great prophet Isaiah:

> Land of Zebulun and land of Naphtali,
> the Way of the Sea, beyond the Jordan,

Galilee of the Gentiles—

the people living in darkness

have seen a great light;

on those living in the land of the shadow of death

a light has dawned. (Mt. 4:15–16)

Conclusion and Summary

Matthew connects the last command of Jesus (go into the world) with the beginning of his ministry (see 4:12); it will be a ministry that brings light to all people in darkness. Isaiah's announcement sights all "Galileans" who dwell in darkness. By execution of the Lord's final command, God's kingdom spreads out into the garden planet. Isaiah further develops this idea with his reference to the Jordan ("the Way to the Sea, beyond the Jordan"). As a river, the Jordan figuratively evokes a spiritual "water image" of scriptural salvation. Further, it serves as a *spiritual boundary* between the "wilderness land" on one side and the "promised land" on the other.

Yet this royal task is not without risk. By designating the Jordan as the pathway to the sea, the sea figuratively presents a danger to those who live near it. Casting the sea as an abode of evil is noted in the book of Revelation: "The dragon stood on the shore of the sea. And I saw a beast coming out of the sea" (13:1). Combined to include Isaiah's prophecy, the sea alludes to a place of grave danger and darkness. N. T. Wright notes: "The sea has become a dark, fearsome, threatening place from which evil emerges, threatening God's people."[12]

The coming and now-being-established kingdom, which is an invisible realm of truth and light, brings God's reign and rule to the nations. This was God's covenant promise to Abraham, a promise whose trajectory is guided by the fulfillment of "blessings to all" (see Gen. 12:1-3). Abraham's blessing is contained in Isaiah's descriptive writing above. Thus, the Messiah comes to a darkened land to bless its captive peoples with the presence of his light. It is that work which the Son, who is the

Light of the world, completes. Further, that work is now given over to his restored servant-rulers. God's original command to "have dominion" and "be fruitful and multiply" finds fulfillment in Jesus' echo-commission to take his authority and make known the name of God to all peoples of the garden planet.

But kingdom does not stand alone; it cannot be separated from the new covenant that is inaugurated at the Passover meal. In the coming chapter we return to covenant. In chapter 7 we follow Jesus and his disciples as they ascend the road to Jerusalem, heading for his final Passover. Along the way a dispute arises. While featured in the *Synoptic* Gospels, by the time we arrive at John's Gospel the story is merged with Christ's foot washing. Here we are faced with a mystery—Why does John leave out of his Gospel mention of the new covenant? —and a question—How does God rule his newly established kingdom? In the coming chapter we will see how these two inquiries combine to further deeper understanding of the **Second** and the **Third Words**.

Chapter 7

A Covenant of Understanding

Indeed, the divine covenants are the means
by which God's rule is established.[1]

In previous chapters, the word "remember," spoken by Jesus and the thief, provided a connection between the Last Supper and Calvary. *Remember* is a key word in Scripture. That word recalls how God is always remembering his covenant commitment to humanity. This was seen in God's promise to Noah in which a sign of remembrance (the rainbow) was placed in the sky. Echoing it is the covenant sign of remembrance signified in the bread and wine instituted by Jesus at the last supper. Moreover, in Exodus we read how God remembered the cries of his people that were in bondage to Pharaoh, which was shown to be an allusion to Adam's race taken captive by the serpent in the garden. In response, God sent a deliverer, Moses, who himself is an allusion to Christ, the "new Moses." All of this "remembrance" is part of a long trending narrative pivot, the focal point being the cross and the thief's **Second Word**. It is an echo that sends readers back to covenant history and its forward rebound in the Upper Room.

In this chapter, the *question of how God rules*—that is, how believers are governed and are to govern in Christ's newly arrived but still invisible kingdom—will be examined through the following process:

1. We begin with a contentious dispute among the disciples concerning greatness. From there its progression is followed through the synoptic narratives to the Upper Room and establishment of the new covenant.

2. John's Gospel, in connection with Luke's, will be most helpful in constructing meaning around this greatness dispute.

3. Arriving at John's Gospel, the mystery of why John omits the symbolic Last Supper will be unlocked (Table 7-1). In its solution comes an answer to how God rules his new covenant kingdom.

The following table sets the stage for this examination on ruling.

Table 7-1:   Gospel Accounts of the New Covenant

Gospel	Summation	Speaks to
Mt. 26:17–30	New Covenant is established	Holy Eucharist (bread and wine)
Mk. 14:12–26	New Covenant is established	Holy Eucharist (bread and wine)
Lk. 22:7–38	New Covenant is established	Holy Eucharist (bread and wine)
Jn. 13:1–30	New Covenant not mentioned	Foot washing

A surprising thing happens when a reader comes to Jesus' final Passover meal (in Christian traditions the Last Supper). The synoptic writers all address the new covenant. Yet John, mysteriously, doesn't speak of it. In his presentation of Jesus' final meal, which John begins by referring to as the "Passover Festival" (13:1) and "the evening meal" (13:2), ironically John doesn't include the symbolic bread and wine. Instead, he attends to how Jesus washes his disciples' feet prior to launching into a lengthy discourse (the farewell address), before concluding the evening—as do Matthew, Mark, and Luke—with the journey to the garden of Gethsemane. The story of why John omits this ceremony, however, may be traced to the disciples as they accompany Jesus on the road up to Jerusalem.

1. A Contentious Conversation: Building Background

An intriguing dispute broke out among the disciples as they journeyed with Jesus on the road *up to Jerusalem*. By using the geographically accurate descriptor "up to Jerusalem," Matthew and Mark figuratively associate this dispute with the cross (on which Jesus will soon be lifted up). Further fueling this association on "the way up" is a background in which Jesus has just announced he will suffer and die, and then most amazingly, be raised up on the third day: "They will condemn him to death ... to be mocked and flogged and crucified. On the third day he will be raised to life" (Mt. 20:17-19).

The story retell below is adapted from Matthew 20, Mark 10, and Luke 9.

> Once again he said it. How many times had he said this before, and how many times did we not get it? This time we were all walking up the road to Jerusalem, along a very dusty portion (what's not dusty on that pathway?), and while it wasn't all that hot it was a sweaty, grimy walk. I guess my mind was wandering when suddenly the Master paused. He began very plainly to tell what was going to soon happen. He was going to be delivered up to the chief priests and be condemned to death. I was fatigued but I know I heard that part. You can't miss hearing when someone starts talking about his coming death. Even though Jesus was speaking in third person, there was no question he was speaking of himself.

As suddenly as he said this, he was off again, striding ever so resolutely as the road steepened. His pace spread us out a bit, but amazingly the Zebedee brothers' mother came right up to him. There she knelt on the hard surface and made the most astounding request: "Grant that one of these two sons of mine may sit at your right and the other your left in your kingdom."

Well, that evening when we were settling down for the night you can bet that conversation went around the group! I'm sorry to say that the reaction was more about the mother's request than how Jesus responded to it. There was some recall, however, that he talked about the way the Gentiles ruled over everyone—of course, he was speaking of the Romans. I kind of wondered if he wasn't going to say something new, like he was going to (finally) accept the crown that all the crowds wanted him to wear and then lead a revolt against the emperor. But that wouldn't really be him. He talked about kingdom service and being last instead of first and serving instead of receiving. I recall his words: "The Son of Man did not come to be served but to serve."

The crux of this dispute is summarized in the following table.

Table 7-2:   Dispute Stories in Synoptic Gospels

Story Detail	Mt. 20:20–28	Mk. 10:32–45	Lk. 9:46–48
Scene	Road up to Jerusalem	Road up to Jerusalem	Not specified; a field below a mountain (?)
Background	Jesus just revealed his coming crucifixion and resurrection.	Jesus just revealed his coming crucifixion and resurrection.	Day following the Transfiguration

Action	A dispute arose over a request to sit on the right and left of Jesus in his kingdom.	A dispute arose over a request to sit on the right and left of Jesus in his glory.	A dispute arose over which of the Twelve was considered the greatest.
Key Line	"Whoever wants to become great among you must be your servant."	"Whoever wants to become great among you must be your servant."	"For it is the one who is least among you all who is the greatest."

Matthew and Mark appear to be telling the same account. However, when comparing Luke's Gospel, the background yields a different location and a different occasion. What is significant, though, is the tendency of the disciples to argue about greatness and positions of honor. Regardless of the number of times the disciples have this argument, Luke presents it at least one more time.[2] That is displayed below, along with the inclusion of foot washing, where in verse 16 John incorporates language used in Luke 22:26 (see also Lk. 9:46-48).

Table 7-3:   Dispute in the Upper Room

Story Detail	Luke 22:24-30	John 13:2-17
Scene	Upper Room	Upper Room
Background	Jesus has just introduced the ceremony of remembrance (i.e., Holy Eucharist).	Jesus has just washed the feet of his disciples.

Action	A dispute arose as to which disciple was considered to be the greatest.	Jesus washes the feet of his disciples.
Key Line	"But I am among you as one who serves."	"You also should wash one another's feet. I have set you an example."

If not for Luke, this dispute story wouldn't figure so prominently into John's mystery of why he neglects to include the ceremony of remembrance in his Gospel. It is in the Upper Room where John's foot-washing story and Luke's dispute story come into play. In Luke's second telling of the story, the setting is no longer a field following the previous day's transfiguration atop a mountain, rather it is Jerusalem and the Upper Room. More so, "the hour has come," so the setting finds the disciples reclining around a Passover meal-table. Richard Foster has an interesting way of telling what happens next:

> Gathered at the Passover feast, the disciples were keenly aware that someone needed to wash the other's feet. The problem was that the only people who washed feet were the least. So there they sat, feet caked with dirt. It was such a sore point that they were not even going to talk about it. No one wanted to be considered the least. Then Jesus took a towel and a basin and redefined greatness.[3]

2. John's Replacement Story

As mentioned at the start of this chapter, John's narrative does not contain the inauguration of the new covenant. He makes no mention of bread or wine as symbols, nor does he use the term new covenant. Rather, John includes the foot washing story described by Foster above. What is important, however, is that John's foot washing contains some of the dialogue found in Luke's dispute story. This connection permits an approximate chronological merger of these two Passover meal stories. Luke's version permits the careful reader to sequence the events in John's presentation.[4] Inferentially, John's foot washing can be located by following Luke's sequence as coming near Jesus' presentation of bread and wine (Luke 22:19–20). John inserts the story of foot washing where the sharing of bread and wine takes place. Since John does not mention the bread and the wine, the foot washing story acts *to replace it.*

The striking omission of the bread and wine from John's Gospel evokes questions of why. Answers will be found in the relational side of John's Gospel rather than within a framework of symbols. While this may also seem strange, given John's preference for double meaning, when the stylistic side of John's writing is stripped away, what remains is a relational core (see 1 Jn. 1:3–4). With this as background we turn now to a story retell of foot washing from John 2:12–17.

For five days the disciples trudge back and forth between Bethany, the hill called the Mount of Olives, and Jerusalem.[5] Jesus spends most of his time in and around the temple. That is risky, especially after he literally threw out the money changers.[6] What a sight that was! But it was not quite the whip lashing folklore made of it over time. Still, he did so explode with righteous anger.

The tables were flipped and coins flew in all directions. Angry voices were heard as everyone scrambled after rolling coins. There was shoving and pushing and plenty of whip cracking, but the sound stung mainly the air as animals crashed away; no one was actually whipped. It looked like a zoo struck by powerful winds. Animals became untethered and doves escaped. It was the zaniest atmosphere ever seen in the outer courtyard of the temple.[6]

That incident put more tension into the week than almost anything. If the temple bosses had their way, they would have dispatched a squad of guards and arrested Jesus on the spot. But how could they? Their spies reported enormous throngs welcoming Jesus into Jerusalem. Shouts of king and hosanna, and every kind of praise rang through the air. No, this year's festival wasn't safe. But now the week was nearly over, and the Twelve, with Jesus, had made their way to a special Upper Room, which mysteriously had been previously arranged.

But now, all were tired and dusty from the week, their feet especially worn by the long journey, not just from walking to Jerusalem, but from three years of travel. And there was tension of what the chief priests might do, and a hoped-for coming announcement: Would Jesus finally stake claim as the people's king? Would he acknowledge the crowds and grant their populous wish? Would he lead this embattled and conquered nation to revolt against Rome and throw off its rotted rule?

Yet as evening neared, and they ascended to the Upper Room, it was good just to get away and finally recline around a table. Not just any table, but the meal table of the Passover Supper. But even then, there still remained unresolved tensions, some stemming from an incident on the way up to Jerusalem. That one produced quite a buzz among the disciples. So, sitting around the table, waiting for the meal, it was easy to recall the outrageous demand of the Zebedee brothers. They had the nerve to ask to be first—to be honored by being permitted to sit at the right and left of Jesus when he came into his kingdom.

Sitting around the table, the idea of greater and lesser took on an uncomfortable meaning. After all, who would clean feet? Custom had to be served. To be honest, part of the controversy over the Zebedee request had more to do with the disciples' own self-perceived pecking order. The arrogance of that request! They coveted the very seats of honor. But still, no one had gotten up to wash even the feet of the person sitting to his right or left. So there they sat, all twelve, waiting. The fast money was on Judas being appointed the job. After all, he had grown sullen of late; it would serve him right to be humbled with such a lowly, menial task. Still they sat and waited, no one budging, not even when the food was passed around and eating commenced. Their feet remained caked with dry, dusty dirt.

Suddenly everyone was grieved, even Judas. Unexpectedly yet not surprisingly, Jesus stood and took off his outer garment. Peter immediately protested. After all, someone had to speak. "Lord, are you going to wash my feet? You shall never wash my feet." Good ole Pete. But the Lord was in no mood for one of his tirades. Jesus quickly cut him down to size—and that's saying a lot. "Unless I wash you, you have no part with me." That set Peter right. And then Jesus said something strange. He was always saying strange things, but this was the most mysterious. "A person who has had a bath needs only to wash his feet; his whole body is clean. And you are clean, though not every one of you."

When Jesus finished, he robed, put aside the filthy water, and asked, "Do you understand what I have done for you?" He talked about serving, and how the one sent—himself—being greater than the others, the messengers. That the messenger is not the master and that we should know this by now. But as always, he softened his statement so that it only hurt but did not cut: "Now that you know these things, you will be blessed if you do them."

3. New Covenant Understanding

Luke's dialogue of the dispute will be referred to rather than John's since it offers more detail. I turn, then, to the Synoptic Gospels to close out this section on how kingdom citizens are expected to act under new covenant rule. Luke reminds readers why Jesus performs foot washing: it is likened to the rule of Romans. That is, as rulers they lord it over everyone. In the Romans' exercise of authority, they have forgotten how to rule a kingdom. In that regard Jesus simply says, "But you are not to be like that." Jesus then transitions to the story's point: "The greatest among you should be like the youngest, and the one who rules like the one who serves For who is greater, the one who is at the table or the one who serves?" (Luke 22:26–27).

Further deepening Jesus' meaning is to pick up Luke's first dispute story, in which children are cited to answer the disciples' question of greatness. Jesus replies, "Whoever welcomes this little child in my name welcomes me; and whoever welcomes me welcomes the one who sent me" (9:48). Whereas Luke uses children, Matthew and Mark fall back on Jesus' statement: "You know that the rulers of the Gentiles lord it over them, and their high officials exercise authority over them. Not so with you. Instead, whoever wants to become great among you must be your servant, and whoever wants to be first must be your slave—just as the Son of Man did not come to be served, but to serve, and give his life as a ransom for many" (Mt. 20:25–28).

By linking these dispute stories together, the reader can plainly hear Jesus elevating the dispute on greatness to an allusion on ruling. By referencing the Gentiles, thus Rome, he notifies his followers that they are not to rule in that manner. They are not to recline at tables and be waited on; no, they are to get up and serve. Thus "the one who rules" is to be "like the one who serves." In this way Jesus constructs an analogy about kingdom rule and kingdom service by placing himself into two roles. As the "greater one," he ought to sit, recline, and be waited on. However, in contradiction to earthly rulers, he disregards that honor, favoring instead abandoning the couch to *rising up* and serving. "But I am among you as one who serves."

Jesus' statement is a radical discourse on rule and power. Through this "living parable" of foot washing, Jesus condemns how mankind rules. When he stands before Pilate at the crucifixion trial his posture and position causes Pilate to ask, "What is truth?" The truth of the matter is that rule of and by mankind is too often characterized as self-serving, vested in reliance on power, intimidation, coercion, and outright violence. Jesus condemns all of this, pointing mankind to a different kind of rule, a different application of power. He says, "But you must not be like that." Instead, he offers himself as an example. By getting up, he repositions himself away from the power seat of reclining at a table, electing rather to wait upon the lesser by service through love rather than manipulation through abusive power and deception.

Table 7-4:   Comparison—Earthly Rulers and Kingdom Rulers

Gospel Accounts	Earthly Rulers	Kingdom Rulers
Lk. 22:24–27	Recline at tables	Get up
	Are waited on	Serve lesser ones
Mt. 20:25–28	"lord it over them"	"must be your servant"

Jesus transforms a dispute "on the way up to Jerusalem," in which he has informed his disciples that the Son of Man will be "mocked and flogged and crucified," to a discourse in the Upper Room on how kingdom authorities' rule. Punctuating all of this is John's treatment of foot washing. Rather than recount the highly symbolic supper with the ceremony of bread and wine, John seemingly elects to replace it with foot washing. The juxtaposition of these two ceremonies is striking. According to John's thinking, when Jesus offers bread and wine, what John remembers is foot washing. And that Jesus, as King of the now in-breaking kingdom, rules not by reclining that he might be waited on, rather he rules by rising up that he may serve.

In the larger sense is the sharp contrast between how children of darkness rule compared to God's children of light. John elects foot washing over rites; he prefers service to being waited on. He understands, as does Mark, who frequently uses the term "on the way." Thus to John, the way of the cross is the way kingdom citizens rule under the new covenant. When Jesus shares bread and wine he inaugurates the new covenant, but what John hears and sees from the lens of foot washing is how kingdom citizens are to conduct themselves as rulers in the coming kingdom. Through the example of foot washing, Jesus instructs that new convent rulers are to serve by rising up. This review of John's Gospel architecture, in which the ceremony of bread and wine is replaced by foot washing, affirms service as answer to Jesus' question, "Do you understand?"

Jesus, through foot washing, acts as Exemplar by offering an example like none other. He is not merely a good man who has come to Jerusalem to serve, but he is the very God of creation. He is the Sovereign Ruler of the kingdom now breaking into the world of darkness and evil. Of him Scripture records: He is the "image of the invisible God," the source of all created, the "beginning and the firstborn from among the dead," and so he is the "fullness" in which "the Deity lives in bodily form." But he is also the one who "emptied himself" that he could be clothed as humankind. Therefore, in Jesus' question, Do you understand? What must be seen is the great humility of this Great God who acts as servant to mankind. When Jesus discusses spiritual poverty, as he does in the beatitudes, it must be seen within the Son's emptying himself of the Divine Being (cf. Phil. 2:6–7). Thus, the ruler, the one who "reclined at table" and then got up to wash dirty feet, is the very one, ironically, at whose feet in a future time all knees will bow (see Phil. 2:10). The jarring, clashing dissonance of this is unimaginable. It is most certainly not the Roman way.

John locates, through Jesus' foot washing demonstration, the essence of the new covenant's "remember me." In this remembrance echo is the core of what the Eucharistic sacrament means. Here in John's Gospel is the relevance of bread and wine as ritual. Here in the action of the Suffering Servant is found the love of God. In the picture of Jesus washing dirty feet is meaning for his words: "For even the Son of Man did not come to be served, but to serve, and to give His life a ransom for many" (Mk. 10:45 NASB). In this picture the richness of irony swirls like a Roman crown submerged in a bowl of dirty water.

Summary

This aspect of servanthood answers the question of covenant rule. It is in foot washing that John provides answers to Jesus' question, "Do you understand?" The new covenant, which is the new way God rules his kingdom, is not driven by personal greatness or lording it over others. It comes not from rubbing elbows with Jesus while sitting at a meal table. Nor does it come from outward expressions based on rites and religious forms. Rather, it is found in true worship done "in spirit and truth." In this kind of worship his followers bathe loving kindness and care upon the "lesser." That is how God's kingdom rulers are to govern under Jesus' new covenant.

While we rightly image the sacrament of bread and wine as representative of the crucifixion, however by turning to John's Gospel and asking why the writer of symbolic language would omit this figurative ceremony, we find God's love-answer through the humility of washing feet. In it is the Son of Man, who, though God, yet he comes as a humble servant. In that vein we understand the true "remembrance" of the Holy Eucharist.

> "If I then, your Lord and Teacher, have washed your feet, you also ought to wash one another's feet." (Jn. 13:14 RSV)

What kind of god stoops to wash dirty feet? Jesus, as creator-ruler who reclines at table but also as servant who rises up asks, "Do you understand?"

In the coming chapter this understanding of covenant rule will be extended from the servant's level to what such acts anticipate: relationships. We will see that it is one's relationship that forms the answer to Jesus' command to remember and his question of understanding.

Chapter 8

COVENANT RULE OF THE COMING HOLY SPIRIT

In the Old Testament, natural objects often become symbols for theological meaning. To illustrate, *sea* represents the abode of evil; *land* signals God's covenant realm of blessings; and *mountains* frequently allude to government and power, the highest associated with God's reign (see Mic. 4:1–3). It is not surprising, therefore, that when Moses is about to die God directs him to go up on a mountain (see Num. 27:12). It is from those heights that Moses views the land long promised, the aim of Israel's exodus out of captivity. Rooted in this mountain image and joined to Israel's entrance into the land that Moses now sees are reasons John Bright casts Moses as a type of Christ. Bright associates Moses with Jesus, the New Moses.[1]

Noteworthy, then, is how the resurrected Jesus, in a parallel act, accompanied by his disciples, comes a final time to the Mount of Olives. It echoes Moses, who having been told of his impending death makes a final request. "Appoint someone over this community to go out and come in before them, one who will lead them out and bring them in, so the LORD's people will not be like sheep without a shepherd" (Num. 27:16–17). As for that man, he is described as one "in whom is the spirit" (v. 18). In naming Joshua to that role, a foreshadowing of the coming Holy Spirit is in view.

In this prefiguring language in which both Moses and Jesus are situated atop a mountain, signaling rule, the disciples are told how they will govern in Christ's newly come yet still invisible kingdom. It will occur as sheep being led by a shepherd, as those directed in their coming-ins and going-outs. It will be accomplished through the indwelling presence of the Holy Spirit. It is the Spirit who will guide and direct the church as it pastures in the land of the new exodus (Acts 1:8).

Reference to the Holy Spirit as the church's guide will be combined in this chapter with Jesus' living parable of foot washing. However, rather than focusing on "Do you understand?" emphasis will come from Jesus' use of the word "*clean*," when he says, "Those who have had a bath need only to wash their feet; their whole body is clean" (John 13:10). This examination will stipulate an essential requirement for Christ's **Third-Word** rulers. **In this chapter** that quest will be directed by a three-fold process:

1. Focus is on the key word *clean* found not only in the foot washing story but also in the parable of the vine (Jn. 15:1-8). A meaning that stands outside the normal interpretation of sin is revealed. Given the narrative context in which *clean* is used I will argue for this meaning.

2. The vine parable is introduced for its admonition to "remain in me." Therefore, an underlying prerequisite for kingdom service is extracted—the necessity of intimate relationship with the resurrected Lord. By seeing *clean* as a ***spatial metaphor*** and the command to "remain in me" as an imperative, the relational outcome of Jesus' question, "Do you understand?" comes into view.

3. This discovery returns to chapter 7's question, How does God rule in the new covenant kingdom? The answer leads to the presence and work of the Holy Spirit. In other words, this chapter is about *servanthood under the relational rule of the Holy Spirit.*

1. Being Made Clean in Ancient Israel

A brief review of the concept clean in ancient Israel provides helpful background. When Jesus washes the feet of his disciples he says to Peter, "Those who have had a bath need only to wash their feet; their whole body is clean And you are clean, though not every one of you" (v. 10). This statement provides an echo to Israel's deep past. At its point of origin stands Moses. The story-retell below is adapted from Exodus 1–3.

Moses was born in a time when a new king has come into power. This new king does not know the story of Joseph for 400 years have passed. (By referring to Pharaoh as the king of Egypt, the biblical narrator establishes a background context contesting God's chosen people against evil's surrogates.) Moses' birth is surrounded by the presence of evil (see 5:2) as the Egyptian king declares death (narratively, a holy war) on Israel's male babies, ordering the midwives to kill them (cf. Mt. 2:16–18). By this means the restorative campaign of God, based in part on the genealogy that runs through Levi to Moses, is threatened (see Ex. 2:1–3). Further, Moses himself is saved from this persecution, hidden among the reeds in a floating basket, a kind of miniature ark made of papyrus and coated with tar and pitch (cf. Gen. 6:14).

Found by a royal daughter, Moses grows up in the house of Pharaoh. Now an adult, after rescuing an Israelite by killing an Egyptian, Moses flees into the wilderness where he comes to live in Midian. Forty years pass. Moses has taken a wife and finds employment as a shepherd. While tending sheep he comes to "Horeb, the mountain of God." Seeing a strange sight from afar, a bush that burns yet is not consumed, Moses approaches. As he does a voice is heard from out of the bush:

> Do not come any closer. Take off your sandals, for the place where you are standing is holy ground. I am the God of your father, the God of Abraham, the God of Isaac and the God of Jacob. (Ex. 3:5–6)

Later, after Moses leads his people out of Egyptian captivity, he comes to Sinai/Horeb, where he receives the Torah (law) and the Decalogue (the Ten Commandments). As recorded in Exodus and Leviticus, the narrator informs Israel how she is to live as God's elect people. Leviticus in particular is informative. One overarching idea is central, of which Alexander writes: "Leviticus is dominated by the topic of holiness."[2]

Holiness emits an echo linking Moses and the removal of his sandals with that of Christ (the new Moses) and the washing of Peter's feet. This nuance is understood in how ancient Israel looked on three interrelated ideas: holiness, clean, and unclean. Jacob Milgrom writes, "Israel is also commanded to distinguish between the holy and the common, as well as between the pure and the impure."[3]

T. Desmond Alexander provides a helpful graphic depicting this concept as a threefold relationship. He illustrates by drawing a horizontal pole. One end is labeled "holiness" while the opposite point is marked "uncleanness/impurity." At midpoint is the status "cleanness." To distinguish the dynamic nature of these three states, we see the label "increasing" with an arrow pointing in either direction, toward holiness or uncleanness. Alexander makes the point: "The further one moves from the middle of this spectrum, the greater the intensity of either holiness or uncleanness. For ancient Israelites, every person, object, place, and period of time can be located somewhere on this spectrum."[4] Alexander previously notes, "Consequently, for the Israelites to enjoy a close and meaningful relationship with God, they must reflect his holiness in their daily lives."[5]

Table 8-1:   Holiness, Clean, Uncleanness (based on Alexander)

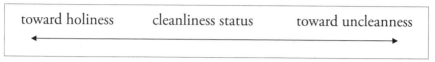

| toward holiness | cleanliness status | toward uncleanness |

At this point we perceive in God's command to Moses, "take off your sandals," the outcome of walking through an unclean land. In Hebrew theology, pollutants abide everywhere: they are on things and are, in some cases, transferable. Moses' journey renders him unclean as he comes into contact with *a **polytheistic*** people who are themselves contaminated and have contaminated the land. To approach God, Moses must be entirely clean. The contagion he bears must be removed. In the metaphor of sandals, it is God's emanating holiness that makes Moses clean (see Table 8-1). He lacks only removal of his unclean sandals, permitting his feet to touch holy ground for his entire being to be saturated with God's holy presence. Visually this can be seen later as Moses withdraws from the Tent of Meeting, his face radiant (see Ex. 34:29).

Punctuating these ideas is the contest between life and death. Milgrom writes in a brief introductory to Leviticus: "Impurity is the realm of death, and only life can be its antidote. Life purges the sanctuary by nullifying, overpowering, and absorbing the Israelites' impurities that adhere to it, allowing the divine presence to remain and Israel to survive."[6]

Much the same occurs in Christ's imperative to Peter, who is attempting to deny Jesus' request ("You shall never wash my feet"). In that way Christ's words ("Unless I wash you, you have no part with me") have the desired effect on Peter ("Not just my feet but my hands and my head as well"). Symmetry is perceived in this echo: how it was with Moses is how it will be with Peter.[7] Not only are both men made clean through contact with God's presence, they are moving toward a state of holiness. Thus, Jesus may say of Peter he is already clean. It is this inward state of moving from being clean to increased holiness that Jesus now desires for Peter. Significantly, both cleansings occur just prior to an exodus.

Through foot washing, Jesus assumes the role of high priest. The text alludes to this by symbolic language. To act as priest, a man must be consecrated by a special ritual, which Alexander notes as "involving water, clothing, and anointing."[8] These symbols of consecration are seen in Christ's ritual-like action concerning his clothing ("took off his outer garments"), to washings ("poured water into a basin" and "began to wash his disciples' feet"), and finally how Jesus has received a special anointing from above at his baptism (see Mt. 3:16–17). All of this corresponds to the sanctification of the Levitical priesthood. However, it is proximity to Jesus in the office of high priest that makes the disciples clean rather than any ritual that might be performed. The closer one comes to God, the more holiness rests on individuals. Again, the comparison of Moses approaching God can be seen in Jesus and Peter as the *spatial distance between them narrows*. Further, as Jesus touches Peter's unclean feet, Christ demonstrates his power over uncleanliness. Jesus acts out what Dempster writes of holiness: "Holiness should radiate from the epicenter of the Holy of Holies through Israelite lives to permeate the entire land."[9] It is no stretch to match Christ, with his many references to the temple, as being the personification of the Holy of Holies (see Ex. 25:40; Heb. 8:5). Richard B. Hays notes: "For John, Jesus becomes, in effect, the Temple."[10]

By this figurative interpretation, John draws his readers back to the ways of ancient Israel, and through foot washing demonstrates its relational impact on Peter and the other disciples. They have been drawn into the sphere of Christ and by his authority as high priest are made clean. In other words, in the dynamic polarity between holiness, cleanness, and uncleanness, Christ's action of foot washing transforms his disciples from clean to holy. In effect, foot washing casts a picture of what the new community, as represented by Mary and John in the **Third Word**, is to become: the fulfillment of the Abrahamic promise to be a holy nation of priests (see Ex. 19:6). Dempster draws together this theme combining covenant rule, a holy people, and kingdom service. "The purpose of this covenant (i.e., at Sinai) is that an obedient Israel may bring God's creation blessing to the world. . . . If Israel becomes a holy nation, it will 'image' God to the nations."[11]

2. From Ancient Ritual to Being Made Clean through Love

Going from this ancient background to the relational rule of the Holy Spirit is the aim of the remainder of this chapter. It is under the Spirit's execution that followers of Christ participate as rulers of the now in-breaking kingdom of God. To do this they must be made clean. The purpose of the text below is to draw a distinction between being made clean because of sin to being made clean from sin's pollutants that contaminate and deprive relationship with a Holy God. It is by being made clean that a believer is able to assume his or her role of servanthood under the new covenant rule of the Holy Spirit.

Servanthood is motivated, in John's Gospel, by the new covenant command to love one another. John ensures this understanding as he topically opens the farewell discourse in chapter 13, writing: "Having loved his own who were in the world he now showed them the full extent of his love" (13:1b). John establishes the love of Christ as the frame over which the foot washing story rests. Similarly, John ends the farewell discourse four chapters later recording that Jesus, having made known the Father's love, desires his disciples to experience this same love that they too "may be brought to complete unity" (17:23). John casts an umbrella of love over the entirety of the farewell discourse.

The Passover meal attended by Jesus and his disciples begins in chapter 13. In the foot washing story, *clean* is a key word: "Those who have had a bath need only to wash their feet; their whole body is clean. And you are clean, though not every one of you" (13:10).

Two things are noted by this usage of clean. One, the overall context is where Jesus addresses his disciples, followers who are already clean (see 15:3). While it is true that even disciples need cleansing from sin, the aim of the story directs toward servanthood, or in other words, acts in which disciples are to be engaged. This passage is not concerned with nonbelievers and their need to be made clean from sin. Rather, given the historical meaning attached to *clean*, the text trends toward holiness and service.

Second, this same emphasis is noted in the vine parable where the Father "trims clean." Here, trimming clean is for the purpose of being fruitful, not so much to cleanse from sin (see 15:1-2). In both parables meaning is directed through use of a spatial metaphor. That is, Peter has already been made clean due to three years living in proximity with Jesus. It is possible for one to be forgiven, hence cleansed from sin, yet remain distant from God. The picture image of both is one of spatial nearness, therefore one of closeness and growing closer in relationship to God. The pruning action of the gardener (God the Father) is one of performing up close and personal work. He is not distant. In the metaphor of gardening, the worker is next to the object of pruning, not far removed from it. While this spatial metaphor ought not exclude the interpretation of cleansing from or pruning away sin habits, sin similarly should not dominate meaning. When Jesus washes Peter's feet, he also is near, up close and present. Both parables are relational in scope and function.

The view in mind is this desired state of holiness, a unity between a believer and the Lord. Such is the case with Peter's remark, signifying he now understands Jesus will have nothing to do with him if he will not permit the Lord to wash his feet. This threatened loss of relationship is more than Peter can bear, so he cries out, "Not just my feet but my hands and my head as well" (13:9). Peter is not worried about the cleanliness of his feet; rather his focus is on the threatened loss of relational closeness to the Lord. Through this living parable of foot washing, the theme of unity through love is overwhelmingly present, as it is in the vine parable. This is due not only to the spatial metaphor but also to the vine parable's repeated use of "remain in me" or "remain in my love."

These two key word phrases, along with the spatial metaphor, merge foot washing and the vine parable together. We have already viewed this aspect in foot washing's use of *clean*. In the vine parable, *clean* is further joined by the key phrase, "remain in me." This phrase, or its derivatives ("remain in my love" or "remain in the vine") saturate the relational vine parable.

Recapping Vine

It is unmistakable what Jesus is now saying to the disciples as they recline around the Passover meal table. They are to "remain in" his love in the same way that he remains in the Father's. The analogy to a vine with its many branches is a transparent picture of Trinitarian oneness. The vine parable acts as precursor to Jesus' farewell prayer (chapter 17), which is a prayer of unity: "Holy Father, protect them (i.e., disciples) by the power of your name, the name you gave me, so that they may be one as we are one" (v. 11b). It is only through the deep unity of remaining in him that a believer may be continually (spatially) cleansed and thus effectively pruned by the Father to bear the fruit of kingdom service (see vv. 1–4). While sin removal is cause for pruning, sin itself is not the only reason pruning occurs. The end goal is to move closer in heart relationship to the Lord (see Deut. 11:13–18).[12]

This is consistent with the purpose of the new covenant, a covenant of heart (see Ezek. 36:26). Here is the expression of Jesus' previously heard message on discipleship. Here repentance for the disciple exists not so much because of sin but because of love for Jesus. Peter's desire to immediately draw closer to the Lord reflects his heart's desire to repent of its distance from the Lord. Repentance for a disciple, therefore, is not so much regret for sin, but acts to narrow the distance between himself and his Lord (see prior discussion in chapter 3, section 3, Kingdom: Repentance and Forgiveness). Narrowing is the point of the spatial metaphor, just as narrowing is the point of Moses removing his sandals. In the end this narrowing results in the whelming presence of the Holy God.

In the vine metaphor, a new-covenant child is one who remains rooted in the vine. Such grounding comes from repeated exposure to Jesus' nurturing word and person. If a disciple remains afar, pruning is difficult. After Jesus shares the vine parable he comes directly to the point.

> As the Father has loved me, so have I loved you. Now *remain in my love*. If you obey my commands, you will remain in my love, just as I have obeyed my Father's commands and *remain in his love*. I have told you this so that my joy may be in you and that your joy may be complete. (Jn. 15:9–11 emphasis added)

Jesus ties together kingdom service rooted in a unifying relationship through new-covenant rule. After Jesus completes foot washing, he asks, "Do you understand what I have done for you?" John answers this question through the affirming parable of the vine in which Jesus concludes: "This I command to you, to love one another" (Jn. 15:17 RSV; also see 13:34). Jesus reduces the new covenant to its essence: it is a relational covenant of love offered by God for humanity, developed within the unity of the Trinitarian God to promote service in his kingdom. John also points to the coming Holy Spirit as part of this covenant bond. He writes, at the conclusion of these two illustrations, "When the Advocate comes, whom I will send to you from the Father—the Spirit of truth who goes out from the Father—he will testify about me" (15:26).

3. The Coming *Rule* of the Holy Spirit

At the outset of this chapter, three tasks were identified as content drivers. Having explored the first two, keyed by "clean" and "remain in me," we now come to the final and overriding task: How does God rule in the new covenant kingdom?

In John's Gospel, his focus on the Cana wedding, on the Last Supper, and on the cross must not be missed. All three are part of his narrative to reveal Jesus as the Son of God. John has evidently structured his Gospel to accomplish this goal. This can be immediately grasped in John's placement of the temple-cleansing story at the front of his Gospel rather than at its close as the Synoptic Gospels report, coming during Passover Week. Such emphasis on story structure causes the careful reader to notice the significance John gives Jesus' message in the farewell discourse, which is on the Holy Spirit and the unity of believers. Table 8-2 illustrates how John's story-structure reinforces the importance of the Holy Spirit.

Table 8-2:   John's Gospel Architecture—Holy Spirit and the Vine Parable

Chapter 14	Chapter 15	Chapter 16
The soon coming Holy Spirit (Ch. 14)	Parable of the Vine and the Branches (Ch. 15)	**The soon coming Holy Spirit (Ch. 16)**

Through means of this gospel architecture (see Table 8-2) the importance of the coming Holy Spirit cannot be stated enough. Graham A. Cole writes: "The divine project involves nothing less than God's people living under God's rule, in God's way in God's place. . . . Pentecost is a crucial event in that story. The people of the Messiah have life in the Spirit."[13] So we see that the Spirit, who comes to the earth below, coming at the request of the Son by the Father's sending, now abides in the Son's absence to conduct the mission and ministry of kingdom reign. Jeremy Treat writes, "God administers his kingdom through the covenants."[14] This administration, now that the Lord has both risen and ascended, falls to the now come Holy Spirit, who takes up kingdom rule within hearts of believers.

Indeed, the parable of the vine is bookended by Jesus' teaching on the Spirit (Table 8-2). John moves his Gospel *from realm* (kingdom) *and rule* (crown) *to relationship* (new covenant, through the unifying and soon coming Holy Spirit) as he begins chapter 14. There Jesus admonishes his followers to "trust in God" even as they have trusted in him. The extent of that trust is likened to a family living together, so Christ speaks of going away to prepare heavenly dwelling places. While his sentence construction is set on a dwelling metaphor (in his Father's house are many rooms, or mansions) he has an eye open to the soon coming and indwelling Spirit, who will take up abode in human tents. This is evident halfway through the fourteenth chapter as Jesus declares: "I will ask the Father, and he will give you another advocate to help you and be with you forever" (14:16).

As the Lord proceeds to speak of the coming Spirit, we must not miss John's textual flow in this multichapter sequence. The coming Holy Spirit is tethered to Jesus just as Jesus is to the Father. Not only does John insert the relational vine parable here, but he wraps the presentation of the Spirit around it (see Table 8-2).

In the vine parable are two sets of triads. Both admonish the imperative "remain in." In the first part of the vine illustration, Jesus speaks three times of "remaining in me." In the second triad, he adds "remain in my love." Of the former, it is defined by the thought: "If you remain in me and my words remain in you, ask whatever you wish, and it will be done for you. This is to my Father's glory, that you bear much fruit, showing yourselves to be my disciples" (15:7–8). Of this remaining in, Sinclair Ferguson comments on the Apostle Paul's use, noting he writes of it nearly 160 times. He claims that it "is the heart and soul of the Spirit's ministry."[15]

Remaining in Christ, which is the imperative message of the vine, can only be accomplished through the mysterious ministry of the indwelling Spirit of God. Remaining in Christ, in effect, is to remain in the love bond of the Trinitarian God. It cannot be effected by study of the Word or by prayer alone. Bible study or time in prayer, without exercise of the Spirit's presence, become mere acts of religiosity, an accepted form of "cheap grace." The new covenant is not an act of works but an act of "costly grace."[16] When Jesus speaks of remaining in him by means of his word, the inclusion is always understood to be through the ministry of the indwelling Spirit. It is the Spirit that brings a believer into Trinitarian relationship (see 3:3–8, 4:23–24).

Once the relational vine parable is spoken, Jesus quickly proceeds to again reference the Helper who comes alongside, that is the Holy Spirit. "When the Advocate comes, whom I will send to you, from the Father—the Spirit of truth who goes out from the Father—he will testify about me; but you also must testify, for you have been with me from the beginning" (15:26–27).

Jesus deepens this thought as he elaborates on the coming Holy Spirit: "Unless I go away, the Advocate will not come to you; but if I go, I will send him to you. . . . But when he, the Spirit of truth, comes, he will guide you into all truth" (16:7–13). A believer experiences the mind of God, then, for the Spirit will "speak only what he hears." This is the same phrase that Jesus so often uses of himself, as one who spoke only what the Father told him and did only what he saw the Father doing. Jesus teaches that to remain in him is to remain within the heart of the Trinitarian God through the indwelling Holy Spirit, "the Spirit of truth." Ferguson is quite clear on this essential matter: "Christ and we are possessed of one and the same Holy Spirit. He is the bond of an unbreakable union."[17] Perhaps Paul best expresses this mystery of kingdom service and the indwelling Spirit: "If the Spirit is the source of our life, let the Spirit also direct its course" (Gal. 5:25 REB).

Summary

The importance of Jesus' social drama, in which he washes dirty feet, undergirds this lengthy narrative begun in the previous chapter on the road up to Jerusalem. In this chapter, literary analysis was applied to the key word *clean*. By tracing a historic meaning attached to the burning bush, we discovered parallels between Moses and Peter. This examination identified both events as spatial metaphors where the distance between Moses and God, as with Peter and Christ, narrowed. Such narrowing vacates uncleanliness, leaving both individuals positioned to be directed by God's Spirit. Therefore, the presence of the Holy Spirit can be seen as the guiding force directing a believer's life. This Spirit leading is particularly evident when disciples engage in the primary task of kingdom life: works of servanthood.

In this multichapter sequence we find a loving God acting in and through the Son of Man, who brings the fullness of God's own being to a musty upper room, only hours away from his sacrificial death. In that epiphany, Jesus opens heaven's window to the soul of God. "Instead, whoever wants to become great among you must be your servant, and whoever wants to be first must be your slave—just as the Son of Man did not come to be served, but to serve, and to give his life as a ransom for many" (Mt. 20:26b–28).

Conclusion Part I: The Narrative Storyline[18]

Examination of Jesus' three statements spoken in the morning through the image of light is now completed. In it the cross discloses royalty and a new covenant; a king and his restored community. This is a gracious king who offers forgiveness and embraces all. And so, he develops not only a new kingdom not of this world, he charters a new covenant of truth through which the Holy Spirit will effect kingdom rule. Of that rule it is accomplished through reigning acts of service. It is in service where is found the express love of God, understood by Christ's illustration of foot washing rather than through ritual ceremony. As believers participate in service acts, they abide in the risen Lord and are made clean, narrowing the holiness gap. *Holiness*, in this narrative landscape, is not just avoidance of sin practices; *it is developed serving the Lord under the relational rule of the Holy Spirit* (see Rom. 12:1).

The crucifixion's first **Three Words**, when read for narrative meaning, express God's forgiveness for humanity's abandonment of his rule. But through the Anointed One, Jesus the Jewish Messiah, the solution to the garden question, "How will Adam and Eve's descendants regain God's community?" is disclosed. This grand story finds a foreshadowing apex in Moses, who stands atop a mountain. His death is imminent. He has led his people out of captivity; they are now poised to enter the land long promised. When read narratively, the story of the exodus is one of liberation and redemption that prefigures the work of the Messiah. Jesus, like Moses, also stands atop a mountain. He has summarily led his followers out of the captivity of darkness. They are ready to enter the realm of God's in-breaking kingdom.

As Moses stands before the LORD, he seeks a shepherd who will go out and come in before the nation. The new Moses too seeks this directionality. Jesus informs his disciples of the coming Advocate who will act to shepherd the church, the visible body of his invisible kingdom. At the inauguration of the new covenant, the new Moses gives instructions through foot washing and demonstrates how his followers are to live under the rule of the Holy Spirit.

The storyline of Christ's last thoughts has progressed from Genesis to Exodus and on to the land long promised. The anticipated rising wave of population commanded in Genesis now finds fulfillment in the liberating work of Jesus, reminiscent of the garden command: "Be fruitful and increase in number; fill the earth and subdue it. Rule over the fish of the sea and the birds of the air and over every living creature that moves on the ground" (Gen. 1:28).

Jesus, now resurrected, stands on a mountain top instructing his newly formed kingdom. He speaks in the light of day as a cloud descends on him. His final words are an extension of the cross message. Imperatively he states:

> All authority in heaven and on earth has been given to me. Therefore go and make disciples of all nations, baptizing them in the name of the Father and of the Son and of the Holy Spirit, and teaching them to obey everything I have commanded you. And surely I will be with you always, to the very end of the age. (Mt. 28:18–20)

Next

Before taking up Part II, an interlude bridges the period of light with the period of darkness. Its purpose is to summarize and synthesize the cross message to prepare the reader for the onset of darkness.

So the Lord God banished him from the Garden of Eden
to work the ground from which he had been taken. After
he drove the man out, he placed on the east side of the
Garden of Eden cherubim and a flaming sword flashing
back and forth to guard the way to the tree of life.

Genesis 3:23–24

Section IV—Interlude

DECEPTION

Narratively, an abrupt, jarring disconnect exists between Christ's morning words and those in the afternoon. This division is demonstrated by the overall tone of the words spoken in light, themselves utterances of hope as Jesus announces forgiveness and makes known God's kingdom. In contrast is the dismaying discouragement of dereliction found in the fourth statement. It comes deep within the period of darkness.

Interlude is a three-segment summary that synthesizes main ideas drawn from the first three words. It functions to bridge morning content with Christ's afternoon utterances. Readers are thus prepared for the coming cosmic battle portended in the garden judgment, itself prefigured by the symbolic dark that covers the Jerusalem countryside.

Read literally, Christ's first three words yield a theme of love (see Jn. 3:16). This is demonstrated through Christ's compassion on the cross toward all humanity. It is there he forgives **(First Word)**, there he warmly welcomes the thief into paradise **(Second Word)**, and there he arranges for the care of his mother **(Third Word)**. However, when the text is read narratively, Christ's literal words transform into a message announcing God's kingdom. Examined from "the beginning," Jesus' first three words take aim at restoring what the serpent stole: God's realm-land and his servants.

Organizationally, the outline below replaces the normal "**In This Chapter**" preview.

> **The First Segment:** Commencing with Genesis' primary theme of light and darkness, discussion centers on how mankind is affected by the pall of darkness.

> **The Second Segment:** Anchored to Matthew chapter 26, key words *betrayed* and *denied* provide a penetrating look at the garden fall, where a conversation on the way to Gethsemane finds parallels to Eden.

> **The Third Segment:** By way of Mark's Gospel, the damage done to creation and man's role as viceroys finds resolution in God's restorative plan.

Interlude—the First Segment

GARDEN IMAGE

"In the beginning God created the heavens and the earth.	and darkness was over the surface of the deep." Gen. 1:1-2 (NASB)

In The Beginning

John's use of *in the beginning* to open his Gospel establishes a Genesis connection. By it he transports readers back to the days of Eden's garden, creation, and even hints at a far more distant time set within the recesses of the Eternal God. As readers, when we too return to Genesis' beginning chapters we are faced with a choice. We can read them as a literal description of creation's six-day account. Or, we can consider how Scripture uses story to convey meaning beyond its literal construction.[1]

In Genesis, God is clearly designated Creator, the one who brought forth the "heavens and the earth." The Apostle John replicates the Genesis opening not only in his Gospel but also in his first epistle, writing: "That which was from the beginning, which we heard, which we have seen with our eyes, which we have looked at and our hands have touched—this we proclaim concerning the Word of life" (1:1). He is not alone in this literary directionality. There is a tendency by New Testament authors to draw readers back "to the beginning" of the story to make clear that which is to come. See for example Mark's opening line: "The beginning of the good news about Jesus the Messiah." Matthew's opening lines, "This is the genealogy of Jesus the Messiah," or Luke's use of genealogy in chapter 3, which ends with the lineages of Seth, Adam, and "the son of God" (3:38), as well as his reference to "beginning" in 1:3.

Biblical Motif: The Primacy of Light and Darkness

This means of symbolic communication—the use of literary elements such as key words and images—to convey underlying truth is perhaps nowhere more artfully developed than in the Genesis creation account. Here is found the first biblical motif: light and darkness. When God surveys the primordial earth, he finds it a place where "darkness was over the surface of the deep." Into that darkness God commands the presence of light. While this account is understood to bring visible light into the void of material darkness (literal reading), it also establishes the grand pattern of theological light and darkness that permeates the biblical story. Thus, we have been reading of the cross hour, "And when the sixth hour had come, *darkness fell over the whole land until the ninth hour.*"

A corollary idea, wedded to light and darkness, is also discovered in the first chapter of Genesis when the text declares life arises. While that life is many and varied, including all manner of plants, insects, fish, and fowl, it rests primarily in the animal kingdom of which man is made supreme. This distinction is drawn as the text announces the creation of animal life as "good" but the tag "very good" is applied once human life is formed. Yet, this corollary is not finished, for man arises on the sixth day, a day Genesis quickly develops as one associated with degradation, destruction, and death.[2] Therefore light and life, with its counterpoint theme of darkness and death, are found in this developing pattern. This twin image of light (good) and darkness (evil) propels the biblical story along dual but antagonistic lines that beg the question, What will God do about the twin demons of darkness and death unleashed in his realm-land of light and life? God answers back, slowly revealing his response through the content of Israel's history.

Table Interlude-1:   Motif of Oppositional Pathways

Twin Demons	Resolution	Reversal
Darkness	Restored to	Light
Death	Redeemed to	Life

Dual Pathways

The dual motifs of light/darkness and life/death are embedded in the prologue of John's Gospel: "He was in the beginning with God; all things were made through him, and without him was not anything made. In him was life, and the life was the light of men" (1:2–4 RSV). Reading further, John adds meaning to this motif as the light shines "in the darkness" but the darkness has neither "overcome" it nor "understood" it.

Later, John's Gospel further reveals the phrase "my time is not yet come" (7:6). And then suddenly, Jesus announces the arrival of his "hour." The time of the cross is here! God's project, though veiled and hidden within the long history of ancient Israel, has suddenly come to fruition and fulfillment in the climatic *sixth* hour of the cross. It is through the cross work of the Suffering Servant that both elements—restoration (targeting light and darkness) and redemption (taking aim at life and death)—are accomplished.

Returning to Genesis, the presence of this dual plotline is first found. On one hand is the treachery of the First Couple. The text discloses their disobedience in taking the forbidden fruit. The second plotline is revealed in the cunning of the snake, of whom Eve declares, "The serpent deceived me, and I ate." Because of this rebellious act, God commits to a project culminating in redemption; he also turns upon the devastation resulting from the snake figure in the thread leading to restoration.[3]

Adam and Eve are removed from the garden on the basis of God's judgment. However, this judgment is lenient, filled with mercy. The promised death (see 3:2–3), which is eternal banishment from God's garden, is commuted to a lesser punishment resulting in physical death (see Mt. 10:28). This act of mercy creates a ray of hope; it comes as God judges the snake: "And I will put enmity between you and the woman, and between your offspring and hers; he will crush your head, and you will strike his heel" (Gen. 3:15).

Over time the vagueness of this prophetic judgment is seen in the conflict between light and darkness, of good and evil. It eventually culminates in the cross attack by Satan. The New Testament makes clear that the final victory in this epochal battle belongs to the Son of Man, whose heel is struck while the snake figure's head is crushed.[4] In that garden account may also be learned something of God's purpose in creating mankind. Humanity is created in God's image and given prominence over all creation with its many life forms. The man and the woman are commissioned to be "fruitful and increase in number; fill the earth and subdue it. Rule over the fish of the sea and the birds of the air and over every living creature that moves on the ground" (1:28).

In this account, however, is an embedment of figurative language that holds a deeper, theological meaning through its commands and images of royalty: increase, fill, subdue, and the royal term "rule." God goes on to say he has "given" to Adam and Eve everything for food and existence. Contextually all of this is tied to "rule over," thus mankind is commanded to exercise authority over "every living creature that moves on the ground." There is more to this authority than just cattle and lions; there is a direct yet veiled reference to the serpent-snake, who in character image slithers across the ground.[5] The First Couple is expected to rule over the snake when he is present in the garden, demonstrating the supremacy of light over darkness (see Gen. 1:16).

Humanity's Purpose

Theologians have taken up the question of man's role in the garden. One line of thought is to perceive the garden as a microcosm of God's earthly realm, acknowledging the earth to be God's footstool (Is. 66:1). This image conveys royal authority. The earth is the physical kingdom of the Creator God. In forming this part of the visible spectrum, humanity is invested as God's proxy. The First Couple is but the initial wave of an anticipated rising population that would advance God's name and his kingdom throughout the vast garden planet. In that way, the race is understood to be God's viceroys. As his image bearers, humanity serves as representatives having all authority to rule this earthly kingdom through his name (see Mk. 6:7).

The notion of mankind as God's royal representatives on earth, as stand-ins, is encountered in some theological manuscripts addressing the Garden of Eden.[6] T. Desmond Alexander sees a connection between the garden and Earth "as a sanctuary," that is, a kind of "temple-garden." "Because they met God face to face in a holy place, we may assume that Adam and Eve had a holy or priestly status."[7] Jeremy Treat labels humanity as a "vicegerency" by which God "reigns through his image-bearing servant-kings."[8] Similarly, Thomas Schreiner uses the phrase "priest-kings," noting they are commanded to "work and keep" (priestly terms) the land (references to Num. 3:7-8, 8:25-26, 18:5-6; 1 Chron. 23:32; and Ezek. 44:14). In his view, their effort is to "extend God's reign over the whole earth."[9]

This perspective of Adam and Eve as servant-kings, or priest-kings, fits within the Genesis motif of light and life. The human rulers are to expand God's earthly kingdom throughout the garden planet, establishing the supremacy of God's throne to the ends of the earth. Their charge to expand and multiply, to rule and have dominion, finds fulfillment in the narrative texture of light and life.

The theme, then, that the earth is God's footstool, his temple where he dwells, the place he desires to place his throne, fits harmoniously within this view of kingdom theology.[10] Treat succinctly states: "The kingdom of God is widely acknowledged as the primary theme of Jesus' preaching, and many argue that it is the unifying motif of the Old Testament, New Testament, and even the Bible as a whole."[11] Thomas Schreiner finds accord as he writes: "God is the sovereign creator who extends his kingship over the world. But he extends his rule through human beings, for as God's image-bearers they must govern the world for God's glory and honor."[12]

It is this kingdom mandate, however, that calls humanity into crisis. How can the now fallen race accomplish God's desire? This paradoxical point has been in view throughout much of this book. We see on one hand that God is sovereign; he is the Creator. Yet, Scripture reveals a powerful undercurrent in the history and works of mankind. Man has "flouted" God's rule.[13] Here is the crux of the problem, and it cries aloud against the backdrop of the paradise garden. In the words of Father Neuhaus: "In the world, in our own lives, something has gone dreadfully wrong and it must be set right."[14] But before considering setting it aright, Matthew chapter 26 helps define the core of this wrongness through the underlying meta-narrative.

Summary

In this opening segment, the key idea that Adam and Eve surrender their loyalty to the serpent was reviewed by accessing Scripture's underlying veiled language. Instead of having dominion over Earth's creatures, in particular the one who "crawled upon the ground," the First Couple abdicate their authority and find themselves banished, separated from their Creator. This rebellion leaves them naked and afraid, but on God's discovery of their crime, he mercifully clothes them, and, in his grace, commutes the harshness of their sentence. While they would yet die, God nevertheless puts into place a distant hope of a coming redemption. The garden-judgment prophecy speaks of a coming clash of titans in which one would be wounded but the other fatally felled. Along with the human aspect of judgment comes a secondary fallout: creation itself comes into decline. God's plan must also include renewal of the good planet.

In the coming two segments, I examine more closely the fall of the First Couple and restoration of both humankind and creation. The second segment specifically looks at God's redemptive project.

Interlude—the Second Segment

GARDEN STUMBLE

"Rise! Let us go!	Here comes my betrayer!"
	Matthew 26:46

Story retell below adapted from Matthew 26:30–35.

> Completing a hymn, the disciples accompany Jesus as he departs the Upper Room. Along the way to the Garden of Gethsemane, Jesus tells the Eleven (Judas has since gone his way) that every one of them will "lose faith because of me" (REB) and "fall away" (NIV). With characteristic bombast, Peter protests on the strength of his own courage and faith: "I will never depart you or lose faith in you." To this exchange Jesus bluntly says, "Truly I tell you, this very night, before the rooster crows, you will disown me three times." To which Peter stammers an unconvincing rebuttal, "I will never disown you."

Genesis chapters 1 through 3 describe not only the creation of the "heavens and the earth," but also convey in broad strokes man's creation and fall. Too often, however, the story of the garden creation and fall is not connected to the next several chapters. In these, the Bible outlines two separate but distinct genealogies. Beginning with the birth of Cain, it follows with Abel and his replacement brother Seth.

Table Interlude-2:   Separate Genealogies (Lines of Darkness and Light)

	Chapter 4	Chapter 5
Lines of Descent	Line of Cain	Line of Abel
Tale of Violence	Cain murders Abel	Abel is replaced by Seth
The lines multiply as they separate	Judgment falls on Cain; he wanders and comes to live in Nod. Cain produces offspring	Ten generations from Adam to Noah are detailed.

An outcome of separation is displayed in Table Interlude-2 as the families of humanity take two oppositional courses, one characterized by darkness, the other by light. This is revealed through the Genesis author's use of the word *separate* (1:4, 6, 14). This use speaks to an overwhelming urgency by the Genesis author to demonstrate, through literal creation language, a theological impulse to separate light from darkness. Genesis' repeated use of separate *anticipates* the coming division of mankind into two lines. How God deals with humanity and this division can be understood through the representational actions of Peter and Judas in Matthew's Gospel.

Two Garden Pathways: Matthew Chapter 26

The verbal sparring by Peter on the road to Gethsemane is in sharp contrast with how Matthew reports Judas' exchange with Christ in the Upper Room. These two conversations (see 26:21 and 26:34) begin similarly ("Truly I tell you"), thus Matthew invites comparison of Peter and Judas through this phrasing. In the case of Peter, he will "disown" the Lord, in contrast to Judas, who will "betray" him.

Significant literary tension, therefore, develops between "betray" and "disown."[15] However, the text is concerned with more than just two people and their response to the cross crisis. There is a subtle yet profound difference in these two words. Narratively, Judas and Peter represent the division of mankind into separate lines described in Table Interlude-2. There are those whose life course is based on betrayal, while the other group is tied to disowning, as we will now discover.

The Bible characterizes Peter's disownment as an act of falling away. Jesus makes this clear when he tells the eleven disciples: "This very night you will all fall away" (26:31). Hence, Peter's disowning is equated to falling away. Matthew is consistent over the remainder of this passage by assigning the word *betray* to Judas and *disown* to Peter. In John's Gospel this continuity of labeling is affirmed (see 18:2–25). Additionally, John also uses the term *traitor* to describe Judas (v. 5). In Matthew 26:45-46, Jesus says summarily to Peter, John, and James at the conclusion of the Gethsemane prayer, "Look, the hour has come, and the Son of Man is delivered into the hands of sinners. Rise! Let us go! Here comes my betrayer!"

Of the word translated "fall" (i.e., "you will all fall away"), the NASB footnotes "stumble." Here, we find Jesus declaring that his followers will all fall away, that is, they will all stumble that very night. This visually graphic word, depicting fall away as stumble, enriches the ensuing dialogue between Jesus and Peter. We have already noted that Peter will deny his Lord. Now we learn that his denial is akin to a stumble, to a misstep, which diverts his course from what he intends ("Even if I must die with you, I will not deny you" [26:35 RSV]). There is discernable theological difference, then, between "disown"—meaning to fall away or stumble—and "betray"—meaning to act traitorously.

Such is not the motivation of Judas. His course of action comes not by way of misstep; it is not because he stumbles. Rather, it is rooted in the depth of his heart's desire as seen in the acceptance of the priests' payment of thirty pieces of silver. This offer comes at Judas' premeditated request: "What will you give me if I deliver him to you?" (26:15 RSV). It is this intent of the heart that separates one who "disowns" from him who "betrays;" from one who "stumbles" or "falls" from one who rebels or becomes a traitor. Like the two thieves on the cross that were narratively perceived to be representational characters, so too are Peter and Judas viewed. Why this characterization of disownment and betrayal is so crucial will now be considered.

The Second Garden Metaphor

With this linguistic and representational groundwork established, Matthew's story following the Last Supper continues. Verse 36 states: "Then Jesus went with his disciples to a place called Gethsemane." This inclusion of garden detail is more than Scripture merely noting a particular setting where Jesus prays and awaits his arrest. It is a flashback trail marker, noting a previous fall by mankind in a previous garden, Eden, which is a prefiguration of Gethsemane. There Adam and Eve are deceived. There they exchange the truth of God's statement for the lie of the devil. Thus, in both gardens—Eden and Gethsemane—is found a parallel exchange of truth for deception.[16] An exchange of allegiance from God to the serpent. It is not mere coincidence that Jesus repeatedly uses the phrase, "Truly I tell you." What Jesus likely has in mind by his incessant reference to truth is the First Couple's rejection of God's truth, exchanging it for the serpent's lie ("You will not surely die").

Adam and Eve disown God's truth and deny God's authority over them, an action akin to Peter's "stumble" as they all "fall away," but not to the degree of a hardened heart, as seen in Judas' action as betrayer. The effects of that stumble result in "God's sovereignty over the earth" being "usurped."[17] Adam and Eve are now subject to the rule of the serpent.

Table Interlude-3:   Comparison—Truth, Betrayal, and Denial in Matthew

Person / Scripture	Statement	Effect
Jesus *Mt. 26:21*	"Truly I tell you, one of you will betray me."	Betrayal leads to rejection of God's truth and authority as sovereign.
Judas *Mt. 26:25*	"Then Judas, the one who would betray him, said, 'Surely you don't mean me, Lord?'"	Betrayal leads to rebellion by willfully exchanging God's truth for Satan's deceptive lie.
Peter *Mt. 26:35*	"Even if I must die with you, I will not deny you" (RSV).	Denial, caused by deception, leads to a stumble, but in the end is reversible (see John 21).[18]

The verbiage describing Peter and Judas is critical to unlocking meaning in Matthew chapter 26. Seen representationally, all mankind may be identified through one of these two responses to Jesus' announcement. First, both men abandon Jesus to the demands of the cross. Peter's comes by way of denial, while Judas' is through outright betrayal.

Second, two outcomes are derived. For Peter, who stumbles against God's truth, believing his own version ("I will never deny you") he must await the resurrection, when the scene shifts to a lakeshore. There the now resurrected Jesus directs some fishermen to throw down their nets on the other side of the boat. Peter, at John's informing "It is the Lord," jumps into the lake and quickly wades ashore. There his thrice established guilt at having denied Jesus is removed in an affectionate threefold counter (see Jn. 21:15–19). Peter's response of disowning ("I don't know the man!") is found to be forgivable, tempered by Jesus' overcoming love (see 1 Pet. 4:8). Peter is redeemed. Judas, on the other hand, carries out an act of betrayal by guiding an armed band to arrest Jesus, despite Jesus' greeting his betrayer as friend: "Do what you came for, friend" (Mt. 26:50).

In these two exchanges, Scripture links humanity's response to God's truth as one of rebellion and abandonment. Ironically, humanity is found derelict of its garden duty. While all (i.e., mankind) turn away from the Messiah as he is lifted up, thus forsaking him, one (group) remorsefully returns. The other remains in a state of abandonment and betrayal. (This is the same representational picture developed through the **Second Word** and the two thieves.) As for the figurative value of the text, Matthew provides no editorializing. He leaves the response choice to each of his readers, who will consume his narrative in the coming millennia. Will they choose disowning God's truth or betrayal? Will they act as Peter does, or remain profane as Judas?

In this two-garden setting, a type of instant replay may be seen, divulging Eden's First Couple as disowning but not acting in total betrayal of the Creator King. By accepting the cunning deceit of the snake figure, Adam and Eve are tricked into the abandonment of their role as priest-kings. By following Satan's lie, they stumble, and thereby disqualifying themselves as God's servant-kings. No longer may they be "fruitful" and "have dominion" over the garden planet, going forth to prepare God's realm as a place of light and life. Judgment follows and in its darkened verdict they are removed from the light of the lush garden. They have not been found dependable. Their allegiance has been reversed. Rather than heed God's words ("Truly I tell") they have chosen to believe the serpent's lie ("You will not die").

The two lines of genealogy outlined in Genesis 4 and 5 (see Table Interlude-2) mirror the two thieves on the cross and their divergent response to forgiveness. One line continues in betrayal; the other finds, like Peter, that they have stumbled. But their stumble comes at the hand of the serpent's deception. In this story of two gardens, Eden and

Gethsemane, symbolic content emerges that coherently sews the meta-story into one large cohesive narrative. Both gardens offer up abandonment to God; both reveal humanity's flight away from the presence of the Creator King. And yet to Adam and Eve, as to Peter, the hope of redemption is communicated. Peter personally finds forgiveness and salvation over a bed of coals containing fish and bread, much as he shared the Passover meal with Jesus in the upper room. There he hears words of his Lord's forgiveness in the thrice asked, "Simon son of John, do you love me?"

This lakeside conversation is an echo reenactment of God's graciousness in Eden's garden toward his now fallen and tarnished image-bearers. Genesis 3:21 states, "The LORD God made garments of skin for Adam and his wife and clothed them." By doing this God reverses the state of the First Couple's now realized nakedness (see 3:10). The hope of a distant redemption is figuratively clothed. The theme of restoration is also in view in this passage. We find it in the judgment of the garden planet itself, over whose land comes a darkened shadow because of humanity's act of falling away (see Mk. 15:33). God declares: "Cursed are you" to the snake. And "cursed is the ground because of you."

Planet earth is substantially changed. No longer is it seen as a peaceful garden where God is accessed. Now the earth morphs into a substantially hostile environment (see Gen. 3:17-19). Its perfect climate is removed; scorching heat and conditions of drought will tear away its fertility. Now the earth will groan and shake as tremors and fault lines merge, and blood like flows of molten rock hemorrhage on its torn surface. The earth is no longer a garden. Creation no longer obeys man's authority, as contrasted with Christ, who commands nature (see Mk. 4:39; Mt. 21:18–22). Now man must submit to its rule and contest other life forms. Now man must forcefully labor to pull from its tortured soil life-giving substance. The garden planet has been poisoned; ironically, its surface sprinkled in violence by its former priestly-rulers, whose blood it will soon ingest (see Gen. 4:10–11).

Summary

God's project to redeem mankind is underway. Through the dual echoes of Eden and Gethsemane we find also dual pathways of rebellion. One, likened to Cain, comes at the expense of a heart-driven betrayal. This can be heard as Cain charges God's inquiry concerning the now slain Abel: "Am I my brother's keeper?" Cain offers no remorse for his deed. The taking of his brother's life is a violation of the sanctity of life. He cares not for God or his created image bearers; he only cares for himself as heard in his wail, "My punishment is more than I can bear."

But not all respond as Cain. To those whose rebellion is laid at the foot of the serpent's deception (Eve's "The serpent deceived me."), like Peter's "falling away," it is a misstep in the eyes of God. Here is a merciful God. Though all have rebelled, God elects to lay the blame at the feet of the serpent and not his image-bearers. Here is understanding for Jesus' prayerful **First Word** ("Forgive them, for they know not what they do."). Adam's knowing not is echoed in Peter's denial, which itself is cast under the shadow of the serpent's deception.

Returning to the representational Cain and Abel, in their progeny is found this underlayment. Abel's line (through Seth), however, though acting rebelliously, gratefully embraces Christ's forgiveness given under the guise of knowing not (see Lk. 23:34). The serpent, who is the first cause of rebellion, is the party of true judgment ("he shall bruise," that is crush, "your head"). In the third and final part of this review, the theme of restoration is taken-up.

Interlude—the Third Segment

GARDEN SYNAGOGUE

1. They came to Capernaum, and on the Sabbath he went to the synagogue and began to teach. The people were amazed ... he taught with a note of authority (Mark 1:1–2 REB).	2. Now there was a man in their synagogue possessed by an unclean spirit. ... Have you come to destroy us (the spirit shrieked)? (vv. 23–24).
3. Jesus rebuked him: "Be silent," he said, "and come out of him" (v. 25).	4. The unclean spirit threw the man into convulsions and with a loud cry left him (v. 26).

Restoration in Mark's Gospel

Mark starts his Gospel, "*The beginning* of the gospel about Jesus Christ, the Son of God." Hence, he immediately connects his biography to Genesis. But what is Mark's message? He speaks directly to the redemptive and restorative work of Christ. Evidently this is on his mind as in verse 2 he draws readers back to Isaiah's proclamation of a coming messiah. Mark confirms John the Baptist as the Voice of Preparation, the one who comes before the Messiah as his front man, announcing and staging the Coming One.

With the Messiah now on scene, Mark captures Jesus' opening proclamation: "The time has come," he said. "The kingdom of God is near. Repent and believe the good news!" After calling the first two pairs of disciples (Simon and Andrew, James and John), Mark establishes that Jesus has come, not only to speak *for* God but to speak *as* God. John claims that Jesus is the Logos, the Word of God. Mark captures Jesus' first engagement of his public ministry as one that takes aim at the restorative objective of the cross work. The setting is Capernaum, the day a Sabbath, the location a synagogue.[19] Properly fixed with theological props, Jesus amazes the populous with his teaching. It is a teaching the people are not acquainted with because "he taught them as one who has authority, not as the teachers of the law" (1:22). The marvel of this day is briefly captured in the short retell below based on 1:21–28.

> On to this Capernaum stage enters a man possessed by an evil spirit. The man, through the occupying voice of that spirit, cries out in fear of Jesus: "I know who you are—the Holy One of God!" Jesus acts swiftly, silencing the spirit, commanding, "Come out!" The witnessing people are dumbstruck. They have never seen the like, especially at the hands of the teachers of the law. They conclude in continued amazement: "What is this? A new teaching—and with authority! He even gives orders to the evil spirits and they obey him."[20]

Coming as this story does at the beginning of Mark's Gospel, the parallel to Genesis is inescapable. First is the reference "in the beginning" (Mk. 1:1). Then is a holy setting—a synagogue—a place of worship, metaphorically a typology of the garden where Adam and Eve, as priest-kings, worshipped God. It comes on a Sabbath, the seventh day, the of God's rest. However, darkness in the form of an evil spirit comes into this synagogue, projecting a backward glance in time as the serpent penetrates the garden abode.

Mark's Gospel reports that an evil spirit takes possession of a certain man; in Eden's garden the serpent takes captive the image-bearers themselves. As the serpent turns Adam and Eve to his kingdom of darkness, he renders their authority void. But now, as Isaiah will prophesy, comes the Messiah. He enters the garden-synagogue and confronts an evil spirit.

Jesus presents his credentials. He speaks with authority, verifying his message as the evil spirit submits to his commands, surrendering in obedience. This reversal by Jesus in the synagogue acts as a microcosm of the garden of Eden, in which Satan spoke and the First Couple obeyed. Capitulation results through their denial of God's truth. But now Jesus comes bent on reversing that outcome and restoring mankind's role as servant-kings. In Jesus, then, is the intended activity of the First Couple who are to be rulers "over the fish of the sea and the birds of the air, over the livestock, over all the earth."

It is significant that this garden commissioning ends not with fowl, fish, and livestock, but includes a special subject—Adam and Eve are to rule "over all the creatures that move along the ground" (Gen. 1:26). Theologically, Genesis ties together Adam and Eve, the snake/serpent/demonic forces, and the mission to rule over those who move along the ground. This is what Mark alludes to in describing Jesus' work of conquering an evil spirit in the synagogue. This story, therefore, illustrates that there is more in view to Mark's Gospel than just an exorcism; in it can be found God's project of restoration as Christ overcomes the powers and rulers of darkness through his manifold truth. The hour to take back the kingdom of God arrives!

Further, to ensure this opening salvo is not missed, Mark adds additional narrative content. He begins with three healings: Peter's mother-in-law (see Mk. 1:29–34), a man with leprosy (see 1:40–45), and a paralytic who is made to walk (see 2:1–12). Alexander notes the theological importance of Jesus' many healings and exorcisms: "Without reproducing their detailed discussion, the significance of Jesus' conflict with demonic forces is reflected in the prominence given to Jesus' rebuttal of Satan's temptations . . . and the recurring references to Jesus driving out 'unclean spirits' . . . and demons."[21] Alexander joins with other writers in pointing out the underlying drama and purpose that is occurring in these spiritual-conflict stories.

What is Mark saying, then, through these opening stories? He is pointing back to "the beginning" by informing his audience that Jesus has now come, come in the *authority* and presence of the Lord, come indeed as the Son of Man to alter the verdict and the outcome of the Garden of Eden. Eden is to be reversed; a new garden is being prepared and man is being set free to do the work he was once commissioned to accomplish. Mark describes this restorative theme: "News about him spread quickly over the whole region of Galilee" (1:28). Into Galilee, land of the Gentiles, land of darkness, comes an expanding light.

This outward-bound projection is further disclosed in the healed leper's response. Although Jesus commands the man to show himself only to the priests to offer sacrifices instituted by Moses, the man, filled with joy, cannot be contained by the law's regulations. He quickly makes known what God has done for him. Thus "he went out and began to talk freely, spreading the news" (1:45). In the healed leper we see a parallel to the intended work of the servant-priests, Adam and Eve. They were directed to "be fruitful and multiply," they were to "fill the earth and subdue it," and to secure "dominion" (see Gen. 1:28 RSV). By fulfilling this outward-bound command, their service was to result in glory and honor to God their King throughout the garden planet, as illustrated by the healed leper.

Interlude Summary

In this three-part review and synthesis is found the need and reason for the cross. It is found in the veiled message illumined in Scripture's symbolic images, key phrases, and figurative language. In other words, it is found in God's meta-story of truth.

The need for the cross, then, grows out of the truth-denying rebellion of Adam and Eve. In that action the First Couple, having been deceived, fall as they deny God's truth. They and their progeny are held prisoners in a kingdom of darkness characterized by deception and lies. This causes forfeiture of Adam and Eve's role as priest-kings, their commissioned authority stripped away. But God, in his mercy, commutes the fullness of their banishment sentence, limiting it to physical death. That was done in view of a great redemptive hope (see Gen. 3:15) that would be brought to fullness in the person of God's Son. Tied to redemption is the restorative theme in which the Satan's works are reversed and mankind returns to God's favor, to live once again as "a chosen people, a royal priesthood, a holy nation, God's special possession . . . who called you out of darkness into his wonderful light" (1 Pet. 2:9).

This fulfillment was seen in the parallel construction of Matthew chapter 26. In it is located Peter's stumble, his denial of truth. But a compassionate Christ reverses the effects of that rebellious fall. To those electing Peter's example, the hope of forgiveness remains through the cross work of Jesus. That work is graciously illustrated through the beautiful imagery of the risen Lord's lakeside meal, baked on "a fire of burning coals . . . with fish on it, and some bread" (Jn. 21:9).

On the other hand, there remains the illustration of Judas. Redemption and restoration await not this division of mankind. Cain's line dead ends, terminating in complete treachery. It is labeled betrayal as Judas, leading a club-wielding contingent, continues to believe "the lie." It ends horribly in his own kind of crucifixion, alone and abandoned, where his death lacks the efficacy of the cross' atonement, his thirty coins of no avail. In the end, this story of stumble and betrayal finds resolution by returning to the beginning message of Jesus. In Mark's Gospel he proclaims: "The time has come . . . the kingdom of God has come near" (1:15).

This three-segment review of Part I provides a biblical framework to contextualize Jesus' statements in the coming period of darkness.

But now, as the study of the morning's first three words closes, the entire mood and what takes place at Calvary is altered beginning with the **Fourth Word**. The day, as is the case with the land, finds itself occupied by darkness. In that somber tone we take up Christ's statements spoken from the sixth to the ninth hour. It is, as John was apt to say, a time of night.

Part II

The Cross in Darkness

Part I illustrates the importance of symbolic language. Particular focus was placed on the image-pattern of light and darkness. Christ's first three words, speaking forgiveness and the formation of God's community, were contextualized by this narrative image. However, as Part II commences, the shadow of darkness descends upon the cross, its nightfall altering the tone of Jesus' words.

Organizationally, three sections comprise the second half of this book. The first, Section V, presents the long-awaited conflict foretold in God's judgment when Adam and Eve failed the serpent's challenge. This may be heard in Jesus' **Fourth** and **Fifth Words**, which themselves yield a story of crisis and resolution.

Rhetorically this prompts the question, What does the cross accomplish? In Part II's middle section, two chapters give reasons why Jesus mounts up on the cross. Interpretation is provided through his state-ment, "It is finished." An *eschatological* look at the **Seventh Word**, in the section's third and final chapter, concludes Section VI.

The book's closing section provides reflection on this study. Theme elements of community and communion, along with a final look at the Bible's literary construction, anchor conclusions.

Jesus' entire life was to proclaim
God's reign as a reign of
compassion, freedom, and peace
against the forces of evil.

Thomas P. Rausch, S.J.

Section V

DARKNESS

Mark's darkness depiction now falls on the crucifixion; with it comes a substantial change in narrative tone. The joy of announcing forgiveness is no longer heard. Now is deep darkness. The cross is silent for nearly three hours as Jesus remains on it. But his enemies' voices are not. He can still hear their taunts, challenging him to quit the cross and "come down." This is the crisis moment. Will Jesus remain on the cross and thereby paradoxically proving his divinity by his death? Or will he come down, preserving his life but abandoning the cause for which he came? Mankind's fate awaits his response.

Organizationally, two chapters bring light to this dark moment. Chapter 9 begins by establishing its tone. Of importance is the brief introduction of the statement: "If you are the Son of God." Resolution of the garden fall and God's insufferably long quest to redeem his people comes in the tenth chapter. It is made known as Jesus echoes an ancient psalm in the **Fifth Word**, the word of thirst.

The image of darkness combined with the cross' symbolic language, revealed through the **Fourth** and **Fifth Words**, propels the reader to discover God's steadfast covenant love as he reclaims his people. Here is the climax of Scripture—the story of God's agape love as the Son's atoning sacrifice restores humanity to pre-fall relationship.

Chapter 9

THE OPPORTUNE TIME

And God saw that the light was good;	and God separated the light from the darkness. Gen. 1:4 (RSV)

In the symbolic language of Scripture when Mark writes, "At the sixth hour darkness came over the whole land until the ninth hour," he does so fulfilling Genesis' statement of separation. It is here on the cross, an instrument bathed in both light and darkness, where God accomplishes (but does not yet inaugurate) the separation of light from darkness for time eternal. The cross is the central moment in the history of mankind; it is the climax of humanity's abandonment of God. It is also, astonishingly, God's resolution to humanity's crisis, and it comes in the **Fifth Word**.

Found one verse down in Mark's Gospel from the statement of darkness is Jesus' shocking cry: "My God, my God, why have you forsaken me?" (15:34). Such proximity textually links the Messiah's despairing cry with the depiction of darkness as it falls on the landscape. Mark's figural darkness looks back on God's creation, where it is displaced by light.[1] It appears that God's purpose at the outset, disclosed by the Genesis author, is this very message now being confirmed on the cross—this removal of darkness from all of God's good creation (see Gen. 1:4; Rev. 22:5).

This chapter's purpose is to establish a narrative tone for the crucifixion that will provide helpful background when we arrive at the resolution of Christ's fourth statement. I begin by (1) examining Scripture's
relentless pattern of contrasting light and darkness. Following (2) is an
introduction of the devil's challenge to Christ, heard in the phrase "If
you are the Son of God." The chapter concludes (3) by considering
the effect Christ's statement of thirst has on the cross. These three sections provide a broad contour for the resolution of the crucifixion story,
which will be examined in the coming chapter.

1. Division of Light and Darkness

The gospels, referencing the word *beginning* in their opening sequences,
recall Genesis' iconic phrase.[2] Genesis' first two chapters establish a
dynamic and harmonious relationship between the Creator God and
his creation. The most important part of creation is the formation of
man, distinguished by the descriptor "very good." However, spoilage
occurs when God's good creation is suddenly torn apart by a horrific
crisis. The image-bearers lie at the heart of the matter. Deceived by
the serpent, they abdicate their appointed role as priest-kings. Further,
through the word *curse* in Genesis chapter 3, the crisis is understood
as creationwide. By aiming at mankind, the serpent succeeds in bringing down not only Adam's race but the created order. Alexander succinctly summarizes: "The story of the fall brings to a bitter end the
harmony that was the hallmark of God's creative activity. In particular
we witness a breakdown in relations between animals and humans,
between men and women, and most important of all, between God
and humanity."[3]

Through Christ's seven words, God's redemptive and restorative
project may be narratively discerned. But it falls to the **Fourth** and **Fifth**
Words where this eons-old catastrophe comes to a clashing climax and
resolution. It is here, set upon a Roman crucifixion, that darkness meets
light, where Satan pits against Christ, and God marshals his forces to
take back a kingdom that was so horribly wrenched away in the First

Couple's abdication. The intertwining of the **Fourth** and **Fifth Words** decisively informs this battle.

When Jesus cries out, "My God, my God, why hast thou forsaken me?" how does this affect the overall project of God to redeem mankind? An answer comes by understanding that Jesus' voice may be interpreted as speaking for all of humanity as well as himself. When viewed representationally, the Messiah's cry is the forlorn heartbeat of mankind.[4] Without God's aid in providing a savior-redeemer, all that humanity can do is utter this hapless cry. Having brought man into being, an existence propelled by the exciting purpose of being named royal proxies to oversee the garden planet, mankind is left to wonder why God has abandoned the apex of his creation.

Humanity is unable to overturn the judgment of death brought by our ancestor's act. It is, after all, as God said it would be: In the moment when the forbidden fruit was taken and eaten, surely the human race died. Our questioning cry, heard on the cross through the voice of Jesus, is rhetorical. We know its answer. We are to die since in our disobedience we breached the separation barrier. To understand this barrier, we return to the beginning, to the opening pages of the creation story.

The word *separate* occurs a minimum of five times in the initial chapter of Genesis, providing a reason to look beyond its literal language. Indeed, this opening chapter transcends even the symbolic, driving to an inexorable theological hint. It suggests that an inherent division is present at the beginning, perhaps even before the creation "clock" counts down the six literal days. The language of separation is intentional, coming as a reaction to a suggested picture of *theological chaos* portrayed in Genesis 1:2, where the primordial earth is described as "formless and empty" with "darkness over the surface of the deep."[5]

This observation that a division is built into the created order— one that divides and separates the forces of good (light) from those of evil (darkness)—is continuously revealed as the biblical narrative goes forward in time. Immediately after the First Couple's fall, we are told that Adam lay with his wife and children are born. This statement in

Genesis 4:1 transitions storyline from Adam and Eve to offspring. For story purposes, we hear no more of man's birthparents. Now the focus zooms in on their children. Cain, the firstborn, and Abel, his younger sibling, are instantly portrayed as adults. Abel is a shepherd; Cain a man of the soil. Apparently, they have been taught by their parents to worship God, and so we find them bringing offerings from their labor. The story acknowledges that God favors Abel's offering from the flock, but of Cain's agricultural harvest there is little regard. In a fit of jealousy, Cain premeditatedly invites his younger brother into his field where, in an opportune moment, he kills his competitor for God's favor.

By following the fourth chapter to its end, we are told of other children that issue from Cain. The chapter concludes when Abel's replacement, a child named Seth, is born. Space won't be used to diagram the divergent lines coming from these two. However, the biblical narrative makes clear they form two lines, two distinct divisions result (see Interlude-2). Cain's progeny follows in the footsteps of their ancestral parent, committing other murders and acts of ungodliness. While Seth's line is not necessarily more "clean," it does result in the birth of Noah, the first man ascribed as being "righteous and blameless." By the end of the eleventh chapter it is evident a separation has formed among mankind. There are those who "call upon the name of the Lord," and there are those who seek their own glorification. This distinction, the backbone of the Tower of Babel story, puts a singular emphasis upon this point.[6] Thus the theological conclusion of separating light and darkness as a narrative image is established.

The importance of this review, where events anticipate the healing work of the cross, is discovered in this division of light and darkness. The Bible conveys understanding that God separates from evil. More so, Adam's race is also sorted on this same basis. A lineage of light in contrast to a progeny of darkness is formed, a line of righteous people compared to an unclean nation.

Given that the cross sits as the centering activity of human history and, furthermore, since the cross itself is depicted by this same image (see Mk. 15:33), its importance cannot be overstated. The centrality of this theme is found when we arrive at the crucifixion. There, amazingly but not unexpectedly, we encounter Mark's description of darkness. Presented in contrast to the morning period of light, darkness appears exactly at the crucifixion's midpoint, which is noon. The cross continues this historical division through Jesus' conversation in the **Second Word** with the thief. By this means the story begun in Genesis comes full loop:

> "And God saw that the light was good;
> and *God separated* the light from the darkness."

The cross is engulfed in prefiguring, primordial *theological light* with its separation from darkness. Thus, the cross reflects creation's initial aspiration; it is, in fact, the culmination of God's intent. Indeed, the morality play of the garden announces that man is created specifically to be a worshipping community of holy priests. It is to be a nation that (a) enjoys fellowship with the Creator-God and (b) receives blessings in the role of vice-regents over the visible realm. However, due to the devastation unleashed in the "darkness fall," this new kingdom is overtaken and occupied by evil; it must be completely severed from God's realm. In the biblical landscape this occurs not only as a separation of darkness from light, but as a judgment curse (see Gen. 3:14–19). Yet, contained in that curse is the pronouncement of a veiled but nonetheless future clash in which the Son of Light collides with a personage of Darkness. The battleground, preestablished by God's prophetic word, is Golgotha. The instrument of battle—the cross.

Given this background, the **Fourth** and **Fifth Words** form both *climax* and *resolution* to this quandary. Paramount is to understand the meaning these two cross-utterances hold for the crucifixion's outcome. Left to their literal intent, these words indicate a Christ who is despondent, exhausted, and beaten. Such is the literal biblical portrayal that haunts the **Fourth Word**: An abandoned and desperate Christ calls out, seeking to know where is the God of mankind? In tone the **Fourth Word** casts as improbable humanity's fate.

As for the Lamb (see Jn. 1:29) nailed to its rough surface, his cry of forsakenness leaves God's entire redemptive restorative project, like his own faith, in grave doubt. This desperate plight, however, is not what it seems. As C. S. Lewis so artfully and delightfully tells, there is yet a "deeper magic" on the horizon.[7] It is a magic for which darkness has no antidote. And it is to be found in the discernment of Christ's **Fifth Word**.

2. The Serpent's Challenge

The gospels make clear that in back of the cross lies a cause that was first encountered in Genesis' garden. Therefore, in the sixth hour, the hour of darkness, is found the snake, uncoiling for its most deadly strike. Now is the time the devil has awaited. This is the time, as Luke records, "When the devil had finished all this tempting, he left him until an opportune time" (4:13).

At the end of forty days, a fasting Christ is confronted by the devil. Three challenges are issued, commonly thought of as temptations. The first aims at Christ's fast, offering him food in exchange for a miracle. The second entices Christ to throw himself down from the heights of the temple, while the final comes in the form of worship. This spiritual-conflict story is often used by the church to teach the necessity of memorizing Scripture to thwart temptation, but the gospel narratives go far beyond that application. The first two challenges explicitly begin: "If you are the Son of God." This phrase reveals a base strategy employed by the Serpent, one we examine in the next chapter. After all, it is humanity that has died, not God; it is humanity that must find a way back to life. But without Christ, Adam's race is doomed. There is no way back. That is the pathos of the **Fourth Word**. It is also mankind's eternal quest: how to accomplish the impossible. The devil challenges Christ, the son of Man: "If you are the Son of God."

Now three years removed from the wilderness fast, Satan engages in the same deception. From the crucifixion comes again this profane echo: "If you are the Son of God" (Mt. 26:63, 27:40). Like a conductor whose choir has hit a wrong note, the narrative reader hears this discordant phrase in the rabble's ranting mock. Satan reveals his own incessant fixation on Jesus' estate as Son of God. It is an honor Satan dearly desires; not so much to be the son but to be God (See Is. 14:12-15). *That is the foundation on which the crucifixion conflict originates.* Using this temptation, the devil batters a now exhausted, depleted Christ in the sixth hour of the crucifixion. "If you are the Son of God, come down. Conclusively prove to all—come down! If you are the Son of God."

3. Depleted

After three hours of darkness, Jesus breaks the stillness of the cross, a silence that has muted Calvary as much as the darkness. He has just issued the desperate cry heard in the **Fourth Word**, after which he gasps: "I thirst" (Jn. 19:28 RSV). These words tell much of his physical condition. They remind readers of what they cannot see—the intolerably bruised, beaten, and bloody body. Nearly bled-out, Jesus reaches a critical state of hydration. His bodily fluids mortally low, his cry of thirst echoes Psalm 22:14–15 (REB):

> My strength drains away like water
> And all my bones are racked.
> My heart has turned to wax
> And melts within me.
> My mouth is dry as a potsherd,
> And my tongue sticks to my gums;
> I am laid low in the dust of death.

Scripture reveals his physical condition prophetically and in real time. The simple statement "I thirst" is painfully easy to understand; yet reference to his physical condition is not the point of its inclusion in the text. Turning to John's Gospel we inquire, Why describe Jesus' thirst? Christ is so apparently dehydrated it seems redundant to state the obvious. In quest of that explanation I elect to examine the **Fifth Word** alongside the **Fourth Word**. One reason is to see this depleted physical condition. The other, and more germane reason is considered in the following chapter. As awful as his physical condition is, worse still is his faith outlook, which is exposed as Jesus charges: "My God, my God, why have you forsaken me?"

This statement produces great angst among his onlookers; they are uncertain what was just said. Both Mark and Matthew report that some think Jesus is calling for the prophet Elijah as he cries, "Eloi, Eloi."[8] Other witnesses are not as sure. These words bring confusion and uncertainty; those hearing do so through a real-time basis without knowing what the future will unfold.

Mark records, "About the ninth hour Jesus cried out in a loud voice." The ninth hour of the day, or three in the afternoon, which is another way to affirm he hung on the cross six hours. It is significant that his cry comes then and not in the eighth hour or even the seventh. Here we come to the interpretative tension between literal text and symbolic. Did Jesus hang on the cross six hours because that was the sum total of time he could last? Does six acquire a symbolic meaning, hinged as it is to the sixth day of creation, the day of man? Or does six point to the number Revelation ascribes to the unholy beast: 666? The Bible makes clear that Jesus' death was preplanned, an event foreseen even prior to the creation of man (see 1 Pet. 1:20–21). Here, then, is the culminating act of the second Adam. Paul confirms:

> In him we have redemption through his blood, the forgiveness of sins, in accordance with the riches of God's grace that he lavished on us. With all wisdom and understanding, he made known to us the mystery of his will according to his good pleasure, which he purposed in Christ, to be put into effect when the times will have reached their fulfillment. (Eph. 1:7–10)

Summary

In this chapter the pervasive background of light and darkness is developed. This tone is often omitted when the church and her teachers turn to the subject of the cross. The crucifixion story *is more* than Paul writing, "Jesus saves." It is a rich texture of not just the gospel story, but, as N. T. Wright reminds his readers, it is a narrative of the "Gospel in the Gospels."[9] Wright's 'gospel in the gospels' in this book is the story of how Israel's history acts figuratively to foreshadow not only the cross, but *expose the crown* through Christ's seven last words.

In the coming chapter, with this backdrop established, Jesus' shocking **Fourth Word** is heard. It is that cry which causes great uncertainty for his hearers. Yet, when perceived through the metaphorical lens of the **Fifth Word,** it becomes the trumpet sound of victory! As we shall see in the tenth chapter, the devil's opportune time is trumped by God's acceptable time.

Chapter 10

AN ACCEPTABLE TIME

When the devil had finished all this tempting, he left him until an *opportune time*. Luke 4:13	But as for me, my prayer is to thee, O LORD. At an *acceptable time*, O God, in the abundance of thy steadfast love answer me. Psalm 69:13 RSV

The tone of the previous chapter establishes the **Fourth** and **Fifth Words** as *climax* and *resolution* of the crucifixion narrative. In this chapter the horrible reality of Jesus' apparent faithless utterance, the cry of abandonment, is taken up. We are shocked by its implication. However, if it understood representationally, it echoes the broken heart of Adam and his children.

Still, the literalness of the fourth utterance suggests otherwise. Jesus, after all, does make this statement. This causes not only the reader to tremble, but to ask, Is it true that Jesus is abandoned on the cross? **This chapter's purpose** is to examine that question. Resolution is sought in (1) the story of the binding of Isaac, which will provide a key to unlocking the terrible implication of the **Fourth Word**.[1] Following (2) is an examination of the nature of Christ, which contains an often-overlooked element of faith with its story tie to "If you are the Son of

God." Conclusion to the chapter and the crisis of the cross comes by (3) examination of the **Fifth Word**.

1. Forsakenness and Abraham's Binding of Isaac

God's plan to restore and redeem mankind takes a gigantic step forward when the reader reaches Genesis 12. Its opening lines powerfully inter-jects the view that humanity must separate itself from darkness. While these words are not found in the text, their thematic presence is evident as the storyline is pushed to new heights. And so we read: "The LORD said to Abram, 'Go from your country and your kindred to the land that I will show you'" (12:1).

This famous call may be likened to Neil Armstrong's lunar step. It is unprecedented. While God has issued instructions before, such as to Noah, this call contains the basis of God's mercy and grace, which is wrapped in the words "I will bless you" and "all the families of the earth" through you. Based on this and many other revelations, Scripture makes known that from the lineage of Abraham will come a Mighty One in whom these promises will be realized. That someone it turns out, is God's only son, the Jewish Messiah, who is given the name Jesus (a.k.a., God Saves or the Lord Saves or simply Savior). Abraham's lin-eage begins, therefore, on the basis of the separation call (i.e., "leave your country").[2] This aspiration is more than the story's literal admoni-tion to relocate to a distant land; veiled in it is the foreshadowing of a future people whose basis for living will be to separate themselves from the deceptive draw of darkness.

Given the overall importance of Abraham to the entire biblical nar-rative, we pick-up his life's climax (told in Genesis 22), which is an allusion to the apex moment of mankind—the crucifixion. It is also a foreshadowing of the **Fourth Word,** the word of doubt and question-ing. The story of Isaac's binding begins with an imperative command: "Take your son, your only son Isaac, whom you love, and go the region of Moriah. Sacrifice him there as a burnt offering on one of the moun-tains I will tell you about" (22:2).[3]

The story retell below is adapted from Genesis 22.

As it turns out, the journey to Moriah was a three-day journey, a relatively short distance for seminomadic people. But for Abraham it was a journey of a lifetime, for in it his life would be forever defined. He was not alone at the start, having taken two servants, and of course, he was accompanied by his only son, the son born of God's promise. Three days give a man a lot of time to think, and that's surely what Abraham did. The task before him, however, was unthinkable. The more he thought about it the more incomprehensible it became. It violated everything he knew about this strange God who kept appearing and reappearing in his life. Why was he even chosen to do this God's bidding? But more so, why now, after the miraculous birth of his son, born to Sarah in her old age, well beyond child bearing years? No matter how he turned it over in his mind, the same answer was there: it did not make sense. True, the people of the land he originated from practiced child sacrifices, as did contemporaries in his new land. But God had never shown any interest in that; he always seemed satisfied by Abraham's altar building and animal offerings. Nothing made sense. Still, the Voice had never failed him —yet. But sacrifice Isaac? His son, his only son, the son he loved who was born of Sarah. No, it could not be.

Suddenly the journey was too short. There in the distance Abraham saw the terrible mountain. Leaving his servants behind, he fixed on his face a mixed mask of bravado and faith, telling them that he and the boy would continue alone to the place of "worship," and then "we will come back for you." With that resolve, Abraham and Isaac climb up the mountain. But now worry has become contagious, heard in Isaac's voice: "Father, the fire and wood are here, but where is the lamb for the burnt offering?" What could Abraham tell his son? He could not bear to say to Isaac, "You are the lamb." But he could not, despite what he wanted to do, take Isaac and flee that terrible mountain. How could he? If he did he would separate himself and his family from the Voice that had miraculously guided his life course since age seventy-five. That Voice had announced Isaac's miraculous birth. But now there is nowhere to turn. He could only say to Isaac what he desperately hoped: "God himself will provide the lamb."

But he didn't; not yet anyway. So Abraham was compelled to bind Isaac, to place him atop the wood pile that would become a funeral pyre for his son. There was but one thing left. Pulling his knife from his robe he lifted it up, high to the heavens above, and then at its apex came the Voice! "Do not lay a hand on the boy. Do not do anything to him."

When this story is broken down by the church, it is most often done as an allusion to the cross and the sacrifice of Jesus. There are so many embedded symbols in the literal text that cross-directionality can hardly be missed. Yet the story is much more than a narrative trail marked by symbols. The story rises and falls on its *representational* value. Thought of this way, Isaac is cast as a type of Christ, the lamb of his question. Abraham, as the father figure, represents the presence of God. This association is fixed by the key phrase, "take your son, your only son Isaac, whom you love" (See Mt. 17:5; Mk. 1:11). Told this way, the narrative becomes an allegory establishing God the Father bearing his only son, Jesus, to the mountain of crucifixion, and there, alone, sacrificing him.

In the loneliness of Abraham is the soulful mourning of yielding his son, his only son, the one he loves most dearly, to the deadly end that results from human sacrifice. The pain that Abraham experiences in this three-day journey, during which he literally recalls every moment of his dear son's life, must have been excruciating. He did not want to do this. Was there not another way out? But after three days the answer was evident: only by the sacrifice of his son could the journey end in true worship.

Therefore, in Isaac, who is cast as Christ, the fear of being the actual sacrifice surfaces. Coming to the mountain top, Isaac glances about; it is barren except for a few thickets. No sign of a ram. Where will the animal come from? There is the knife and there is the fire; but no animal. There is only himself. Heard through this typecasting is the boy's fearful question: Where is the lamb for the burnt offering? With no animal in sight, Isaac feels the love of his father slipping away. He feels betrayed. How could his father, the one he loves and the one who loves him, do this awful thing? How could he be left here to die? He asks his father, "Why have you forsaken me?"

In the pathos of that cry is an eternity of pain. As the boy asks this question, he sees no other sacrificial victim. Truly he is alone. His vision narrows, his sightlines shorten. None are there to rescue. Two servants are below, but they are too distant to see what is about to transpire, and even if they could see, they are too far away to prevent his sacrifice.[4] Father, Father, why have you forsaken me?

What is often missed as Christians interpret this "story of the cross" is the Father's role and his presence. Isaac, as it turns out, is not alone; he is not abandoned. He is accompanied by Father Abraham every step of the way along the three-day journey. When Jesus is nailed to the cross, and his followers have fled, he too apparently is alone. Therefore, when he cries out the wail of abandonment, does he cry it for himself or for mankind?

Certainly, it is for mankind. But is it also for himself? That is the real question the **Fourth Word** asks. But the life of Abraham isn't unknown to Jesus; he knows it well (cf. Lk. 16:19–31). Therefore, on the cross, when he mournfully questions his Father-God, does he not do so with the sure knowledge that the Father has been and is with him every step of the way on his own three-day journey? Just as Father Abraham was with Isaac, so too must be Jesus' Abba-Father.

With this story of Abraham and Isaac acting as background rehearsal for the cross, we turn now to the **Fifth Word**, the word of thirst. We do so in search of a conclusive answer to the doubt heard in Jesus' cry, to the question of dereliction. But first we must see the story of Isaac and his father for what it is—a story of faith. To aid this understanding, a frequent question by the gospel writers is recalled: Who is Jesus?

2. The Nature of Christ

Christology is a branch of theology devoted to the identity of Christ and his life. From it comes an incontrovertible truth: Jesus is God, but he is also man.[5] This conclusion, that Jesus is both man and God, is accepted today within Christianity. But that was not the case when Jesus presented himself throughout his home region and eventually to the temple priesthood at Jerusalem. The gospels, disclosing this struggle, may be read from two perspectives: the biblical authors' editorial views, which hold Jesus to be the Son of God, but also a narrative view in which people encountering Jesus must contend with this question. At issue is the challenge faced by the Twelve: Who is this one called Jesus? (see Mk. 4:41). The synoptic accounts reveal a transition as followers become believers, disciples become servants, and, in John's Gospel, confused men eventually say with conviction: "my Lord and my God." Summarily, the portrayal of the centurion at the foot of the cross climaxes Mark's Gospel as the Roman soldier declares, "Surely this man was the Son of God!"

The following summary is drawn from the passion narratives.

> Answers to the twin questions, when and how did Jesus come to ascertain his own divinity, are not explicitly told in the gospel accounts of Jesus' life. There is no carefully crafted story in which the reader is given insight into how Jesus comes to conclude that he is the Son of God. However, careful reading of the text draws a reader into an implied understanding that Jesus too must discover his own faith as the Divine Son (the Messiah). Such a statement may seem outlandish, perhaps even heretical, today. But if believers are to hold the duality

that Christ is *both* man and God, then Jesus must be permitted, as are all humans, the pathways of individual growth and
faith development. He is born of Mary, the alleged son of
Joseph, though Matthew and Luke quickly imbue the role of
Joseph as father figure rather than father in fact.

As Mary's son, Jesus finds in her the first and most reliable
witness to his unique personage: his birth story. He is not
like his childhood playmates. How does Mary tell Jesus of
his birth? Scripture provides no answer other than the iconic
"his mother treasured all these things in her heart" (Lk. 2:51).
The family flees Herod's persecution when Jesus is not more
than two, ironically going down to Egypt, the motif-land of
slavery. From there, the story advances to the death of Herod
and the tiny family is called "out of Egypt" (Hos. 11:1).[6] All
this time Jesus is growing "in stature," culminating in the
twelve-year old's three-day domicile in the temple. After that
we hear no more of childhood or early adult years.

This brief sketch returns us to the question: Did Jesus "just know"
he was the Son of God? Or was it through biographical sound bites
and other unstated life experiences that he gradually came to a faith-
conclusion that he was not only Mary's son, but God's son as well?
There is scriptural evidence to suggest that by age twelve, Jesus thought
of himself as God's son (e.g., "my Father's house," see Lk. 2:49). But it is
his baptism at the River Jordan that a voice from heaven announces him
so, confirming Jesus' earlier identity awareness.[7] Significantly, all four
gospel writers elect to record this event. The three synoptic biographers
do so from a third-person view, most likely adopting Mark's language
in 1:10: "he saw heaven being torn open and the Spirit descending on
him like a dove" (see Mt. 3:16–17; Lk. 3:21–22).[8] John's Gospel tells
this story from the testifying voice of the one who baptizes Jesus. We
are told that John the Baptist witnesses the descent of the Holy Spirit

and hears a voice proclaiming Jesus as Son of God (see Jn. 1:32–34). The baptismal event, therefore, concludes Jesus' personal quest to affirm what Mary was told: "The virgin will be with child and will give birth to a son, and they will call him Immanuel (which means, 'God with us')" (Mt. 1:23).

By the time Jesus turns thirty he is fully convinced he is God's son. Furthermore, readers of the sacred text also know this salient information. It is only those who walk alongside Jesus and encounter him in the byways of life that have yet to discover this meaning, which, it seems, is an objective of the writers (see Jn. 20:30–31; Acts 1:1–2).

While this subtext feature (Is Jesus the Son of God? Along with the query, How and when does he acquire divinity's self-awareness?) is not often the subject of pulpit preaching, its relentless presence in the gospels is one that should not be missed.[9] Its significance is found in the devil's temptation challenge, "If you are the Son of God." This narrative hammer commences straightaway after Jesus is confirmed as God's son. It is not accidental that Matthew and Luke reveal an immediate challenge to Jesus' now confirmed belief that he is the Son of God. In Matthew's version, only two verses separate baptism from temptation. Luke wedges a lengthy genealogical listing (see Lk. 3:23–38) between Jesus' authentication and the devil's temptation. If not for this inclusion, which acts to draw attention to sonship, then a mere three verses separate this story chain. Common to both Matthew (4:3) and Luke (4:3) is the devil's opening statement: "If you are the Son of God."[10]

Jesus' unique nature figures in the devil's attack on the cross. Therefore, the purpose of this review of Christology is to present background on which the cross-battle is fought. For three years, Christ has been plagued by this Son-of-God question. It starts at the conclusion of his forty-day fast when the devil appears and challenges Jesus directly: If you are the Son of God, do such and such. This questioning of Jesus' personal faith continues throughout his three years of public ministry. Thomas Rausch writes: "Until the end of Mark's Gospel, the real identity of Jesus is not recognized. . . . It is known only to the reader, and to the unclean spirits who recognize him as 'the Holy One of God' (Mark 1:24), 'the Son of God' (Mark 3:11), and 'Son of the Most High God' (Mark 5:7)."[11]

During this three-year period, Jesus will seek confirmation of how his followers comprehend him. Thus he asks, "Who do people say the Son of Man is?" (Mt. 16:13). Even John the Baptist inquires, "Are you the one who was to come, or should we expect someone else?" (Mt. 11:3). In Matthew's Gospel, the narrative sequence surrounding this question provides a skeletal framework on which the opening story of Christ is told. It begins in 1:1, as Matthew outlines Christ's genealogy, beginning with its suggestive "Jesus Christ the son of David, the son of Abraham." Then follows the miraculous birth story with the child's name as "Immanuel (which means 'God with us')." Quickly the story advances to Jesus' baptism, when a voice from heaven declares, "This is my Son." Matthew next introduces the wilderness temptation and Satan's mocking faith challenge, "If you are the Son of God."

This challenge of faith not only resides in Christ's divinity, it defines him as human. As man, he is subjected to all the frailties of flesh and blood. Contrary to the sweetness of some Christmas carols, heard for example in the hymn "Away in the Manger," Jesus does, in fact, cry. As a toddler he falls, scrapes his knee, and bumps his head; he gets slivers in his fingers as he pokes around his father's carpentry shop. He knows joy, laughter, and sorrow (the absence of Joseph in the biblical story). And as Mary's child he must grow, learn, and develop. By age twelve he has so mastered the ancient scrolls that he can hold his own with the great teachers of Torah: "Everyone who heard him was amazed at his understanding and his answers. . . . And Jesus grew in wisdom and stature, and in favor with God and man" (Lk. 2:47–52).

The relevance of this climaxes at the cross. There Jesus must ascend it as man; he cannot mount it as God. Though his is the "DNA" of divinity (cf. Mt. 1:18), it is not negated by his human birth but rather suspended at his incarnation (see Php. 2:5–11; Col. 1:15).

And so on the cross, as throughout his entire life, he is fully man. He must, as is the case with all humanity, approach God by faith.

When Jesus was a child he had to grow into the belief that he was the Son of God. While this was confirmed in many ways, nevertheless he had to embrace and fully believe his own uniqueness and divinity. Thus, the narrative subtext presses this faith question: "If you are the Son of God."

This narrative question of faith is one of great challenge to Jesus, the Divine man, as he lay nailed to the cross. In the backdrop he can hear this lifelong inquiry as the religious leaders and the rabble mock, "If you are the Son of God" (cf. Mt. 26:63, 27:40; Lk. 22:67). This challenge is orchestrated by the Deceiver, who uses it to challenge the Messiah to "come down" (see Mt. 27:39–44; Lk. 23:35–37). Faced with this test, Jesus can miraculously come down (see Lk. 4:9–11). Doing so will conclusively prove his divinity. But it will also forfeit his atoning role. No longer will he be the sacrificial lamb (see Is. 53:6), the Isaac test case.[12] God cannot be that lamb. God did not fall in Eden. Man did. Jesus must resist this challenge to come down. Only by remaining on the cross can he prove, by its atoning work, that he is the Son of God. In that way he completes God's love work, a work that only the Son of Man, in the person of God's Son, can accomplish. This is Isaiah's "stricken" lamb, the one on whom "he was crushed for our iniquities; the punishment that brought us peace;" and through the cross "we are healed" (see Isa. 53:5; Jn. 1:36).

The faith connection to this challenge, therefore, is heard in Jesus' woeful cry of forsakenness, the **Fourth Word**. Here is a replay of Isaac: "Father . . . but where is the lamb?" Here is Isaac's loneliness, in which we sense the child's fear of being abandoned. Isaac feels his father's love slipping away as Abraham binds him to the woodpile and lifts high his blade, ready to strike its death blow into his tender body. He wonders: Why have you forsaken me, me the son of your love, your only son? And so too Jesus cries out: "My God, my God, why have you forsaken me?" which encourages the devil and causes believers to quake.

Rausch writes of the **Fourth Word**, embedding it within a look at Psalm 22, which prophetically begins:

> My God, my God, why have you forsaken me?
> Why are you so far from saving me,
>   so far from the cries of my anguish?
> O my God, I cry out *by day*, but you do not answer,
>   *by night*, but I find no rest. (vv. 1–2 emphasis added)

Rausch offers two views on this psalm's interpretation. To some this cry is one of despair; but to others it "represents an expression of hope."[13] More so, in our examination of the cross, Christ's apparent dereliction cry finds resolution in the **Fifth Word**, which it turns out is a word of faith. It is to this optic we now turn.

3. The Fifth Word

Abraham's binding of Isaac, acting as cross rehearsal, along with the devil's statement, "If you are the Son of God," questions Christ's faith. It prepares the reader by foreshadowing the **Fourth Word's** apparent abandonment. Narratively, two ancient psalms serve to pivot the crisis away from its apparent despair and defeat to rejoicing and victory by unlocking its resolution, found in the **Fifth Word.**

Two Ancient Psalms

A few excerpts from Psalm 69 (RSV) demonstrate its prophetic application to the cross.

> Save me, O God (v. 1). . . .

> I am weary with my crying;
>   my throat is parched.

> My eyes grow dim
>   with waiting for my God (v. 3). . . .

> mighty are those who would destroy me,
> those who attack me with lies (v. 4). . . .
>
> For it is for thy sake that I have borne reproach,
> that shame has covered my face (v. 7). . . .
>
> But as for me, my prayer is to thee, O LORD,
> At an acceptable time, O God,
> in the abundance of thy steadfast love answer me (v. 13). . . .
>
> Hide not thy face from thy servant;
> for I am in distress, make haste to answer me (v. 17). . . .
>
> They gave me poison for food,
> and for my thirst they gave me vinegar to drink (v. 21).

The psalmist begins with words of faith; he cries out his dependence on God to save him. The content of the psalm is strikingly like the setting of the cross. Further, it brings a godly alternative to Satan's "opportune time" heard in the phrase "acceptable time."[14] This gives rise to the expectation that the cross is God's acceptable moment to overcome the work of evil. Further, verses 3 and 21 alert the reader to a great thirst. This psalm leads to a conclusion that the cross is the acceptable time, the right moment for God to conclusively answer the psalmist's plea "save me." Thus, in this "acceptable time," we find this article of faith, and it comes within the great thirst of the One who bears mankind's reproach.

> Why are you cast down, O my soul? . . . (Ps. 42:5 RSV)
>
> I say to God, my rock,
> "Why hast thou forgotten me?
> Why go I mourning,
> because of the oppression of the enemy?"
> As with a deadly wound in my body,
> my adversaries taunt me,

> while they say to me continually,
> "Where is your God?" . . .
> Hope in God; for I shall again praise him. (vv. 9–11)

Like Psalm 69, Psalm 42 finds the psalmist under attack and discouraged. God's whereabouts are questioned, heard in a cross-like echo, "Where is your God?" Here is the taunt from the onlookers as they challenge the crucified Messiah to come down from the cross (see Mk. 15:32; Mt. 27:42). This questioning symmetry and faith attack, however, are countered by the palmist's thirst response:

> As a heart (deer, NIV) longs for flowing streams, so longs
>   my soul for thee, O God. (Ps. 42:1 RSV)
> My soul thirsts for God, for the living God. (v. 2)

Psalms 69 and 42 provide a link to the **Fourth** and **Fifth Words.** Previously the question, Why does John include Christ's statement of thirst when the synoptic accounts do not? was raised. Other than to confirm the demands of prophecy, it seems so unnecessary to speak of his thirst. This is particularly magnified by its scriptural sequence, coming as the fifth statement. If John truly wants to show Jesus' great thirst and dehydration, then why does he do so now, at the very end of the crucifixion? Why does Jesus cry out at a time when something to drink comes too late to be of aid? An answer is to understand Jesus' statement, "I thirst," (RSV) as a metaphorical expression of truth.

Psalm 42, like much of what Jesus taught, comes from the voice of metaphor. It begins with a simile, tying together a deer with its referent, the parched soul thirsting after God. Jesus similarly uses thirst when he encounters a Samaritan woman at Jacob's well. There the Lord develops the daily ritual of drawing water to metaphorically transform a conversation between himself and the women into a spiritual dimension. Jesus likens himself to a spring of water, one that wells up to eternal life. "If you knew the gift of God and who it is that asks you for a drink, you would have asked him and he would have given you living water" (Jn. 4:10). We see this same construction in Psalm 42, where the psalmist writes how his soul's thirst, like a panting deer, longs for God, echoing the cry of Jesus' thirsty heart heard in the **Fifth Word**.

Psalm 42 informs how thirst, as a spiritual metaphor, can hold significant meaning for how Jesus uses it from the cross when divorced of its literal meaning. John's story of the Samaritan woman demonstrates Jesus' tendency to make connections between actual thirst and spiritual thirsting. Indeed, as William Willimon writes, thirst is a biblical metaphor.[15] With this as backdrop, we may again turn to the cross and find meaning behind the apparent real-time cry of thirst.

The twin statements "My God, my God" and "I thirst" powerfully connect what otherwise could be taken as two separate remarks made in an afternoon's darkened sky. However, forsakenness and thirst now suddenly combine into a relational plea as the Lord witnesses the horridness of sin's effect to divide the bond between mankind and God. In Jesus' statement of thirst, we hear an intense desire to fully unite with the Father. John writes, confirming Jesus' meal-table discourse in the Upper Room, "Father, just as you are in me and I am in you" (17:21). This affirmation on the part of Jesus is more than just a post-dinner conversation; it acts to prefigure the challenge of the coming crucifixion. Further, it symbolically acts as an antidote to Satan's challenge, "If you are the Son of God." Thus, both at the meal table and later at the cross, Jesus stridently denies a rift between himself and the Father.

That Jesus should use the language of picture-framing words while on the cross should not be a surprise. Much of his communication over the past three years was done through parables and painting word images using natural scenes. He spoke of farming and animal husbandry; of the sea and fishing; and in particular he was fond of images and words associated with I AM, such as the gate, the vine, and the bread. To the woman at the well in Samaria he used water as a metaphor to transcend what would not only be a socially awkward situation but one that was clearly out of bounds for a holy man and rabbi into one of insight and spirituality through well-water imagery.

We find Jesus on the cross thoroughly dehydrated, down to the final minutes of life. In this exhausted physical condition, but more so in an apparently depleted spiritual state—abandoned and forsaken—he now phrases an exact representation of his most stringent inner desire: to be with the Father. His life energies gone, he looks to heaven and affirms his entire being is God centered. He declares not the **Fourth Word's** forsakenness, but rather announces the *thirst* he holds for his Father. His cry is not one of abandonment; rather it is an affirmation of faith, a counter to the lifelong question "If you are the son of God?" It is a declaration of unshakable unity that exists now, as it always has, between the Son and his Abba-Father. Most significantly, as the Son of Man, he speaks representationally. Jesus cries out humanity's great thirst for God, for the Creator mankind once abandoned. This, then, is the great reversal Scripture has so long held in view. Jesus does not cave to the Tempter's deception, "If you are the Son of God."

Read this way, Jesus completes the allegorical message drawn from the binding of Isaac. Just as Father Abraham strode every step of the way during the three-day journey, and just as Father Abraham was there at the altar of sacrifice on Moriah, so too Jesus loudly proclaims that his Abba-Father is also at the cross altar. He is forsaken not! He is the "Son of God."

The story behind the **Fourth** and **Fifth Words** is revealed as a story of unparalleled faith. By means of the metaphorical **Fifth Word**, through Jesus' own statement of hungering and thirsting (see Mt. 5:6), he forever demonstrates the oneness that unites Father and Son. Jesus' utterance of thirst nullifies all claims of abandonment; it decisively dismisses the Tempter and his empty words, "If you are the Son of God." In this exemplary act Jesus responds as humanity was expected to from the beginning (see Jer. 29:13; Deut. 4:29).

Summary

Use of the **Fifth Word** as metaphor quenches forever the profane challenge heard in the devil's mockery, "If you are the Son of God." Thus, Jesus proclaims victory on the cross. He does not yield to the deceitful, crafty temptation *to believe the lie of being abandoned*. He knows that his Abba-Father, as in the days of Abraham and Isaac, is with him. Jesus asserts an unshakable faith that the Father always has and forever will be in his accompaniment. This declaration at long last concludes the separation of light from darkness found in the creation story. No longer must mankind be separated from the Father's kingdom (see Gen. 3:24). No longer must the Spirit of God hover over the waters of darkness to separate them (see Gen. 1:6). Now, in the sacrificial work of the cross, there is nothing but unifying light.

With the **Fourth** and **Fifth Words** the cross turns from disaster and deceit to triumph and truth as Jesus crushes the massively evil ego of the Deceiver. Mistakenly thinking he is on the verge of victory (the despairing **Fourth Word**), the Deceiver now finds (through the **Fifth Word**) that it is himself who has been deceived! In this scene the drama that began with the serpent's deception of Eve turns full force on the Deceiver, crushing and bruising his manic ego (see Gen. 3:15). What royal irony![16] The "opportune time" has become the "acceptable time;" the hour of the cross.[17]

Psalms 42 and 69 not only provide an answer to humanity's cry, "Save me, O God," they reveal Jesus' defeat of the Tempter, thereby restoring mankind to the garden realm. This emphasis on restoration is further echoed in the psalmist's words, "What I did not steal must I now restore?" (69:4 RSV). The psalmist's question, prophetically the voice of the Messiah, finds resolution in Christ's reversing action as the kingdom is returned to God.[18] And with it comes return of man's original trajectory as servant-kings.

Section V Conclusion

The importance of reading the Bible from the symbolic lens is demonstrated in this two-chapter sequence. Heard literally, the **Fourth Word** cry of Jesus is one of discouragement, of dereliction of duty. However, when the ancient stories are consulted, the echoing effect of richly veiled and representational language turns apparent despair to rejoicing. The crucifixion account, when understood meta-narratively through the **Fourth** and **Fifth Words**, is both climax and resolution.

The **Fourth Word** locates mankind on the cross. But in the **Fifth Word**, Jesus demonstrates he is the Son of God. By not heeding the temptation to prove his sonship by miraculously "coming down," but instead remaining on the cross he establishes not only his humanity, but answers with finality the gospel subtext, "If you are the Son of God." The act of remaining ensures his reign; it negates the Tempter's challenge to prove sonship by throwing himself down (see Lk. 4:9). Rather, in this reversal, it is Satan who is cast down. It is the beginning of the final end of Satan's usurping reign over humanity. And it comes by word of truth as the God-man, Jesus the Jewish Messiah, declares humanity's great thirst for this ever-accompanying God (see Gen. 22).

One final observation about the **Fourth** and **Fifth Words**. Like the morning's three, they also form a cross conversation. However, unlike the morning statements, their primary audience is not mankind. These are words Jesus reserves for his Heavenly Father, further nuancing the message of oneness and sonship. As we transition to the **Sixth** and **Seventh Words,** we discover that this heavenly audience remains.

Section VI

LIGHT

The seven words spoken from the cross comprise a narrative story, a sermon in capsule form. What Jesus says yields broad understanding for mankind; it answers eternal questions. In the crucifixion saga, highpoint comes in the intertwining **Fourth** and **Fifth Words.** In them the climax of man's garden crisis and its solution is found. But now the reader comes to Jesus' **Sixth Word**, the most significant of all. Ironically, it does not focus on those eternal questions; rather, it points to answers. Jesus' sixth proclamation informs humanity what God accomplishes through the crucifixion.

Organizationally, Section VI presents, in summary form, *a few* of the numerous attainments that occur because the Son of God came as the Incarnate One and was crucified. Three chapters make-up this segment. The first, chapter 11, concerns man's basic problem, the rebellion in the beginning as mankind adopts violence as its creed, abandoning the God of peace. What follows in chapter 12 is the long quest by God to effect separation from darkness for humanity. Section closure comes in chapter 13 and the **Seventh Word**. It builds an eschatological conclusion as God embraces his image-bearers in a faith-sponsored communion.

Chapter 11

SWORDS OF VIOLENCE

The Sixth Word: "It is finished!"
If the crucifixion were an epic novel, its setting, characters, and plot would be introduced in the first **Three Words**. Over time, as generations, centuries, and millennia pass, all drive toward a penultimate climax heard in the angst of the **Fourth Word**. Resolution comes in an allegorical understanding of the **Fifth Word**. The **Sixth Word**, as saga summary, discloses how God blesses the human community. An eschatological exclamation point, the **Seventh Word**, foreshadows a light-filled communion with God.
"And the Word became flesh and dwelt among us, full of grace and truth."   (Jn. 1:14 RSV)

The **Sixth Word** can be understood in two dimensions. The first is that the crucifixion is over. It is synonymous with Christ's dying breath. On the other hand, it leads to debate over not just what it is Christ finishes but what he accomplishes.[1]

Stanley Hauerwas expresses this divide over the sixth statement.

"It is finished" is not a death gurgle. "It is finished" is not "I am done for." "It is finished" will not be, as we know from the tradition of the ordering of these words from the cross, the last words of Jesus. "It is finished" is a cry of victory. "It is finished" is the triumphant cry that what I came to do has been done. All is accomplished, completed, fulfilled work.[2]

Many, such as Hauerwas, understand *finished* to mean "accomplished," including the translators of the REB. Christ's work, while done, is more than done work. It is work that achieves. The question is not so much what does *finished* mean, but how does this work change the tarnished created order? What are these now-finished works?

In this chapter, a more widely spread look at the cross and its outcomes is taken than is commonly understood in the phrase, "Jesus saves." Therefore, this chapter takes aim at this question of accomplishment.[3] I do so by splitting this chapter into two sections. The first examines (1) an apparent contradiction concerning violence in the commands of Jesus in the hours just prior to his crucifixion. On the one hand, he condemns violence when he is taken captive in the Garden of Gethsemane. But on the other, he appears to support it when he gives his disciples a final marching order. The word (2) *sword* brings these two oppositional teachings together. Combined (3) with garden imagery, resolution to this question of violence with its apparent contradiction is gained. The second section examines the cross work with implication for sacrifice and scapegoating, both acts of violence. Thematically, this chapter provides important concepts on violence when linked to the cross and Jesus' **Sixth Word**.

THE FIRST SECTION: THE END OF VIOLENCE

The sixth statement finds related echoes in ancient Israel's past and mankind's future. In John's book of Revelation, a phrase nearly identical with that of the **Sixth Word** is found. John writes of seven angels that pour out God's judgment wrath on Earth (see Rev. 16). After the seventh angel's work is completed, Scripture records: "Out of the temple came a loud voice from the throne, saying, 'It is done!'" (21:6). What follows are signs—flashing lightening and rumbling thunder—that end in a mighty earthquake. Couched in this depiction is another cross image: darkness. This is presented by the fifth angel's bowl of wrath when John writes: "The fifth angel poured out his bowl on the throne of the beast, and its kingdom was plunged into darkness" (16:10; cf. Mk. 15:33). Further, this kingdom of darkness is contextualized in the following two chapters of Revelation, which focus on Babylon and its fall, captured by the phrase, "Fallen! Fallen is Babylon the Great!" (18:2).

The story being drawn is one of violence undone through God's judgments. This reversal is understood as a "mighty angel picked up a boulder the size of a large millstone and threw it into the sea, and said: 'With such violence the great city of Babylon will be thrown down'" (18:21). Further, this allusion to violence as a hallmark of evil is heard in the rejoicing of heaven's multitudes. "Hallelujah! Salvation and glory and power belong to our God, for true and just are his judgments. . . . He has avenged on [Babylon] the blood of his servants" (19:1–2).

1. Swords of Violence

We now turn to see how this future without violence fits into Christ's **Sixth Word**. Mel Gibson's movie *The Passion of the Christ* is infamously known for the brutalizing of Jesus. No other movie has shown the crucifixion's sheer violence in such abject, graphic detail. Though violence permeates the crucifixion story, in real time it begins, astonishingly, with Christ and his followers. The short story retell below is from all four gospels.[4]

> Just prior to his arrest Jesus takes his disciples into the Garden of Gethsemane. Having eaten a full meal and a beheld a lengthy discourse, their eyes are heavy; they are not prepared for what is to come. Knowing this, Jesus instructs: "Sit here

while I go over there and pray." However, the Lord takes with him Peter, John, and James. He gives them further instructions: "Stay here and watch with me." But the text goes on to inform that the disciples fall asleep. Twice more Jesus awakens the slumbering men: "Are you still sleeping and resting? Look, the hour is near, and the Son of Man is betrayed into the hands of sinners. Rise, let us go! Here comes my betrayer."

Scripture tells us that a large crowd armed with "swords and clubs" moves in and surrounds the small band of disciples. At this point one of them (John identifies Peter) draws his sword and strikes, slashing the right ear of the high priest's servant.

Jesus is appalled by this thrust. Instantly he commands: "Put your sword back in its place." Luke's Gospel goes on to recount two things of this incident. First, he quotes Jesus as further saying, "No more of this!" Followed by the Lord's final miracle, as he touches the man's ear and effects healing.

Peter must be puzzled by Jesus' condemnation of his action. After all, only an hour or so before the Lord once again spoke strangely. That conversation began shortly after the meal concluded in which Jesus established the new covenant. He had just recalled the past three years, in particular the times he sent out the Twelve and others on training missions. He asked, "When I sent you without purse, bag, or sandals, did you lack anything?" Affirming this, the Messiah added, "But now if you have a purse, take it, and also a bag; and if you don't have a sword, sell your cloak and buy one." To this the disciples replied, "See, Lord, here are two swords." Jesus says, "That is enough."

How strange is this conversation? Here is Jesus, the man of peace and peaceful means, the one who tells crowds to "turn the other cheek."

But now at the hour of his crucifixion, does he alter the course of his message? Why does he evoke a command to buy a sword, accepting the two the disciples proffered? Yet only moments later Peter, seemingly in response to these instructions, is vehemently told to put his sword back as he viciously attacks one of the mob. Jesus hesitates not: "No more of this."

One thing is certain: the crucifixion is filled with violence. It begins here in Gethsemane, moves on to Christ's arrest and subsequent clubbing before the chief priests, and then he is savagely beaten by the Roman soldiers before large spikes horribly pin him to the cross. This hour of violence ends once solders pierce his "side with a spear, bringing a sudden flow of blood and water" (Jn. 19:34).

The crucifixion story is filled with violence; yet, does the reader discover a jarring contradiction as he hears Christ's commands to "take up a sword" but also his exclamation to abandon its use? The apparent oppositional direction of Jesus' two instructions is intriguing. Table 11-1 reviews this stunning sequence.

Table 11-1:   Dual Sword Orders in Luke 22

Jesus	1.) "If you don't have a sword, sell your cloak and buy one." (v. 36)	2.) The disciples said, "See, Lord, here are two swords." (v. 38)
Disciples	3.) "Lord, should we strike with our swords?" And one of them struck the servant of the high priest, cutting off his ear. (vv. 49–50)	4.) But Jesus answered, "No more of this!" And he touched the man's ear and healed him. (v. 51)

The contrariness of these two commands—one to buy a sword, the other to put away the sword's violence—forms a crucifixion mystery. What does Jesus mean when he tells the disciples to buy swords and take them as they go to proclaim his message of peace? If he means for disciples to actually purchase swords—and thus take up the way of the sword—why then does he stridently condemn Peter's obedience as he slashes the servant's ear? This oppositional teaching sounds vaguely familiar to a time when Jesus pronounced he has come to divide a family from itself—and that with a "sword" (see Mt. 10:34–36). In other words, its essence is found not in a literal presentation but rather as a metaphorical communication.

To grasp what Jesus is driving at as he shouts, "It is finished," it is helpful to return to Genesis, where swords and other forms of inflicting violence are first encountered. If Adam and Eve's original sin is discounted, coming as it does by way of the Tempter's deception, the first recorded sin outside of the garden is when Cain slays his brother Abel (see Gen. 4:8). While this sin of murder comes not by the sword, it does come violently and premeditatedly. It is indeed the start of mankind's violent ways. It should not surprise humanity, therefore, to find atop the Ten Commandments list of "thou shalt nots" this imperative against killing.[5]

Intriguingly, in the preceding story, is the presence of cherubim who swirl "a flaming sword flashing back and forth" (3:24). We shall return momentarily to this sword. Yet Scripture's narrative point is made clear: when man fell, he fell into absolute and utter darkness. There was nothing halfway about it. The first sin is violent murder.

This is a horrendous reversal from the emphasis on creating life. Here, the terror that sin will become is immediately forced onto the biblical reader, as if the writer of Genesis wants to contest humanity with Cain's question: "Am I my brother's keeper?"[6] That Cain asks this question, coming only nine verses from the cherubim's sword-wielding presence, is arresting. After all, the purpose of this celestial being is to guard the tree of life. In this way Scripture takes aim at the inviolable gift which is life, and the special kind of sacredness that is all life, not just human. In that regard all forms of violence, whether they result in death or not, come under Christ's prohibition, "No more of this."

The use of swords in gardens should not escape our attention either. In Eden, we find the message that life is priceless. It must be guarded, a task that falls to the cherubim's posting at the tree of life. But in Gethsemane, the biblical reader is confronted with this imperative against violence as we hear Christ's condemnation of Peter as he slashes the servant's ear.

These story details—the cherubim holding a sword as he guards the way to the tree of life, Peter's flailing use of a sword, and the soldiers piercing of Jesus' side—combine to answer Cain's question, "Am I my brother's keeper?" Without a doubt, putting an end to violence and violent death, such as Abel experienced, is one thing Jesus holds in mind as he says, "It is finished." Therefore, the **Sixth Word**, which in number form is associated with both the death of mankind and with the sixth commandment's prohibition against killing, forms an intriguing Scriptural symmetry.

2. Meaning of Swords

The key to this quandary is discerning what Scripture means when it speaks of swords. While often times there is an all-too-literal application of swords as instruments of violence in the Bible's pages, the narrative use of swords holds symbolic meaning. Authority for viewing swords metaphorically comes by understanding how New Testament writers often treat this word. An apparent use surfaces in the *apocalyptic* writings of John as he writes of heaven standing open and sees a rider on a white horse. Crowned with many crowns and costumed in a robe dipped in blood, this rider bears the name "Word of God." John writes: "The armies of heaven were following him, riding on white horses and dressed in fine linen, white and clean. Out of his mouth comes a sharp sword with which to strike down the nations. 'He will rule them with an iron scepter'" (Rev. 19:14–15).

Pictured is a biblical sword, it is sharp and ready to strike mankind. In John's portrayal, this sword is an instrument of violence set in context of a military campaign. Its apparent use is to subdue the wayward line of mankind so that the rider on the white horse may "rule" (v. 15). A clarifying phrase follows in which this campaign is seen as a holy war to determine whether God or the "beast" and its "false prophet" (v. 20) will rule heaven. John writes of the rider on the white horse: "KING OF KINGS AND LORD OF LORDS" (v. 16).

What is occurring, then, is God's final and eventual victory over all usurpers for his kingdom. John's apocalyptic writing sets this end-time event on a warfare image. Yet the type of warfare alluded to is not common to mankind. John's images of battle are not based on weapons of violence, rather they are set on weapons that can defeat deception. We read in verse 20 about the "false prophet," who, along with the "beast," had "performed signs [that] deluded those who had received the mark of the beast and worshiped its image."[8] Given this overall context, which includes the words *false* and *deluded*, the sword the rider on the white horse brandishes—significantly it comes out of its mouth—is the word of truth. Truth is God's chosen weapon to combat the delusions and deceptions of his enemies. God fights not in the gutter, he hits back not with the power of actual physical force, but rather through the glorious might of his truth.

Reversing course, we leave Revelation and come to an earlier writing by Paul, his epistle to the Ephesians. Many scholars believe this letter and three others were written while Paul was in prison (hence, the letters are termed the prison epistles). Written from either Rome or Caesarea, Paul is most likely under house arrest. A Roman guard is always nearby.[7] Given this situation, in this set of letters it is understandable that Paul would use military metaphors, such as the passage known as the armor of God: "Put on the full armor of God so that you can take your stand against the devil's schemes. For our struggle is not against flesh and blood, but against the rulers, against the authorities, against the powers of this dark world and against the spiritual forces of evil in the heavenly realms" (Eph. 6:11–12; Paul may also have drawn on Isaiah's usage in 59:17).

Found in this listing of armor is the admonition to, "Take the helmet of salvation and the sword of the Spirit, which is the word of God" (v. 17). As seen previously in Revelation, the reference to *sword* is metaphorical. Its powerful and deadly use is employed as an instrument of truth against the "devil's schemes." This is the biblical admonition of how to fight a holy war.

The writer of Hebrews also calls upon this image:

> The word of God is living and active. Sharper than any double-edged sword, it penetrates even to dividing soul and spirit, joints and marrow; it judges the thoughts and attitudes of the heart. Nothing in all creation is hidden from God's sight. Everything is uncovered and laid bare before the eyes of him to whom we must give account. (4:12–13)

In the consistent image language of Scripture, once again *sword* is chosen to present a picture of truth. In this case, the sword is not composed of metal, rather it is "living and active;" it is used to discern falsehood by "uncovering" deception and lies that are "laid bare." From all of these accounts comes the important understanding that in God's realm, weapons of warfare are words of truth.

3. Resolution of Contradiction

With this in mind, we now return to the cherubim of Genesis 3, posted on the east side of the Garden of Eden with his "flaming sword flashing back and forth" as he guards the tree of life. He wards off all invaders by discerning their intent and causes retreat as he defeats them through God's weapon of truth.

Seen this way, a metaphorical meaning for sword emerges. Swords frame out as instruments of offense. That is, in battle they are weapons that can lead to victory. When Jesus instructs his disciples that a time is coming for them to take the message of the kingdom to the world, in that context he commands the purchase of swords. Of the two that are offered, he says "That is enough." Jesus does not mean their actual use, as Peter wrongly infers, striking the priest's servant. The Lord says, "No more of this!" The kind of swords Jesus holds in mind are not 'swords' as instruments of violence, but 'swords' as instruments of truth.

As for the "two swords" that Jesus affirms are enough, several meanings exist. One is to understand them as kingdom instruments. In this view they present God's truth to the Hebrew people who, like the high priests, have failed to clearly hear (*shema*) Jesus' kingdom message. The second of the two swords may indicate its use upon the Gentile world. In either event, Christ's cry to take up swords falls in line with the general contour of Scripture where swords are hailed as offensive instruments to battle evil and deception. But they are not instruments to slay another, as was the case in mankind's first sin. Of that violence, Jesus imperatively commands, "No more!"

THE SECOND SECTION

SCAPGOATING AND
VIOLENCE—THE LAST SACRIFICE

In this section, the end of violence described above finds focus in scapegoating and altar sacrifice. The sacrifice of Jesus brings these twin evils together. Here I take up (1) the prophetic proclamation of the high priest (it is better for one man to die than a whole nation) which sets in motion the crucifixion. Aided by S. Mark Heim's work, we will see how the twin evils are understood within a framework of redemptive sacrifice. Secondly, closure is gained by (2) relating violence to our society and Jesus' imperative command, "No more."

Intertwined with the termination of violent actions comes an end of scapegoating and sacrifice. Of these two subjects, the idea that Jesus' is the last sacrifice finds doctrinal agreement in the Christian community.

This is a theme the writer to Hebrews expresses as he compares the superiority of Jesus to period practices of ritual-based altars. In chapter 10 the author takes specific aim at the sacrificial system. He notes that "the sacrifices made endlessly year after year" can never "make perfect" those who employ them (10:1). He concludes it is God's intent they end because of the "sacrifice of the body of Jesus Christ once for all" (v. 10). Hebrews forcefully states, referring to Jesus: "But when this priest had offered for all time one sacrifice for sins, he sat down at the right hand of God. . . . By one sacrifice he has made perfect forever those who are being made holy" (vv. 12–14). He summarily writes, "Christ was sacrificed once to take away the sins of many people" (9:28).

Yet not all see Jesus as a friend of God and a source of good for the nation. Those invested in ancient ways with temple practices are severely threatened by this itinerant rabbi who wanders the territory's towns and villages. After three years of teaching, his message is spreading as untold numbers throng to him. This is clearly demonstrated by the coronation parade as Jesus enters Jerusalem in advance of Passover. The following short retell is adapted from chapters 11 and 12 of John's Gospel.

> The popularity of Jesus is unquestionable. But so is his divisiveness. Many of the common folk love him. They thrill at his poetic teachings, his pointed remarks aimed at the teachers of the law, and his condemnation of a corrupt religious system that profits from a crooked exchange of temple currency. Systems of taxes, both religious and political, are outrageous.[8] No wonder so many seek in Jesus a new order, a new way of doing things. It is no wonder so many want him to wear David's crown.
>
> But that is not the case with the religious hierarchy and those devoted to its traditions. In Jesus they foresee a threat of immense proportions; indeed, it is their view that his continued existence will bring down the national life. How dare

he counterclaim the law of Moses with his "you have heard it was said" sayings! As Jesus' popularity increases, he faces an oppositional response by traditionalists who urge temple leaders and council members to do something about this heresy. John's Gospel affirms this political and religious alliance: "What are we accomplishing? Here is this man performing many miraculous signs. If we let him go on like this, everyone will believe in him, and then the Romans will come and take away both our place and our nation." Faced with this charge the high priest suggests: "It is better for you that one man die for the people than that the whole nation perish." Thus, he offers a redemptive national sacrifice to maintain the existing political and religious order.

Jesus becomes an intended scapegoat to serve the nation's traditions and its leaders. It is their desire that his death provide the classic outcome of scapegoating, preserving ancient ways and power structures through victimization. In *Saved From Sacrifice*, S. Mark Heim looks at scapegoating as a form of violence against an innocent. In his view, violence is overwhelmingly present in societies, and by its application those in power use it to maintain cultural norms and values. "The Gospels make clear that it is Jesus' antagonists who view his death as a redemptive sacrifice, one life given for many. . . . It is intended to unite the community, to prevent the outbreak of escalating violence between occupier and occupied, to keep the peace."[9] Applied to the Jewish religious community and the Roman Empire, this reflects their perception of Jesus as a threat to the peaceful ways of the standard norm or power structure.

In Heim's theology, which finds roots in the anthropological work of René Girard, the cross becomes the means to end the evil of human scapegoating inherent in victimizing an innocent for the "greater good" of another. While Heim's book, with its thesis of redemptive scapegoating, is controversial, it nevertheless produces a surprising consistency with traditional cross views.[10] In his conclusion Heim writes, "We are saved from sacrifice because God suffered it. . . . The passion (i.e., the cross) is a divine act revealing, reversing, and replacing our redemptive violence, which we so long and tenaciously hid from ourselves in the very name of the sacred. When our sin had so separated us from God and built our peace on blood, God was willing to come and die for us, to bear our sin and suffer the condemnation that we visit upon our victims (i.e., scapegoats) and so deserve ourselves."[11]

When Jesus utters the **Sixth Word**, it is beneficial to recall how it echoes not only an end to violence but to violence perpetrated by a powerful class on its less-powerful members. As the author of Hebrews states, in the sacrifice of Jesus there is an end to all forms of religious sacrifice. Jesus' sacrifice is the last sacrifice. "But he has appeared once for all at the culmination of the ages to do away with sin by the sacrifice of himself" (9:26).

Summary

In this first of three chapters on Christ's accomplishments from the cross, we have sighted a neglected aspect of the cross work: to end violence. Whether violence occurs religiously, such as in ancient rites; or in everyday living, when dying violently occurs frequently, as it did to Abel; or through devious and self-centered victimizing of the lesser (through scapegoating, most often found in political motives or corporate intrigue), we must hear Christ's words: "No more." Further we must hear these words as they relate to all forms of violence that humanity perpetrates on itself. To document this daily tragedy seems unnecessary, especially when there are so many instances on which to draw. Yet, I offer as one illustration the following news report from Chicago in the summer of 2016.

> Thirteen people were shot to death over the Labor Day weekend, making it the deadliest holiday weekend of one of the deadliest summers the city has experienced in decades. The 13 were among 43 people who were shot over the weekend.

The deaths pushed to 488 the total for the year—surpassing the 481 homicides last year.[12, 13]

Moreover, violence is wholly condemned by Jesus' seemingly contradictory teaching about swords. God's desire is that violence ends not by a counterstrike of more violence but by the sword of truth.

The biblical system of sacrifice contains, with its emphasis on blood, both a historical cause (the violent death of Abel, the first sin) and a redemptive solution (the atoning blood of Christ). Through such narrative use of swords, the biblical story forges a theological connection. It is fitting, therefore, as the Roman soldiers come to Jesus but find him dead, nevertheless they pierce him with a sword, an act of unneeded violence. This results in Jesus' blood flowing out and falling on the earth (cf. Gen. 4:10). In God's all-encompassing redemptive work, even the garden planet's surface is not forgotten of its need to be cleansed from the toxic poison of mankind's continual acts of violence. To all these Jesus says, "No more." In the end, God forsakes his own might to forcefully overcome evil. He does not engage in violence to end violence; rather he uses the might of truth, in the person of his only Son, to overcome evil and so end violence.

To refer again to Heim: "Abel's blood called for vengeance, and sparked the cycles of retaliation that we have contained only with more blood, the blood of sacrifice. Christ's death speaks a different, better word than this."[14]

Seen from this lens of violence, the story of sacrifice, which on its surface appears as a system based on death, finds its resolution in an opposite direction based on life. John Sailhamer aids in understanding this reversal. He refers to Leviticus: "the *life* of a creature is in the blood" (17:11). Sailhamer writes, "Consequently, though the blood was the life of the animal, when it was shed it signified the loss of its life and hence the animal's death."[15] Thus it was the life force of the now dead animal that "made atonement" (Ex. 17:11).

By this means it is not the animal's death that made atonement, rather its atoning effect is representationally held by this life force, that is, its blood. Sailhamer adds: "It was a substitution. In God's grace the offering of a substitute atoned for Israel's sins."[16] Yet, as the writer to Hebrews underscores, that former system based on animal blood was ineffectual. Its sole purpose was to serve as a temporary placeholder until the authentic life force, which is the Lord, could wash away the effect of sin, cleanse forever, and provide an eternal, once-and-for-all redemption through its conquest of death. Hebrews notes: "It is impossible for the blood of bulls and goats to take away sins" (10:4) In such sacrifices—with their burnt offerings and sin offerings—God was not pleased (see vv. 5–10; Is. 1:11–14).

It is this life force that John holds in mind, recording the Roman soldiers piercing Jesus' body. From out of such violence flows "blood and water." As Christ's life force issues out and saturates the planet's soil, it provides not only redemption for all of man's inhumane treatment against mankind, but cleanses the garden planet as well (cf. Gen. 4:11–12). "No more," Jesus orders. His is the last sacrifice.

However, it must be asked, if Christ puts an end to violence through his sacrifice, then why does violence and oppression, often in the mode of scapegoating, still persist? A biblical answer may be found as we look at another set of accomplishments in the coming chapter.

Chapter 12

OF TWO AGES

The Sixth Word: *"It is finished."*

"But as it is, he has appeared once for all at the *end of the age* to put away sin by the sacrifice of himself." (Heb. 9:26b RSV)	"Grace to you and peace from God the Father and our Lord Jesus Christ, who gave himself for our sins to deliver us from *the present evil age,* according to the will of our God and Father." (Gal. 1:3-4 RSV, emphasis added)

Mark's strange depiction of darkness that fell on the Jerusalem landscape presents challenges for interpretation. The easiest is the literal view in which a reader understands that nightfall came to Jerusalem on that awful cross day. A metaphorical view gives rise to various meanings, such as God's judgment of mankind. Comprehending Jerusalem's darkness as a biblical motif offers yet another avenue of understanding.

When this latter, symbolic motif is applied, Mark's statement transforms into a stunning graphic image. Viewed as biblical theology, this image pattern splits the crucifixion into two distinct, yet cohesive segments of three hours each. More so, when Hebrews 9:26 is applied, the phrasing "at the end of the age" pushes Mark's description beyond literal intent or metaphor. There is something theological about the coming together of "the end of the age" and "darkness fell over the whole land" that demands attention.

In this chapter we consider the role of the cross in bringing to conclusion "this present evil age" and the coming a new age of God's heavenly kingdom. As this duality of ages unfolds, the cross is seen as a cleaver, splitting them asunder. While one age sunsets, the other arises. This chapter takes aim at how the cross accomplishes this cosmic dance.

Organizationally, this chapter is comprised of two sections. The first considers (1) the cross' impact on these biblical ages. Then, (2) Mark's statement of darkness is interpreted with these ages in mind. Finally, (3) Christ's role in these two ages is further examined. **In the second** section the mystery of these ages—why both still continue even though one retreats —is examined in light of the coming throne of God.

THE FIRST SECTION: OF TWO AGES

1. Two Ages and the Cross

Biblical time references can have various meanings. For example, metaphorically as in Christ's "hour;" or literally, such as the six hours he was on the cross. Such duality may be applied to Mark's description of darkness. There can be no argument that the strange darkness that fell on the land from the sixth to the ninth hour casts a metaphorical shadow; a possible interpretation is that it pictures the wrath of God. It may be equally argued that Mark's description of darkness is real; thereby Mark records how a great darkness obscures Jerusalem.

Yet these two interpretative approaches seem to fail when compared to the starkness of the biblical image we have been pursuing throughout this book. There is something about this strange darkness that transcends both literal description and metaphor. More so, a broader meaning may be discovered through a narrative reading. With regard to that, Scripture notes existence of an evil age and an "age to come." The latter is the epoch when evil is finally overthrown, and a new heaven and a new earth appear.

John Bright anchors these two ages squarely on the coming of Christ and his kingdom (see Lk. 18:29–30). Bright sees the New Testament announcing that "the New Age of God, proclaimed by the prophets, had begun."[1] Like Bright, Sinclair Ferguson addresses these two ages, but through a dual-covenant framework: "The anticipation of the new covenant experience viewed from within the old covenant setting is that the new age will bring the fulfilment of what was commanded, namely 'law in the heart.'"[2] Thus both Bright and Ferguson see the new age as synonymous with the coming new covenant.

These two views, however, when rendered in light of Mark's statement, are more than just cementing old and new, of joining former with later. They are, in fact, a cleavage of time itself. Jeremy Treat captures this idea by fixing on Hebrews 9:26 the end of one age and the start of another: "The cross of the resurrected Christ, therefore, falls precisely in the middle of the two ages of redemptive history, and it is in this capacity that we can speak of the *centrality* of the cross. . . . The cross, therefore, is the climatic midpoint of redemptive history, the hinge on which the eons turn."[3]

2. Mark's Statement of Darkness

With this understanding of the two ages set, Mark's statement may be read not as metaphor or as an actual moment when darkness occupied the land. Rather, it points to an accurate and authentic theological chronology of restorative and redemptive history itself. "And when the sixth hour came, *darkness fell* over the whole land until the ninth hour" (15:33 NASB, emphasis added). Graphically, this statement may be pictured in Table 12-1.

Table 12-1:   The Fall of Darkness

"And when the sixth hour came
darkness fell
over the whole land until the ninth hour."

This statement is suggestive that not only did night fall, thus obscuring vision, but that *darkness itself—as an evil force—fell.* Mark's use of the sixth hour shades interpretation toward the biblical period of darkness rather than its literal understanding.[4] Thus, the era of the "present evil age" (which, it may be argued, is the age of rebellious mankind under the usurping influence of the devil) is now literally falling. Further, it is being replaced by the kingdom of light and life, which is a prophetic fulfillment of God's Anointed One (see Jn. 1:4). In this way, Mark's statement of darkness may be applied to the long-standing biblical motif of light and darkness as well as Jesus' sixth utterance, "It is finished." Mark seems to be indicating that the *age of darkness* has fallen! That the present evil age is passing away. *It* is done.

Treat describes a biblical two-age scenario: "In the two-age eschatological timeline, the cross plays a central role."[5] This notion of two ages is not only disclosed by the symmetry of light and darkness, it is revealed in Mark's statement, which is visualized in Table 12-2.

Table 12-2:   Cross Symmetry—The Two Ages of Biblical History

AGE OF DARKNESS (descending)	AGE OF LIGHT (Ascending)
"And when the sixth hour came, *darkness fell* over the whole land until the ninth hour." (Mk. 15:33 NASB)	"I have come into the world as a light, so that no one who believes in me should stay in darkness." (Jn. 12:46 NIV)

The morning three-hour cross conversation discloses that the kingdom of heaven—the ascending branch in Table 12-2—has commenced. This kingdom is one of life and light; it now enters fully into the darkened world of humanity (see Is. 9:1–2). As it does it displaces the age of darkness—that age which failed to comprehend it (see Jn. 1:5). The rule of darkness is ending; the reign of life and light is beginning. Consummation of the past "evil age" comes in the sixth hour of the crucifixion.

The age of the devil and man's rebellion is now being thrown out as the kingdom of God breaks in, ushering with it the age of grace and truth. The writer to Hebrews expresses this in terms of the two covenants: "By calling this covenant 'new,' he has made the first one obsolete; and what is obsolete and outdated will soon disappear" (8:13). The age under law finds fulfillment in the coming age of grace.

3. Christ and the Coming Age

Of this new age, Isaiah prophesizes by referencing Galilee of the Gentiles. This well-known prophecy is displayed in Table 12-3.

Table 12-3:   Prophetic Symmetry of the Two Ages

Land of Zebulun and land of Naphtali, the way of the sea, beyond the Jordan, Galilee of the Gentiles— the people living in darkness	have seen a great light; on those living in the land of the shadow of death a light has dawned. (Mt. 4:15–16; Is. 9:2)

Isaiah not only pinpoints the actual geographical center of the Messiah's early ministry (see Mk. 1:14), he prophetically addresses the two ages. There is the age of darkness, in which the people of Galilee dwell; yet there is also a coming age of light heralded by Jesus' arrival (see v. 15).

Further, the symbolic and actual geographical symmetry of these ages is disclosed by the exactness of the cross' chronology. The cross hour commences at the third hour, concludes at the ninth hour, and finds its midpoint at the sixth hour. Graphically and theologically, the sixth hour is both the halfway point of the crucifixion and the transition point of the two ages. The sixth hour is both an actual time and an epochal, cosmological fulcrum when "darkness fell."

Table 12-4:   Midpoint of The Two Ages—The Fall of Darkness

3ʳᵈ Hour of the Cross	6ᵗʰ Hour of the Cross	9ᵗʰ Hour of the Cross
Crucifixion commences – "Present Evil Age" Satan's Kingdom of Darkness	Midpoint of crucifixion – Transition of Two Ages	Conclusion of crucifixion – "Coming Age" Christ's Kingdom of Light & Life

Summary: Constructing Meaning through Biblical Images

This book opened the crucifixion story by reviewing the wedding at Cana. It began as Jesus denies his mother's request to help with a wine crisis. She notifies, "They have no more wine." He replies, "My time has not yet come." But now, on the cross, his time, a time of wine, has come. In the Upper Room during his last discourse he prays, "Father, the time has come." Of the coming Passover, John writes, "Jesus knew that the time had come for him to leave this world and go to the Father" (Jn. 13:1). It is for this hour that Jesus said, "I have come into the world as a light, so that no one who believes in me should stay in darkness" (12:46).

These are words of image—of light and darkness—and these are also words of theological reality and what is finished on the cross. Jesus is light and brings light into the world. Where light exists darkness may not. This is a replay of the original primordial creation in which the Spirit of God hovers over darkened waters as God speaks, "Let there be light." This statement is more than creation history. As symbolic imagery, seen through a narrative examination, God's creation command ("Let there be") *anticipates* the spread of his light and truth throughout the planet realm. In that way it acknowledges a time when the era of darkness will be removed from the garden planet. It is a time when the Spirit of God will no longer need to hover over darkness as a warden over captives. In this coming age, the prisoners are freed!

Just as actual darkness is displaced by light, so too does Christ's light evict the devil's domain of deceit. These two powerful forces, like matter and anti-matter, cannot coexist. The cross therefore brings light in the form of a new exodus, a new covenant, and a new kingdom. In doing so it closes the door on the world's present evil age, which is an age of captivity, legalism, and bondage. Christ ends this evil age through the illumination of his in-breaking kingdom. The man from above enters into the darkened world below (see Jn. 8:23). He brings with him the coming age of heaven, which is an age of light and life, displacing this present age of darkness and death.

In concluding this segment on cross accomplishments, we turn to Father Neuhaus.

> At the cross point, everything is retrieved from the past and everything is anticipated for the future, and the cross is the point of entry to the heart of God from whom and for whom, quite simply, everything is. Here is the beginning and the end come together, along with everything along the way from the beginning to the end.[6]

But if Jesus does in fact usher in a new age and thereby destroy the works and the age of the devil, how is it that the present evil age continues? The observable fact that evil is seemingly everywhere and that it throws a heavy weight of destruction and death in its wake is as incontestable as the death of Christ. Of this question more is considered below.

THE SECOND SECTION: BATTLE for THE AGES

In this section, the topic of (1) the battle between light and darkness is taken up before asking (2) "If light is victorious then why are hurt, harm, and suffering so prevalent?" Conclusion comes (3) with a big-picture look at why.

1. The Battle between Light and Darkness

The contest between Jesus and Satan is staged at the final meal table. In John's Gospel, this conflict is never far from sight. During the farewell discourse, Jesus talks mainly of the new kingdom, its symbols and relational construction; and of the love and unity the Father has for the Son and the Son for the Father. Still, darkness looms. A coming battle is prefigured "because the prince of this world now stands condemned" (16:11). And then later John writes of Jesus, "But take heart! I have overcome the world" (v. 33).

At the meal table Jesus spends little time with the subject of darkness; it is still a time for the message of light. Clarification of darkness is left to his followers, such as the Apostle Paul, who adds to this framework: "For he has rescued us from the dominion of darkness and brought us into the kingdom of the Son he loves, in whom we have redemption, the forgiveness of sins" (Col. 1:13–14). Still, the hour of darkness comes, stealing in on the Lord through Judas' betrayal, the subsequent arrest and trial, and finally the crucifixion. In the gospels the period of darkness is filled with symbolic words and images, all depicting a climactic battle waged over the Messiah's crown.

John provides insight into this battle. There at the very meal table is the counterfeit angel of light. John writes: "As soon as Judas took the bread, Satan entered into him" (13:27).[7] And there in the garden is Peter, mistakenly brandishing his sword only to be dismissed by the words, "Put your sword away! Shall I not drink the cup the Father has given me?" (18:11). Then there is Caiaphas' misguidance designating Jesus as the nation's scapegoat, followed by more of Peter, this time his denial. Jesus stands bound before Pilate who asks, "Are you the king of the Jews?" (18:33). And so a crown of thorns is forced upon this king's head, a purple robe adorns his whipped and lashed body, and he is mocked: "Hail, O king of the Jews!" (19:3).

Verses as these evidence a cosmological battle between light and darkness, between Christ and Satan. It is at this point that we must recall what Luke says of the wilderness temptation: "When the devil had finished all this tempting, he left him until an opportune time." The cross is that time. Calvary is the decisive moment in the cataclysmic battle of the ages. Of that outcome, hear again the words of the Messiah: "But take heart! I have overcome the world." On the cross, Jesus secures the future of all followers of light. He is the Light and in the cross battle he decisively defeats death and Satan (see Col. 2:9; v. 15).

2. A Reason Why

Anticipating a chorus of "yeah, but" questions, Father Neuhaus writes: "It is finished, yet it is not over."[8] Of that halfwayness, other writers have taken note. Schreiner writes:

> In every instance there is an *"already but not yet"* dynamic. Salvation is inaugurated but not yet consummated. The kingdom has penetrated this present evil age, but the kingdom has not come in all its fullness.[9]

Schreiner correctly raises the observation of an "already but not yet" reality. It is the elephant in the room of biblical theology; it questions the certainty of Christ's triumph. A glance at the daily newspaper or social media provides reasons to wonder about the decisiveness of Christ's victory, even to question the victory itself. The news from both this nation and around the world indicates anything but the defeat of darkness. It seems that since the terrorist attacks of Sept. 11, 2001, the power and forces of evil have grown, not diminished. If that is so, how can the Bible declare Jesus triumphant? To the world it seems that

Satan, not Christ—that darkness rather than light—reigns supreme. It is for this reason that Neuhaus declares this battle as completed, yet still "contested."[10]

We long to ask Neuhaus: Why, if Christ triumphs on the cross does evil and darkness still prowl about, like a roaring lion, seeking to devour any and all? While the Bible may not tell all, it does disclose some of the reasons for this condition. We begin with Jesus. Who else is better positioned than the One who suffered and endured the cross to explain its outcomes? Turning to his kingdom parables understanding is sought.

Mark, like the other gospel writers, has carefully considered both content and arrangement in his narrative. In his third chapter we learn that Jesus designates twelve followers as apostles, thus Jesus begins to marshal his army of the future. Immediately following, Mark inserts the teaching of the strong man and the divided house, in which Jesus refutes those claiming his miraculous powers are owed to Satan (i.e., Beelzebub): "By the prince of demons he is driving out demons" (3:22). In chapter 4, Mark records four kingdom parables. These instruct, first, that the kingdom of God has come contesting the kingdom of evil. Second, in each parable a teaching on the importance of doing the will of God is discovered. The one who does the will of God is the one who participates in this contest between the kingdoms of darkness and light. Collectively, these four parables provide specific information about the kingdom of God. First, it is likened to seeds. Next, it is portrayed as a light, set out so that all can see. This is followed by the need at harvest time to separate the good crop from the weeds. Finally comes the mustard seed, where the kingdom is likened to "the smallest seed you plant in the ground" (v. 31) that "grows and becomes the largest of all garden plants" (v. 32).

It is impossible not to notice the progression of this chain. The kingdom starts out small, but over time grows into something enormous. Relating this to the cross as the turning point on which the two ages pivot, we are to understand that the kingdom begins remarkably small (see the opening chapters of Acts) but then it rapidly sprouts, takes roots, and grows (see the end of Acts). This is precisely what Jesus has in mind when he metaphorically uses fishermen to instruct the coming church mission. His point is best discerned after the cross is finished, for there is found its application. Of that Matthew writes: "'Come, follow me,' Jesus said, 'and I will make you fishers of men'" (Mt. 4:19).

This image of men fishing for men, of women casting nets of grace, is bound up in Jesus' final discourse, when he prays for such fishermen and their catch (see Jn. 17:20). It is on behalf of all future catches that God holds in abeyance the final moment of Jesus' decisive conquest over darkness. He holds it until the net is full and all who are destined for adoption into the kingdom of his Son have been brought in.[11] He holds it until "It is finished, yet it is not over" becomes "It is finished and it is done!"

2. Why in the Big Picture of Theology

Still, some may say, that is fine; let men be fishers of men. But why must all the hurt and tragedy go along with it? Why must the 9/11s, police and domestic shootings, and urban killings continue? Why must terror seize the world with its calamitous body counts? How can God permit such evil? Why must there exist a great wealth divide between a country's citizens, or conflict shred ethnicities? Why must walls and rhetoric divide nations? In truth, such questions are bigger than the scope of this work, but a quick refresher is to understand all of this as an outcome of rebellion with its inevitable consequence of violence, scapegoating, and death (see Gen. 3:14–19).

Once the garden fall occurs, from that point on, if mankind is to remain a free moral agent, even to the point that rebellion is allowed to continue, then with that decision comes all of the rest. All of the evil, hurt, and ill; all of the tragedy attached to man's insistence on piloting his course through a cosmos in which he knows so little. This continual desire to rule is a biblical replay of Israel revolting under the leadership of her many judges. That historic period is summarized in the book of Judges: "In those days Israel had no king; everyone did as they saw fit"

(21:25). In that period Israel dwelt in an age of evil. Although she has passed over the Jordan and attained the land of promise, yet the people do not know God as sovereign. In spite of God's desire to be in their midst, too often Israel rejected the Creator's presence.

But now, as Jesus comes to Israel, indeed to the world, he is presented as king (see Jn. 18:31–37). He is the long-awaited "king of the Jews" (Mt. 27:11), the coming king of the world. He is the fulfillment of Abraham's seed of blessings to all (see Gen. 12:2–3, 17:15–16). He takes up the cross of suffering, fulfilling the most ironic and paradoxical of all prophecies—the king suffers serving his human subjects. He suffers shoulder to shoulder with mankind, that through his suffering all may be healed.

As the garden rebellion unfolds God has two choices. Either end mankind's history at its beginning, or allow man's history, and thus his insufferable bent on harm, to fully run its course. To continue, but not forever. Thomas Schreiner remarks:

> Human history could have ended there, with the death of Adam and Eve. But the Lord in his grace promised that the offspring of the woman would triumph over the serpent and his offspring (Gen. 3:15). God's reign over the world would be reestablished, the world would be reclaimed through conflict; a titanic struggle between good and evil would ensue. The outcome, though, is guaranteed from the outset.[12]

In biblical *cosmology* there is something hidden in the garden story that exceeds the history of humanity. And so God permits suffering to achieve a bigger ambition than what is normally seen in the literal story of Israel. Under God's providence the present evil age continues until all the nets that were to be cast have been cast, and all the fish that were intended to be caught are caught. Then and only then will the time of pain and suffering come to end. Then even will death itself cease, for then will come the eternal reign and rule of Christ (see Rev. 22:1–5).

In that future eschatological time, evil will be vanquished from God's realm (see Rev. 20: 7–10). For in that time God will (finally) realize what the ancient creation story long anticipates: the separation of light from darkness (see Gen. 1:4; Rev. 21:5-8).

Christ's in-bringing of God's kingdom into the domain of darkness is the fulcrum point of the cross. This is the final divide, this end point of choice between life and death. This is the already and once played-out drama faced by the nation of Israel as its people were about to enter into the land of promise during the exodus. Theologically, Israel was at its own halfway point between captivity in Egypt and freedom in the land of promise. Moses emphatically declares:

> See, I set before you today life and prosperity, death and destruction. For I command you today to love the LORD your God, to walk in obedience to him, and to keep his commands, decrees and laws; then you will live and increase, and the LORD your God will bless you in the land you are entering to possess. . . . Now choose life, so that you and your children may live and that you may love the LORD your God, listen to his voice, and hold fast to him. For the LORD is your life. (Deut. 30:15–20)

To those dwelling in the cross' future, a time of new exodus, the net of grace remains yet open; fishermen still cast it upon the sea of humanity. Darkness also continues its assault and rage, yet its reign is temporal though its scope unmerciful, bloodied by man's insistence on violence. Still hope remains, this hope of the cross and the fruit it bears (see Num. 13:23; 27; Deut. 26:1-4; Mt. 26:29).

Therefore, Paul writes of a more excellent way: "And now these three remain: faith, hope and love" (1 Cor. 13:13). The age of evil ends. This is the great hope of kingdom citizens. This hope is based on faith. At present, the Messiah-King is absent from his earthly realm. His kingdom remains an invisible kingdom, a kingdom of the spirit (see Lk.

224 Last Words of Christ

17:20–21). But the kingdom advances through visible manifestations of the church; it grows and expands and fills the land. This is the great message the writer to Hebrews speaks: "Now faith is being sure of what we hope for and certain of what we do not see" (11:1). This faith, then, that believes with certainty the coming age of the new creation.

Summary

The cross, set in this visually stunning image of the fall of darkness, not only discloses but accomplishes this eschatological end. It is the terminus of the "present evil age" and beginning of the kingdom era; an age that even now is pivoting on the midpoint of the cross—"the climax of history." With it comes the end of sacrifices and the beginning of community redemption, but more so the restoration of God's kingdom as evil's kingdom of winter relinquishes its hold. A new springtime, portended by the Seventh Word, is examined in the following chapter.

Chapter 13

In View:
A New Dimension

The Seventh Word: "Father, into thy hands I commit my spirit."
(Lk. 23:46 RSV)

"If there is a natural body, there is also a spiritual body." 1 Cor. 15:44b	"After six days . . . He was transfigured before them. His face shone like the sun, and his clothes became as white as the light." Mt. 17:1–2

The **Seventh Word** is the strangest of Christ's cross utterances. It is strange because as humans we have little experience to construct its meaning. In his **First Word**, the utterance of forgiveness, while all may not seek it, all understand it. Regarding the thief, all know what it means to be repentant, yet all do not repent.[1] Forsakenness is so very human; who has not experienced alienation? The same can be said of all his statements; there is an equivalent but not equal life experience for each.

But when the seventh statement is considered, an experiential chasm opens. When Jesus commits his spirit into his father's hands, how is this statement to be understood? Jesus does not say, as we would comprehend, "Father, into thy hands I commit my *body.*" Body would be understandable; we live in a body, it is our companion, our framework, our containment. The word *spirit* is different. Paul uses it on occasion, such as the close to his second letter to Timothy when he writes, "The Lord be with your spirit." Still, there is something unknown about this.

In this chapter Jesus' statement of committing his spirit will be considered.[2] The goal is not to put a definitive touch on the seventh utterance; rather its pursuit will be a gateway into a coming new dimension of life. The purpose of this chapter, then, is to be evocative but not provocative. **In this chapter** the concept of (1) a death-to-life progression is considered. This is followed by (2) a scriptural review of the coming new life. The chapter concludes by examining (3) four dimensions that constitute that new life.

1. Death-to-Life Progression

Scripture introduces a death-to-life progression as an outcome of the garden fall. When the First Couple ate what was forbidden, they immediately passed from life to death. In that moment they died spiritually. That was the ultimate meaning behind God's warning, which the serpent distorted as he lied, "You will not surely die." Part of that deception is discovered in the fact that Adam and Eve continued to live. However, as the creation story concludes, the cherubim's posting signals Adam and Eve's passage into spiritual death. Still, it would be a death not without hope.

That hope comes in the strange words they hear their Creator speak. Words he has never used before. They are frightening words, statements telling of "crushing and striking," more so words that surely put a chill into Eve's soul: "I will put enmity between you (the serpent) and the woman." Evidently Eve's children would square off in some future battleground with the children of the snake. It was a ghastly prospect. Having spoken that ominous pronouncement, the Creator replaces their fig leaf coverings: "The LORD God made garments of skin for Adam and his wife and clothed them." This provision, filled with theological considerations, was done in anticipation of a future clothing wrapped in righteousness. In the passage of time, Christ would become that garment for Adam's race (see Gal. 3:27).

2. Scriptural Foundation of Death into Life

Paul takes up the matter of death and life in his second letter to the Corinthians. He contrasts the life lived in our bodies with the life to come through the figure of a tent. By comparison, Paul says if our tent is torn down, that is our body destroyed, we have another house, another building from God. In this tent-like metaphor we find a connection to the **Seventh Word's** use of *spirit*: "For while we are in this tent, we groan and are burdened, because we do not wish to be unclothed but to be clothed with our heavenly dwelling, so that what is mortal may be swallowed up by life" (5:4). Jesus first, then humanity, is that mortality now about to be swallowed up by life (see 1 Cor. 15:20–23).

That Paul ends his statement with "life" rather than an expected "swallowing up by death" is shocking. After all, when humans die, they enter the domain of death, not life. Death is the conventional understanding; the world holds that life precedes death. But no, Paul indicates the natural state (i.e., redeemed state) of humanity is to gain life, not death, as mortality expires. In this way he can say of mortality that it is swallowed up by life. He teaches that our earthly tent is exchanged for a "heavenly dwelling." There is another body awaiting redeemed humanity. There is a *spirit-tent* on the horizon for all believers. Three Bible verses, listed below, present this view:

  a. God provides a future, eschatological body. "If there is a natural body there is a spiritual body." (See 1 Cor. 15:35–44)

b. This new body is available for those who have died "in Christ." "If we have been united with him in his death, we will certainly also be united with him in his resurrection." (See Rom. 6:1–5)

c. This new body will be like Christ. "But we know that when he appears, we shall be like him, for we will see him as he is." (See 1 Jn. 3:2–3)

3. The Coming New Life

With that background we approach Paul who writes, "We are of good courage, I say, and prefer rather to be absent from the body and to be at home with the Lord" (2 Cor. 5:8 NASB). Through such language Paul introduces the absenting of our earthly tent for another. It is this other body that Christ has in view when he says, "I commit my spirit." He is after all from heaven, not from earth below. But it is to this word *spirit* which, being dwellers in a physical body, a body comprised of earth's dust and chemicals and water, we have no suitable basis for understanding. We can see and touch and hold our bodies; but we cannot see, or touch or hold our spirits. Yet it is for reason of this spirit-body that the meta-narrative has been driving since the garden.

In his informing work on the Holy Spirit, Sinclair B. Ferguson writes of this question. He picks up the language of Paul's "first Adam" and "second Adam." Adam and Eve are portrayed as the First Couple, while the second Adam figuratively refers to Christ. Ferguson hypothesizes:

> The first Adam was created as the image of God. The knowledge of God and communion with him in righteousness and holiness were the hallmarks of his life (Eph. 4:10; Col. 3:24). Yet he was created for a condition or state beyond his present one; otherwise, the testing conditions which he underwent in the context of Eden serves no purpose. . . . Although unspecified, many indications are given to suggest that his final condition was one of glory.[3]

Ferguson anticipates a changed body and an increased change in status for Adam and Eve. The primary point of interest here is the suggestion that the First Couple's final destiny was interwoven with glory. That is also the case with Jesus as he speaks of the commitment of his spirit. This unquestionably is in his mind when he addresses, in the farewell discourse, his return to the Father and the subsequent sharing of his father's glory: "Father, the time has come. Glorify your Son, that your Son may glorify you" (Jn. 17:1).

Glorification is a state; the Father may receive glory because of the Son's work. But glory may also be a covering; it may cover one just as clothes cover our bodies. While we understand how glory, figuratively, may cover, such as through a heroic action, but in another dimension of being it may be just as real as our bodies are real to us. Ferguson explores that dimension. "The startling significance of this might be plainer if we expressed it thus: the Spirit is given to glorify us; not just to 'add' glory as a crown to what we are, but actually to *transform the very constitution of our being* so that we become glorious" (emphasis added).[4]

Paul writes: "Now the Lord is the Spirit; and where the Spirit of the Lord is, *there* is liberty. But we all, with unveiled face beholding as in a mirror the glory of the Lord, are being transformed into the same image from glory to glory, just as from the Lord, the Spirit" (2 Cor. 3:17–18 NASB). In this regard, Paul notes a transformational aspect contained in "glory." It is more than just a state of exaltation. At a core level, it may approach essence. In this regard Scripture can say, "God is love." Or of Jesus, he "is life." Or of the Spirit, he is the "Spirit of Truth." While we tend to think of all these as attributes, we may also need to reconsider them in light of what Christ taught concerning his kingdom. It is an invisible kingdom; it is from above, therefore it is of another *life dimension* as totally foreign to us as is the concept of death to God. After all, God is Life; actual LIFE. It is impossible for God not to be life; it is impossible for him to be dead, because his constituent make-up is *life*. This can also be said of light.

We think of light in figurative terms, thus Jesus brings light into a darkened world. But God is described in the Bible as light. Not just figurative light, but actual light, which stems from his glory. Revelation informs us that the new Jerusalem "shone with the glory of God" (21:11). "The city does not need the sun or moon to shine on it, for the glory of God gives it light, *and the Lamb is its lamp*" (21:23, emphasis added). This is not figurative language; rather it is stated as a fact. The Lamb is compared to a light source. The light of the Lamb *is the source* of light for the New Jerusalem. In some manner, by some means, *light emanates* from the transfigured Christ (see Mt. 17:2). Thus, Jesus may authentically say, "I am the *light* of the world" (Jn. 9:5, emphasis added).

In our struggle to understand such concepts as how one can be light or glory, it is at this point that we must recall origins. We are of below. We are of the earth, of biological matter; our cosmology rests within that dimension. But Christ comes from above, comes as the Son of God. He comes as one whose "kingdom is not of this world," whose kingdom is entirely different than our earthly centers of power. We cannot comprehend him because, as God, we are not formed as he is. He is life, and love, and truth; not in an abstract, figurative way, but in actuality. In an essence-like manner, he is life, love, and truth, glory and holiness. His very make-up, how he is formed and constituted, is completely, utterly strange to our way of thinking and having our being.

When Jesus says to his father, "into thy hands I commit my spirit," he is saying something about his very nature. His essence. He is Spirit. Paul addresses this paradigm shift in thinking in 1 Corinthians.[5]

> If there is a natural body, there is also a spiritual body. So it is written: "The first man Adam became a living being;" the last Adam, a life-giving spirit. The spiritual did not come first, but the natural, and after that the spiritual. The first man was of the dust of the earth, the second man from heaven. As was

the earthly man, so are those who are of the earth; and as is the man from heaven, so also are those who are of heaven. And just as we have borne the likeness of the earthly man, *so shall we bear* the likeness of the man from heaven. (15:44–49 emphasis added)

Paul's language is not, at this point, metaphoric. He is writing literally. We are created in God's image, but not yet fully formed into that image. This is the same for the age in which Christians live: the kingdom has come, yet it is not fully here. Further, our created image has become tarnished by man's fall in the garden.[5] However, God so constituted us that our destiny is to bear his likeness, but not to be God. To bear his image means to become not God—as the serpent implied in its lie—but to be possessors of his actual image. Scripture says, we are becoming transformed into his likenesses and that by glory unto glory. While living on Earth this transformation is more figurative, anticipating an actual transformation yet to come. This is not to say, however, that we are not already substantially transformed for we have the indwelling Spirit.

Paul is speaking not only of the future, but paradigmatically; that is, he is speaking of a whole new dimension of life. Of a new way of thinking about and conceiving human existence. This is noted when he states: "For the Lord himself will come down from heaven, with a loud command, with the voice of the archangel and with the trumpet call of God, and the dead in Christ will rise first. After that, we who are still alive and are left *will be caught up with them in the clouds* to meet the Lord in the air" (1 Th. 4:16–17, emphasis added).

What Paul says is a shocking declaration. The simple fact is that humans cannot be caught up in the air. Gravity won't permit it. The natural laws of physics and nature preclude such an event. But these restrictive laws we observe are laws from below, from this universe. Yet Paul, knowing all this, writes with full assurance anyway.

Given this new paradigm, believers must also think not so much outside the box as outside the body. God intends to vest mankind with a new body, a spiritual body. Paul states in his first letter to the Corinthians:

> What you sow does not come to life unless it dies. When you sow, you do not plant the body that will be, but just a seed, perhaps of wheat or of something else. But God gives it a body as he has determined. (1 Cor. 15:36–38)

Paul then writes of this death to life progression:

> So it will be with the resurrection of the dead. The body that is sown is perishable, it is raised imperishable; it is sown in dishonor, it is raised in glory; it is sown in weakness, it is raised in power; it is sown a natural body, *it is raised a spiritual body*. (vv. 42–44; cf. Jn. 12:23–26)

4. Four Dimensions of the Coming New Life

First, it is an unseen dimension. It is spiritually discerned. Jesus can say to the Jews, "I am the light of the world." He demonstrates that light by way of miraculous signs, such as granting sight to the blind. By such means he metaphorically makes known the invisible. But for Jesus himself, the invisible is always in view. Jesus frequently says he can only do what he *sees* the invisible Father doing; he can only say what he hears the invisible Father saying. To Jesus, it is as if a window into the invisible domain of heaven is always open. That such a view exists may be understood in Stephen's death. "But Stephen, full of the Holy spirit, looked up to heaven and saw the glory of God, and Jesus standing at the right hand of God. 'Look,' he said, 'I see heaven open and the Son of Man standing'" (Acts 7:55–56; cf. Mk. 1:10).[6]

Second, in a conversation with a Samaritan woman (see Jn. 4:1–26), Jesus refers to those who worship in spirit and truth as being "the kind of worshipers the Father seeks" (v. 23). It is possible when Jesus says "the kind" he is expressing two meanings. After all, how many times did Jesus speak in dualities? The most apparent meaning is what the text declares: they are the kind of worshipers the Father desires. But if Jesus does hold two meanings for this phrase, then he is informing the woman of something of singular importance. His use of *kind* may itself be an echo back to Genesis and the creation of life. In Genesis 1 there is an intentional use of the word *kind*. For example: "The land produced vegetation: plants bearing seed according to their kinds and trees bearing fruit with seed in it according to their kinds." Further, "God made the wild animals according to their kinds, the livestock according to their kinds, and all creatures that move along the ground according to their kinds."

In this regard, we find in Scripture the concept of "kinds bearing life after their own kinds." Most importantly, however, this pattern is broken once human life is introduced. Scripture reports: "Let us make mankind *in our image*, in our likeness. . . . So God created mankind in his own *image*, in the image of God he created them; male and female he created them" (vv. 26–27, emphasis added).

While humanity can clearly reproduce itself biologically, bearing its own kind, the Genesis narrative moves to another dimension by noting that humanity is not the outcome of God creating man as his own kind but rather "in *his image*." True worshipers cannot be those whose physiology comes by way of kinds, that is, as direct biological reproductions. But they *come by way of spiritual reproductions,* that is, regeneration, reproduction by image (cf. Jn. 3:3; 1 Pet. 1:3). Those who are born again of this spirit image are the authentic worshipers the Father desires.[7]

Third, in this holistic conversation—considering the words of Paul, of Jesus, and of the Holy Spirit as expressed through the biblical narrative—there is extraordinary symmetry. While mankind is birthed in flesh by means of kinds, yet in death, when raised up in Christ Jesus, humanity is clothed not with a perishable body but an imperishable one of *image*. In other words, a spiritual body. This 'body' which Paul refers to is fashioned not after its own fleshly *kind* but rather in the *image* of God; therefore, it is of spirit. Since God will not create another in his kind, he elects instead to create humanity in his own image. Hence, we hear Jesus teaching Nicodemus that a man must be "born from above."

God therefore first creates humanity after his image but within a body. If Ferguson is correct, then God had something else in view for Adam and Eve in a future time. That something, apparently, is what redeemed mankind is now being transformed into from "glory unto glory." Eventually humanity, which is a progeny of light, is to be fully transformed into the spirit image of God. So, Jesus may say with foresight: "God is spirit, and his worshipers must worship in spirit and truth" (Jn. 4:24). As to that comparison, John previously wrote: "God is light; in him there is no darkness at all" (1 Jn. 1:5)

Fourth, we ask, What will this spirit/body be like? John aids understanding when he writes in his first epistle chapter 3: "Dear friends, we are now God's children; what we shall be has not yet been disclosed, but we know that when Christ appears *we shall be like him*, because we shall see him as he is" (1 Jn. 3:2 REB, emphasis added). Since Christ, "the last Adam," is "a life-giving spirit" (1 Cor. 15:45), we are his recipients. For we too shall "bear the image of the heavenly man" (v. 49).

The Bible gives some glimpses of Christ after the resurrection but before his ascension into heaven, presumably before his complete glorification (see Jn. 20:17), the glorification he had with the Father before his incarnation, when he laid aside his equality with God (see Php. 2:6–7). Turning to John's Gospel we read: "On the evening of that first day of the week, when the disciples were together, with the doors locked for fear of the Jews, Jesus came and stood among them" (20:19). A week later, Jesus once more visits the disciples in the same room, once more with the doors locked. In this instance Thomas is invited to "Reach here with your finger, and see My hands; and reach here your hand and put it into My side" (v. 27 NASB). Even the NASB, which more strictly renders a word-for-word translation, records this verse the same: "put it *into* My side." Then there is the account of Peter and Christ by the lake. In it, as previously noted, Jesus thrice forgives Peter over a breakfast of fish and bread (see Jn. 21:12). So, we must wonder about Jesus and his new body. This body that once dying can no longer die. We wonder about this body that has been "swallowed up by life."

Paul's first letter to the Thessalonians instructs us concerning a future eschatological time: "For the Lord himself will come down from heaven, with a loud command, with the voice of the archangel and with the trumpet call of God, and the dead in Christ will rise first. After that, we who are still alive and are left will be *caught up* with them in the clouds to meet the Lord in the air" (4:16–17). Paul writes nearly the same thing in his first letter to the Corinthians: "I declare to you brothers and sisters, that flesh and blood cannot inherit the kingdom of God, nor does the perishable inherit the imperishable. Listen, I tell you a mystery: We will not all sleep, but we will all be changed—in a flash, in the twinkling of an eye, at the last trumpet. . . . For the perishable must clothe itself with the imperishable, and the mortal with immortality" (15:50–53).

These brief glimpses indicate a radical change is in view for regenerated humanity. How radical, or what will be the final composition of the redeemed body has not, as Scripture declares, been "disclosed." However, what we can be sure of is the paradigm represented through the Jewish temple. The temple in Scripture is more than a real-time object, even more than metaphor. It expresses an authentic look forward to the coming Holy Spirit, and, eventually, to the new dimension of the unseen world. Jesus taught that after his death and resurrection, the Holy Spirit would indwell each believer.

Such residence is the fulfillment of Old Testament imagery of God's Spirit as he came on the temple structure of ancient Israel. In doing so, it held in view this post resurrection abiding of the Spirit within believing humanity. If believers are, as Scripture alludes, *being transformed by glory into glory* in the likeness of Christ, then the future body is unimaginably outside the present paradigm of a sensory biological body. The composition that comes into view is this spiritual body (see Rom. 8:10–11). If believers are to take on God's image in a very real and full state, then they must take on the resurrected, glorified body. Thus, Jesus' final word may be pondered: "Father, into your hands I commit my spirit."

Chapter Summary

Seven statements from the cross have been examined. As noted, the last word is most peculiar. It leaves us with ambiguity yet certainty. The trail of Scriptures followed in this chapter leads to an also veiled, yet image-rich look at the coming spirit-body of regenerated disciples. As Paul says, Christians are baptized into Christ's death so that they might be resurrected, not only into newness of life but into a new dimension of living. That dimension is disclosed through the symbolic image of the ancient tabernacle as the tent bearing the glory and Spirit of the Lord. This is made known as the book of Exodus ends: "Then the cloud covered the tent of meeting, and the glory of the LORD filled the tabernacle" (Ex. 40:34).

In this way the Spirit of God foreshadows his coming and indwelling presence, not only in the life of the believer, but also eschatologically in the coming new dimension.

Section VI: Conclusion

Two statements, Jesus' **Sixth** and **Seventh Words**, were examined in this section. They lie in sharp contrast to the **Fourth** and **Fifth Words**.

These are words of light. Though spoken in the literal darkness of that awful day, they bear no shadow to their counterparts. Rather, their literary use finds employment as narrative summation and eschatological exclamation point. These are words of fulfillment; words of a still yet-to-come kingdom future. These words counterbalance the deep darkness of despair and defeat. These words rise up above death and degradation and proclaim the sovereignty of God and his power to change and transform the human body and spirit; indeed, the human heart and soul.

Afternoon Conversation: Theme Elements

Paralleling the three statements from the morning hour are the afternoon's utterances. They too, like their counterparts spoken in light, offer up a conversation. Christ's afternoon discourse, unlike the morning's, speaks directly to his Abba Father. Table 13-1 discloses statements four through seven as theme elements.

Table 13-1:   Afternoon Conversation—Theme Elements

Hours on the cross	Theme Element 4th Word	Theme Element 5th Word	Theme Element 6th and 7th Word
3 (period of darkness)	*"Eloi, Eloi lema sabachthani?"*	*"I am thirsty."*	*"It is finished."* (And) *"Father, into your hands I commit my spirit!"*
	Forsaken / Broken >>>	*Thirsting / Seeking >>>*	*Reconciled / United >>>*

PART II   CONCLUSION

In Part II, the climax of the crucifixion and its accomplishments were presented. The angst of the **Fourth Word** appeared to doom Jesus' fate and mission. But that awful utterance, colored in bleak hues of darkness, was amazingly reversed when Jesus proclaimed the **Fifth Word**, the word of triumph.

Previously the question, How will God deal with the twin demons of death and darkness unleashed in the garden? was raised. Answers to that inquiry were sought through Scripture's literary devices. Such an approach differs from today's norm in which believers are taught to "go deep," to drill down into a passage, to exegete fully. Yet, such deep drilling frequently misses the broad contours of the Bible. In the end, drilling deeply often produces an overly narrow understanding of the meta-story. This study discloses that by reading broadly rather than deeply, by reading horizontally rather than vertically, Scripture's *shallow-depths*, like a broad cresting wave washing up on a shore, deposit a treasure trove scoured from its deeper fathoms.

In this quest to discern how God answers the twin-demons question, two threads were constantly on display. Intertwined, they laid out a cross blueprint displaying an architecture of vertical and horizontal beams. On one cross piece was located death; the other held darkness. In chapter ten, the story of how Christ vindicated humanity by defeating the devil was told. That victory emerged out of Christ's reliance on truth.[8] When confronted by truth, Satan's deceptive ways, his lying and cunning, became the source for his doom and defeat. With darkness dispatched, chapter 13 examined a dimension of the coming new life.

Christ's cross victory unhinged the present evil age. As that age now descends, fittingly, into its own descriptive horror, God's kingdom of life and light ascends. More so, the Holy Spirit, as temple dweller, anticipates a regenerated community. It is the Spirit who fulfills Moses' request to be the "one who will lead them out and bring them in"

(Num. 27:17) as the church navigates the waters of life while darkness still floods destruction over the face of the deep.

In the next chapter, answers of how to read the Bible, which are found in the tension between literal language and its symbolic counterpart, are affirmed. Also highlighted are the objectives of this study, which were (1) to examine and construct theological meaning for Jesus' final statements; and (2) to reveal the importance of reading the Bible narratively, as inspired literature.

Section VII:

WORDS

In this section, the project to examine and construct meaning of Jesus' seven last words closes. Three summative conclusions are described. One is the significance of reading the Bible as inspired literature; the other two orbit the book's examination of the meta-narrative and the study's two major cross themes.

Immediately following is an appendix listing tools used in developing meaning of Christ's thoughts on the cross.

Chapter 14

AFTERWORD

After all the nails have punctured Jesus' flesh and pierced his bones. After all the rabble have mocked his incarnational divinity. After all of Jesus' last words have been heard. After all that there remains this question: What has been learned from his final thoughts?

In this book's introduction, I described a tradition where cross-authors and pastors often approach the Lenten season by commenting on Jesus' last words. When they do, generally they consider each word as if it has no connection to its neighboring word. In such a view, the first word lacks coherence with the third, or the fourth finds no relationship to the fifth. If I were to name that pathway to understanding, I would call it Fragmentary Lane.

I have not traveled that well-worn trail. Instead, I have jogged up Scriptural Street, a neighborhood with houses themed by related hues, where lawns are trimmed alike, whose flowers blossom in spring, and sprinklers fountain in summer. There, autumn leaves landscape residences, informing all that this community exists by planning, design, and intent. Jesus' words, in my view, best belong on Scriptural Street. It is there, in the overarching community of the meta-narrative, where his statements are best understood, formed as they are out of the deep, contextualizing backdrop of the Old Testament.

In my search for meaning, I started looking where Scriptural Street begins—the opening pages of Genesis. There I discovered what many know, but paradoxically seldom teach, that the Bible is a literary document. A reading of its initial chapters immediately presents a challenge to modern thinking. Does its descriptions detail how God literally created, or does it convey meaning based on how an ancient culture thought about God, about themselves as a chosen people, and how the divine Creator elected to present himself to them? In other words, did the God of creation reveal himself in a way common to ancient times and customs—through story composed of embedded metaphorical language?[1]

For some reason, twenty-first century believers find themselves locked in mortal combat over this issue: Is the Bible literal, thinking, if it cannot be literal it cannot be true. If it is not literal, then how can it be trusted?

A stroll up Scriptural Street reveals otherwise. Its welcoming neighborhood discloses the Bible as more than a history book, more than a cookbook account of creation. *How this ties in with Christ's last words is strikingly important.* If Genesis is read literally, then its symbolic voice is dampened, even muted. But what if Genesis is more than literal text? What if its language not only informs readers about God and his community but more so provides a key to its own understanding? The contention of *Last Words of Christ* is that such an interpretative key exists. Further, it is discovered when the Bible is read as *inspired literature.*

This path less traveled—this jog up Scriptural Street where harmony and coherence are its lampposts, where attention is focused by a unifying storyline—begins immediately when a reader opens Genesis to hear the text proclaim that God made the heavens and earth. While it goes on to describe a literal six-day creation, in its literary process Scripture does something quite extraordinary. Something that is contained in the first day's account, which is uncovered as God commands: "Let there be light," and then most remarkably the biblical author adds, God "separated the light from the darkness" (Gen. 1:3–4 NASB). Not just light or darkness but "*the* light and *the* darkness." Further, the word "separate" occurs not only once on the first day, but twice on the second day, and then twice again on the fourth day. Five times in the first four days is found this emphasis on separating. Surely, the author of Genesis is drawing a theological bullseye.

Such obvious targeting acts like a magnet, pulling readers into this descriptive divide. By doing so, the biblical author provides an important clue to understanding the mystery of Genesis' poetic-like creation prose. He aims to install a strategy by which a reader may unlock meaning, not only in the creation account but most certainly the first eleven chapters. And quite possibly beyond, encompassing minimally the Pentateuch and likely extending its influence far beyond.

This call to understanding acts like a blinking traffic light on Scriptural Street. Its cautionary yellow causes the observant reader to slow down and scan for more signs, to look broadly, to ponder creation's numerical emphasis. In the original language of the Jewish Bible, numbers comport a scriptural cadence. This dance begins dramatically in Genesis 1:1. There, the most recognizable verse in the Bible, "In the beginning God created the heavens and the earth," consumes ten English words. But in Hebrew, the statement is done in *seven*. Immediately symmetry rises out of the narrative. It is there, in that originating language, where an embracement of symbolism common among ancient cultures appears:

Seven—number of opening words

Seven—creation account days

Seven—number of cross words

Careful Bible readers and serious scholars alike have long noted the importance of this number to the biblical text. Gordon J. Wenham writes, "(Gen.) 1:1 consists of seven words, 1:2 of fourteen (7 x 2), and 2:1–3 of thirty-five (7 x 5) words." He adds additional details too numerous to list here surrounding the number seven's presence before concluding: "Seven is of course a sacred number throughout the Old Testament."[2]

When the sacred and symbolic use of seven is merged with the text's emphasis on "separated," the reader is left with a substantial clue in how to read the Bible. It appears that the surface-level text is written to permit a veiled yet symbolic voice to be heard. This voice (*shema*, O Israel!) lies just beneath the surface. In *Last Words of Christ*, I have examined Scripture's encoded symmetry from the lens of literary language. When Mark writes that at noon the midday sun was banished and darkness covered the whole land, he is describing more than just the weather. He is narrating symbolically, using the same style as Genesis. And that is the first lesson from the crucifixion story. The gospel writers' use of this descriptive image—light and darkness—to surround the cross is the same image depicted by the Genesis author. Thus, the cross echoes back to Genesis a parallel act of recreation.

The literary nature of the Bible has drawn much attention lately. James K. Hoffmeir clarifies: "Literary or rhetorical approaches seek to examine the broad tapestry of the text rather than simply isolating threads. . . . In recent years, exciting developments have been made in the literary study of Genesis, an approach that treats the book as literature."[3]

In *Reading Backwards*, Richard B. Hays writes, "If we learn from them (e.g., OT and NT) how to read, we will approach the reading of Scripture with a heightened awareness *of story, metaphor, prefiguration, allusion, echo, reversal, and irony*."[4] Hays' point to understanding the Bible is to read it with both old and new testaments in view, drawing them together so that one informs the other. The key is to read them for their figural narrative rather than just historical and "plodding literalism."[5]

The point at hand is to realize the importance of reading the Bible as inspired literature. Far too long biblical scholarship, more so the church's teachers and pulpit pastors, have avoided this salient point.

But of late, focus on final form, which attends to the Bible's literary construction and its many genres, has gained sustaining momentum. It is not surprising, therefore, to read a comment by Charles Halton, general editor of the *Counterpoints* series, who writes: "We don't read Gen 1–11 in the same ways as the early church mothers and fathers. For the most part, they were interested in reading Genesis allegorically, that is symbolically. By and large, we don't approach the Bible that way."[6] While Halton is aiming at a discussion comparing ancient cultures and how they communicated compared to our modern, technologically driven culture, the *significance of what he says regarding first-century believers should not be lost*: reading Scripture "allegorically, that is symbolically." Such awareness is leading to a growing trend in which the laity is returning to historic roots by reading and interpreting Scripture as literature overlaid with symbolic meaning.[7] In this way the interpretative strategy implanted in Genesis' literal language is being rediscovered.

Conclusions

Three questions hovered over this book, directing its content and paving its conclusions. **In this chapter,** those questions guide the book's final findings: (1) What is the message of the Bible's meta-story? (2) What is the theological meaning of Jesus' last words? And, (3) What is the significance of reading and interpreting the Bible in its final, inspired, and literary form?

1. Message of the Meta-narrative

Obviously, there are many ways to read and reflect on the message of the Bible.[8] When an answer to that is sought in the cross narrative, there is an overwhelming tone: *king and kingdom*. Jesus immediately initiates this when he opens his public ministry, announcing: "'The time has come,' he said. '*The kingdom of God* has come near. Repent and believe the good news!'" (Mk. 1:15, emphasis added).

That statement proves key to understanding the meta-narrative's message. Much of the Lord's teaching orbits it, thus his parables frequently hold a kingdom strand. Further, in Matthew's Gospel, in the telling of the Christ child's birth, wise men come from the east bearing gifts. One is gold, a king's symbol. At the express order of Pilate, who is the ranking Roman official in and around Jerusalem, a sign nailed to the cross shouts: "JESUS OF NAZARETH, THE KING OF THE JEWS" (Jn. 19:19). This origination comes as Pilate, stunned and confused by Jesus' claims, can only exclaim: "You are a king, then!" (18:37).

In the Old Testament, Isaiah's voice rises above his message of social justice, anticipating a coming ruler: "Of the greatness of his government and peace there will be no end. He will reign on David's throne and over his kingdom, establishing and upholding it with justice and righteousness from that time on and forever" (Isa. 9:7).

Isaiah is not the first nor will he be the last to proclaim this message. God informs Abraham, Israel's patriarch of patriarchs, of this intention as he gives the covenant promise. Of Abraham's wife, Sarah, God states: "I will bless her and will surely give you a son by her. I will bless her so that she will be the mother of nations; kings of peoples will come from her" (Gen. 17:16).

These are only a few of the Bible's nearly inexhaustible references to what many scholars find: the kingdom reign of the Messiah is the Bible's primary message. It is this arc of a coming kingdom in which God's Anointed will reign, that holds the biblical story together.

Last Words of Christ's affirms that conclusion. Whether the reader starts in Genesis, sampling the Torah with its many beginnings, invests the Prophets by hearing their pleas for social justice and righteousness, or rejoices in the Writings' wisdom literature, a prevailing meta-story emerges from all three sections of the Hebrew Bible. It is one of kingdom and God's reign. Leapfrogging past Jesus' kingdom parables, we find the same message in the New Testament. Coming on the final book,

Revelation, we hear John's conclusion. He paints a picture of heaven's multitudes, now viewed as an infinite worshiping cloud of voices. Their collective praise echoes the Bible's epic message:

> Hallelujah!
> For our Lord God Almighty reigns.
> Let us rejoice and be glad
> and give him glory! (19:6–7)

Conclusively, the meta-narrative can be summed up as this: God, who is king, has come to dwell and reign among mankind. This is the primary affirmation of *Last Words of Christ*. That King is Jesus, Israel's Davidic Messiah. As Revelation announces in its closing verses, this king is coming once again:

> I, Jesus, have sent my angel to give you this testimony for the churches. I am the Root and the Offspring of David, and the bright Morning Star. . . . Amen. Come, Lord Jesus. (22:16–20)

2. Crucifixion Theological Message

If we return to Fragmentary Lane, we are bound to read Christ's last words as separate statements, divided from one another. Such a reading would move us in the exact opposite direction of Jesus' teaching. He came to unify mankind by joining Jew and Gentile into one worshiping community by virtue of his agape love.

In contrast to a fragmentary approach, this study found how a literary reading of the first three words produces a cohesive message. Rather than disjointed statements, his words echo the heart of the gospel. They address humanity's need to be forgiven and to forgive, to be accepted and to accept, and to be embraced and to embrace. His words forge a forgiven people into the nexus of a new community (**Third Word**).

Viewed biblically, Jesus is calling Israel to understand that God has fulfilled his covenant promise to Abraham. A promise that extends God's
outstretched hand to bless, to have children in such numbers as to rival
the starry sky, and to be given a promised land in which they may dwell
securely.

The words spoken in darkness also fit this framework of theme-
elements. The **Fourth Word** begins with a troublesome rumble: "My
God, my God, why hast thou forsaken me?" Its resolution, however,
quickly crescendos in Jesus' actual yet metaphorical cry of thirst. It is
this thirst, spoken representationally for mankind, which paves the way
for not only the climax of the cross, but terminates in the great desire
of God to dwell in communion among mankind (**Seventh Word**). The
words spoken in darkness, therefore, give rise to Jesus' afternoon cross
message: forsaken/broken, thirsting/hungering, and reconciled/united.
Collectively, they proclaim God's relational communion with his image
bearers.

Table 14-1:   Message of the Cross Words

Time Period	Theme Elements	Theological Message
Light	Forgiven Accepted Embraced	Reunited in God's *kingdom community* through forgiveness
Darkness	Forsaken Thirsting Reconciled	Joined *in communion* with the Father through Christ's cross work

3. Literary Significance

In *Last Words of Christ*, I sponsored the idea that the Bible's unseen
author inserted important keys to aid understanding and develop interpretation of Scripture's many stories. Of those numerous keys, one was
highlighted throughout this book: attention to symbolic language.

By applying literary tools to the Bible's ancient language, a fresh understanding of Christ's final thoughts emerges. When read from that optic, two findings dominate: the reign and rule of Christ has come to earth, and God's long sought desire to dwell in communion with his image bearers has been realized. The cross is for God an instrument of re-creation, restoring Eden's garden and redeeming his broken and stolen community.

NARRATIVE CULMINATION

Application of Mark's statement regarding darkness falling on the Jerusalem landscape discloses a narrative and interpretative key to understanding Jesus' last thoughts. Through a literary analysis, more than a biblical exegesis, the dominant scriptural image of light and darkness, first encountered in the foreshadowing creation language, is found to anticipate a coming Person of Light who, in the power of the Holy Spirit, extinguishes and replaces darkness, leaving humanity and the garden planet bathed in God's glorious light.

Appendix A

Literary Tools

Listed below are literary tools used to interpret and develop meaning and understanding of Christ's last words.

Table A-1: Literature Elements

LITERATURE AS	ELEMENTS
Story Narrative	Setting Plot Characters Crisis and Conflict Climax and Resolution Summary and Conclusion Meta-narrative, or Meta-story Theme Author's Purpose and Style
Construction	Metaphor Simile Tone and Tempo Symmetry Key Words and Phrases Number Meaning

Language	Repetition • Word • Numbers Literal Symbolic • Images • Echoes • Foreshadowing • Prefiguration • Figural • Types, or Typology
Biblical Presupposition	The Bible is a vast collection of material, existing today in a literary final form. Scripture's content, though, is nearly inexhaustible, which challenges readers to reduce it to one, overriding view, often referred to as the meta-narrative (or meta-story). While unanimity is not found among students and scholars as to what constitutes this primary thrust, the view proposed in this book is that of *king and kingdom*. This spearheading theme is further informed when the Bible's pages, particularly those of the Old Testament, are read as inspired literature featuring a host of symbolic devises. For the laity, this holds promise for a robust interpretative strategy given the overseeing authorship of the Holy Spirit. Further, this arc is most clearly discerned when the cross is held in view.

Appendix B

GLOSSARY

Apocalypse (apocalyptic): refers to a writing style associated with the end of the world; used biblically, the Apocalypse refers to the book of Revelation.

Atonement: a religious act or rite that repairs a broken relationship; in the Judeo-Christian tradition, atonement results in the reconciliation of man to God; specific to Christianity is the saving work of Christ.

Canon (canonical): derived from the Greek, it notes an official and accepted collection of books. In this case, the canon of Scriptures that form the Old Testament and the New. While there is general agreement on this list of books, the Protestant world and the Catholic universe do not have equal lists.

Cosmology: study of beginnings; a scientific, or in this book theological, investigation into origins.

Dereliction: as used in this book, it describes one who is abandoned and the giving up of one's duty or responsibility.

Eschatological: theology concerned with the future, especially death, judgment, and coming life.

Epistle: biblically, a letter as part of the authorized documents in the Bible.

Figural: interpretation of two (or more), separate biblical events in which each informs the other; leads to synthesis producing greater understanding than separate parts.

Hebrew Bible: written mainly in the ancient Hebrew language, the book is composed of three sections. These are determined by the word's three consonant sounds: T, N, K. Thus: 'T' for the Torah, 'N' for the Prophets, and 'K' for the Writings. This three-fold ordering varies from typical Protestant Bibles, which order and organize Old Testament materials differently. Catholic Bibles may include materials many Protestants consider extra-biblical (e.g., the Apocrypha).

Hermeneutic: having to do with interpretation strategies; applied narratively, the guiding principle that the Bible is the best interpreter of itself emerges.

Holy Eucharist: in Christian traditions, a sacrament in which the celebration of the death and resurrection of Christ is remembered through a representational rite employing bread and wine.

Messiah: in Jewish traditions, the hoped-for anointed one, appointed by God as the savior of his people. Christian beliefs hold that Jesus Christ is that person.

Meta-story or meta-narrative: the understanding that the Bible presents one overall story that can be discerned through all its books. It is the meta-narrative (or meta-story) that sews together the various books of the Bible.

Motif: an overall pattern; in scriptural application, the existence of repeating, dominant patterns, such as light, or an overuse of numbers, such as 40.

Pentateuch: the first five books of the Bible; in the Hebrew Bible constitutes the Law (or Torah).

Polytheistic: belief in more than one god; plural gods.

Scapegoating: a practice in which one segment of society preys on another segment; a weaker or innocent party, on which blame and harm or true violence occurs to preserve or strengthen the dominant party's hold over a community.

Spatial Metaphor: draws meaning by comparison of nearness from one object to another. Physical distance becomes a measuring stick to understand the metaphor.

Synoptic: when used biblically the term is associated with the Gospels of Mathew, Mark, and Luke as they present similar (but not exact) summaries of the life of Christ.

Theology: from *theo*, that is, of God or relating to Divinity; and *ology*, that is, to study about.

Type or typology: a representational view in which one person or historic event is source material as an allusion to another and yet-to-come person or event.

NOTES

Preface

1. Klink and Lockett, p. 13.

Introduction

2. Wright summarizes this question in his preface postulating, "We have all forgotten what the four gospels are about" (p. x) before coming to the point: "It isn't that we've all misread the gospels, though I think that's broadly true. It is more that we haven't really read them at all" (p. 10). By the close of his work he has developed this thesis, noting that "the themes of the kingdom and the cross" according to the ways we've been "conditioned to read the gospels," might well be "held at arm's length" (p. 212).

3. *The Story: Getting to the heart of God's Story*, by Randy Frazee, Zondervan, © 2011.

Prelude

4. Of the relationship between literal text and symbolic, that is its allusion to or anticipation of a yet to come event, John Sailhamer writes: "Thus the (biblical) author views past events with an eye to the present, and often assumes that the narrative would be read in that way" (Sailhamer, p. 31).

5. Adapted from *Webster's II New Riverside Dictionary*, (1984), s.v. "symmetry."

6. Walter Brueggemann addresses symmetry: "Second, the primary pattern of indictment and sentence, a rather symmetrical conventional model, is filtered through Jeremiah's acute personal experience of God" (p. 33). Here, Brueggemann suggests that one way to read and understand Jeremiah is to observe in it a symmetrical pattern, in this instance, handing out indictments and revealing corresponding punishments. This is a much broader look at symmetry than illustrated in the Genesis and John passage comparison (See Brueggemann in bibliography).

7. This quote is a familiar refrain as the disciples continually wonder what his parables mean. Jesus' use of parables is explained in Mt. 13:13-15.

Chapter 1

1. Rutledge, p. 7.

2. The word *shattering* is used by Stanley Hauerwas in *Cross Shattered Christ.*

3. The idea that Jesus prays or meditates on the psalms during his six hours of agony is supported by many cross authors.

4. Richard Neuhaus writes of this temptation and Jesus' resistance to it in the context of the Messiah's mission: "Only as he remains on the cross to the death does Jesus prove that he is indeed the Son of God" (p. 111).

Chronology

1. The RSV was chosen to list Jesus' final words because the translation in phrasing and cadence is likely familiar to most readers.

Chapter 2

1. Of *typology* David Limbaugh notes: "Typology has been defined as 'a method of biblical interpretation by which a person, event, or institution ("type") in the Old Testament corresponds to another

one ("antitype") in the New Testament within the framework of salvation history.' This means that God uses the Old Testament type in some redemptive activity for His people, and it foreshadows or prefigures what He would perfectly fulfill in Christ." From David Limbaugh, p. 155. Quote attributed to Friedbert Ninow in *Eerdmans Dictionary of the Bible*, (p. 1341).

2. In *How God Became King*, N. T. Wright describes "the story of Jesus as *the story of the kingdom of* God clashing with the kingdom of Caesar" (p. 127). He says later, "It is clear that all four gospels regard the story of Jesus not only as the *confrontation* between God's kingdom and Caesar's kingdom, but as the *victory* of the former over the latter" (p. 204).

3. As seen in Mark 3:31–35, the use of notable Bible characters such as Mary and John as representational figures is not without precedent. Jesus, when told his mother and brothers were outside, takes the opportunity to use them to express that whoever does the will of God is his brother, sister, and mother.

4. For a deeper look at the concepts of insider and outsider see Frank Spina's *The Faith of the Outsider: Exclusion and Inclusion in the Biblical Story*.

5. Concerning the symbolism of Mary and John, Thomas Rausch writes that Jesus' expression has the effect of transforming relationships from clan-based to relational. Thus Jesus' disciples come to be seen as his "family" (pp. 69–70).

6. Rutledge, pp. 31–32.

Chapter 3

1. Jones, p. 102.

2. Wright, *Luke* p. 74.

3. Rausch comments on the strategic importance of the phrase "the finger of God." Referring to J. P. Meier, the point is made that Jesus' use of it must lead to a Jewish conclusion that "the

presence of the kingdom in Jesus' ministry" is realized. Rausch, p. 86.

4. In Deuteronomy 9:10 is found the originating model for Jesus as he bends down and writes with his finger on the ground. In Deuteronomy, God writes the commandments for a second time with his finger. Forgiveness is explicitly implied. When Moses smashed the first set of stone tablets, it signaled the breaking of the covenant. Now, by issuing a second set, God signals forgiveness. The use of God's finger links the passages in Deuteronomy and John.

5. The term *living parable* is used from time to time to indicate an actual event that is told in such a way as to foster a literary-like feeling or tone. In presentation it is like a story being dramatized.

6. Jones, p. 16, emphasis added.

7. Commenting on the Third Word, Father Neuhaus reminds the Protestant world of the importance of Mary. Not just as the mother of the Lord, but being "the first of the disciples that Mary is to be honored." In a balanced chapter between the Protestant world and the Catholic, Neuhaus bridges the role of motherhood and discipleship. He maintains she is "the icon of the disciple-church." He writes: "Mary is the model of discipleship in her total availability to the will of God" (pp. 78–90).

8. Jones, p. 61.

9. Some Christians, who are used to treating repentance as a norm, a kind of required formula part of an altar call's ritual, there is often little theological thought given to its deeper, OT origins. Continually Israel's prophets call for repentance, yet it is almost always a national embrace they seek, such as heard in Jeremiah 14:19 in which God is asked: "Have you rejected Judah completely?" And then, in verse 20 comes the reply: "O LORD, we acknowledge our wickedness and the guilt of our fathers; we have

indeed sinned against you. ... Do not dishonor your glorious throne. Remember your covenant with us and do not break it."

10. Barclay, *Matthew*, p. 84.

11. The Sermon on the Mount begins "and [Jesus] began to teach them." *Them* refers to the Lord's disciples mentioned in this same verse. Matthew is careful to distinguish disciples from "the crowds" of the previous verse (see Mt. 5:1–2).

12. The biblical section generally encompassed under the heading "The Sermon on the Mount" begins with the subsection labeled "The Beatitudes" in the NIV. However, the overriding context is found in Mt. 4:12, in which Jesus is presented as a light to a darkened world. In verse 17 his ministry is described: "From that time on Jesus began to preach, '*Repent*, for the kingdom of heaven has come near'" (emphasis added). What follows is the Sermon on the Mount. Thus, a textual link is drawn from Jesus' message of repentance (v. 17) to Matthew's placement of the Beatitudes (5:2). By this means repentance is not only textually linked to the Beatitudes, but it may be seen to subsume it.

13. Jones, p. 16.

Chapter 4

1. Dempster, p. 94, emphasis added.

2. Alexander, *Eden*, p. 20.

3. Spina, p. 55.

4. Bright, p. 67.

5. There is an interesting parallel between this statement in Samuel and the word choice *forsaken*, in which Jesus uses in the **Fourth Word**.

6. Cole, p. 120.

7. Bright, pp. 127, 130.

8. Ibid, pp. 145, 169.

9. While David functions at times as a type of Christ, his kingship foreshadows the coming kingdom of God, as seen in its inclusive embrace of non-Israelites. Some RSV editions at 2 Sam. 15:32 contain the footnote, "Under David's inclusive policy, various non-Israelite groups (Hittites, Philistines, Canaanites, and the like) became naturalized."

10. Cole, p. 121.

11. There are innumerable proofs for Christ's kingdom bringing. Matthew's Gospel, for example, overwhelmingly confirms the kingdom. See 2:11, 4:17, 7:21, 10:7. There are also the many and varied kingdom parables. See N. T. Wright and his treatment of kingdom in *How God Became King*.

12. Treat, p. 139.

13. N. T. Wright, *How God Became King*, pp. 220, 246.

14. In classic biblical irony, the text employs the voice of a thief to announce what was stolen by the serpent out of the garden—the earthy kingdom (see Ps. 69:4).

Chapter 5

1. *Oxford Online Dictionary*, s.v. "covenant." http://www.oxforddictionaries.com/us/

2. Barclay, *Letter to Hebrews*, pp. 90–94.

3. Koenig, p. 42.

4. Barclay, *Letter to Hebrews*, p. 91.

5. Lamech is a grandson in Cain's lineage. See Gen. 4:17-18.

6. Scripture records in Genesis 9:14-15 that God promises to "remember my covenant." This is the point of origin of the "remembrance *echo*." This echoing sound (remember/remembrance) resonates throughout the Hebrew Bible, finally striking accord in Jesus'

Passover meal-table statement (Lk. 22:19; see Table 5-1). This is what the thief volleys back as he asks Jesus to *"remember me."*

7. Genesis 17 records God changing Abram's name to Abraham (meaning "father of many").

8. Schreiner, p. 17.

9. Like Noah, Abraham too is a man of the "tenth generation." By this means, Scripture continues to signal God's work of a "new thing," of a new creation (see Gen. 11:10-27. Also, Dempster, p. 75).

10. Schreiner, p. 18.

Chapter 6

1. Many scholars, such as Thomas Schreiner, comment on the apparent role reversal as Jesus controls the trial. Schreiner, p. 524.

2. John's use of time nay be more symbolic than literal. Or it may reference six in the morning.

3. In Schreiner's view, Pilate overcomes his reluctance to put Jesus to death due to his fear of the Roman Emperor. To wit: "Jesus was a rival king to Caesar" (Jn. 19:12). Schreiner, p. 510.

4. Alexander, *Eden*, p. 78.

5. Cole, p. 115. Cole's use of the term "ruptures" is derived from Jacquews Ellul, 1985, chapter 7 taken from *The Humiliation of the Word*.

6. Cole describes the intent of the Triune God as one "to reclaim his creation in general and his image-bearers in particular. The protoevangelium of Genesis 3:15 signals as much." Cole, p. 117.

7. The theological application of this description of Satan should not be missed. As evil's prince, his pseudo-kingdom not only is filled with lies and intrigues, but is totally oppositional to Christ's kingdom. This teaching must be a source of soul searching for believers today who find themselves caught up in a society that

treats so lightly truth, and so avidly embraces figures who masquerade as kingdom citizens, often using guile to gain political rulership.

8. Treat, p. 44.

9. Bright, p. 203.

10. Dempster, p. 59.

11. Ibid, p. 58.

12. Wright, *Surprised*, p. 109. See pp. 108–109 where he refers to Noah and the flood threat; the same concept is repeated in Israel's watery passage in her escape from Egypt; see also Daniel 7:1–3.

Chapter 7

1. Schreiner, p. xiv.

2. The disciples engage in disputes over greatness more than charted in this chapter. See, for example, Mt. 19:13 and 18:1–14.

3. Foster, p. 126.

4. *Halley's Bible Handbook* describes the Passover meal as being two parts: the actual Passover supper, and then the Lord's Supper (p. 610). *Eerdmans' Handbook to the Bible* notes that a typical Jewish Passover meal featured four cups of wine. During the first cup the story of Passover is told and then a second cup is shared around. *Eerdman's* identifies this second cup as the one depicted in Luke 22:17. Following this, the guests would wash their hands, thanksgiving would be said, and the bread broken. Following the roasted lamb, "Jesus instituted the Lord's Supper, breaking the bread laid aside earlier and passing round the third cup of wine, the 'cup of blessing'" (pp. 492–493).

5. Mt. 21:17, Mk. 14:1-3, and Lk. 21:37 give some indication of where Jesus spent his days and nights that last week. *Eerdmans' Handbook to the Bible* notes confusion between Matthew and Luke. On the slopes of the Mount of Olives was "Gethsemane"

with the "village of Bethany ... on the far side." The Mount itself "overlooked Jerusalem" (p. 674).

6. While John locates the temple cleansing at the beginning of his Gospel, I have elected to reference it here, during Passover Week, following the synoptic tradition of putting it at the end of Jesus' ministry.

Chapter 8

1. Bright, p. 203.

2. Alexander, *Paradise*, p. 237. The centrality of holiness is also contained in Exodus. John Sailhamer notes that "the idea of God's holiness is a central theme" in Exodus (p. 245). Holiness ties these two **canonical** books together.

3. Milgrom, p. 107.

4. Alexander, *Paradise*, p. 243.

5. Ibid, p. 237.

6. Milgrom, p. 101.

7. The symmetry of these two men is striking. In Moses' case, holiness occurs through the removal of sandals, hence his contaminated feet are made clean. This echo finds its forward rebound as Christ washes Peter's sandal-less feet. Both men come into contact with God's presence; the result is one of nearness and being bathed in God's emanating holiness.

8. Alexander, *Paradise*, p. 238.

9. Dempster, p. 109.

10. Hays, p. 82.

11. Dempster, p. 101.

12. Verses 13, 16, and 18, each referring to Israel's *heart*, anticipate Deuteronomy's command in chapter 12:2 for ancient Israel to "destroy" the practices of the occupying people of the Promised

Land. By extension, nothing is to come between Israel's heart and the Lord God.

13. Cole, p. 209.

14. Treat, p. 129.

15. Ferguson, p. 100.

16. The terms *cheap grace* and *costly grace* are adapted from Dietrich Bonhoeffer. For a short review of his life, see Michael Van Dyke, *The Story of Dietrich Bonhoeffer.*

17. Ferguson, p. 107.

18. The word *storyline* is uniquely employed by Stephen G. Dempster in his work *Dominion and Dynasty*. In a visual chart, *storyline* is contrasted with *commentary* (p. 51). His use of these terms provides a helpful linguistic structure to outline the Hebrew Bible. *Storyline* relates to books of the Old Testament that tell the tale of ancient Israel, while *commentary* provides pause by which other OT books address Israel from God's view—often declaring displeasure at how a covenant people have departed from his ways.

Interlude

1. The question of literal or figurative is a source of longstanding biblical debate among some Christians. After all, Scripture is "sacred" and "inspired." The point contended in this manuscript is one that would not limit the narrator's freedom to express meaning—whether that meaning is accomplished through literal history or a figuratively rich story. In their guide to teaching the Bible, Wall and Nienhuis write: "The question of whether we should take the Bible literally or figuratively is sometimes asked to disguise the more honest question: Is the Bible for real or is it just another religious fiction? People think that because a fiction never really happened, it has no relevance in the reader's search for truth. . . . Myths, fiction, and stories are compelling because

they convey significance and meaning about the human experience. The same is true with the Bible: its significance does not rest strictly on the historicity of all its claims." Frank Spina broaches this contour when he writes in his introductory chapter, "More than anything else, I have attempted to concentrate on the stories themselves in this book. The story is, after all, the issue. By allowing the stories to speak for themselves, we give the biblical material in all its richness an opportunity to surface" (pp. 12–13). The overriding context for these authors is their focus on the biblical meta-story. Wall and Nienhuis state, "A metanarrative, then, is a big, overarching story that takes a group of smaller, different stories and provides a framework for understanding how they all fit together. The Bible is made up of lots of different stories, but when considered as a whole there is a discernible, overarching 'big story,' the 'metanarrative'" (p. 27). My intent rests not upon this debate of literal versus figurative language but on examining the broader, more thoughtful meanings found within the Bible's symbolically laden story trove.

2. This is a primary theme of Genesis 4–11.

3. By referring to these features as a dual plan I do not mean to imply a distinct separation exists in God's project. While that may be overly clinical, nevertheless it helps clarify the biblical mandate.

4. Reference to "striking his heel" is normally accorded to Jesus on the cross. However, when viewed narratively, this image may be suggestive of a figurative heel associated with "God's footstool." Thus, the heel that is struck is God's footstool, that is his reign over creation and mankind. The serpent is understood to strike against God's realm. As for the snake's "head crushing," that awaits later development in this narrative.

5. Of the word *snake*, which I use in a literary sense, being the common image ascribed to it in modern religious culture, it is hardly

used in Scripture. In Genesis, *snake* is more correctly cast as "serpent" (see NASB, NIV, KJV, REB). After the gospel accounts were written and the time of Christ on the cross was over, few references to *snake* are found outside of Revelation. In Acts 28:3, Paul is bitten by a "viper" (NASB, NIV, KJV, and REB). In verses 4 and 5, the word is translated "creature" (NASB), "venomous beast" (v. 4) and "beast" (v. 5 KJV). However, the NIV, after using "viper" in verse 3 renders "snake" in 4 and 5. Similarly does the REB. In Revelation 12:7–9 "dragon" is found and restated as "serpent" (verse 9; NASB). Thus also does the KJV, the NIV, and the REB render this word. The point at hand is subtle but bears out the reluctance of the biblical authors to address the devil but infrequently. After Jesus has died and risen, *serpent* virtually disappears other than in Revelation's garden echo. In that way, the prophecy of the serpent striking the heel of the woman's offspring while the serpent's head is crushed is borne out. The New Testament, after the cross, treats the serpent as though it is dead.

6. Indeed, the New Testament also takes up this concept. In 2 Corinthians 5:20, Paul describes Christians as Christ's "ambassadors."

7. Alexander, p. 25, *Eden*.

8. Treat, p. 42.

9. Schreiner, pp. 6–7.

10. We must recall that when Adam and Eve are commissioned, they have yet to fall. They are, theologically, a species without sin. They have "authority" to command any they encounter, either inside or outside the garden. Thereby it is God's intention that they move outside Eden, preparing the garden planet for God's eventual visitation and establishment of his throne. However, their fall disrupts (i.e., ruptures) this ambition; but it does not untrack God, resulting in God's project to restore humanity and his good creation to his original intent.

11. Treat, p. 40.

12. Schreiner, p. 6.

13. Ibid, p. xiii.

14. Neuhaus, pp. 10–11.

15. While *disown* is translated in the NIV—the RSV, NASB, and REB prefer *deny*.

16. To clarify, Peter's deception is self-deception. He believes his own statement ("I will never disown you.") rather than the truth of his Lord's ("This very night you will all fall away." and "This very night, before the roster crows, you will disown me three times.").

17. Alexander, *Eden*, p. 102.

18. Through this comparison it is possible to view Adam and Eve's rebellion in the garden more like Peter's stumble than out right betrayal. This is because their stumble occurs in the face of the snake's deception; it was not the intent of their heart to rebel against God. Thus God mercifully initiates a course that offers the possibility of reversal (i.e., redemptive and restorative pathways).

19. I am indebted to T. Desmond Alexander's writings on this passage. From it I drew this insight: "In the light of this, the location (a synagogue) and the timing (on a Sabbath) underline the extent of the enemy's control." (see *Eden*, pp. 112–113).

20. This oft repeated reference to Jesus as having "authority" addresses what mankind lost in the garden—authority over the planet and its life forms. Kings have authority; they command and it is done. But now Adam and Eve, as exiled priest-kings, have lost their voice of authority. They have forfeited the right commensurate with God's granted authority to have dominion over the garden planet and to rule over those life forms dwelling in it. Among them is a snake which "creeps upon the earth" (Gen. 1:26 RSV).

The First Couple has lost authority over darkness, evil, and the serpent (see Mt. 28:18, 19).

21. Alexander, *Eden*, p. 112.

Chapter 9

1. Richard B. Hays uses "figural" in the subtitle of his book, *Reading Backwards: Figural Christology and the Fourfold Gospel Witness.*

2. Matthew's reference to beginning comes in the form of his gene-alogy, by which the gospel reader is transported back to Genesis' opening chapters. See Tenney, p. 143. Also see "biblos geneseos" in Schreiner, p. 433. The other three gospel writers use *beginning* in their opening statements.

3. Alexander, *From Paradise*, p. 149.

4. Refence to the word *forsaken* is a characteristic hallmark of some of Israel's ancient prophets. The word itself acts as a soundboard to launch man's desperate cry, heard for example in Jeremiah's portrayal of Israel's questioning: "Why has the LORD decreed such a great disaster against us? What wrong have we done?" An answer resounds back from the voice of God: "It is because your fathers forsook me ... and followed other gods and served and worshiped them. They forsook me ..." (16:10-11). Often this word, *forsook* (forsaken), occurs in a *reversal context*, heard here as the prophet voices God's counterpoint: "However, the days are coming ...." when Israel shall say "As surely as the LORD lives, who brought the Israelites up out of Egypt, but they will say, 'As surely as the LORD lives, who brought the Israelites up out of the land of the north and out of all the countries where he had banished them. For I will restore them to the land I gave their forefathers.'" Textual interchanges such as these call the careful reader of Israel's ancient scrolls to the cross and Christ's Fourth Word. In this forward rebound, its echo strikes squarely on the cross, foreshadowing God's long held reversal.

5. Use of the term '*theological chaos*' is intentional; it is not the same as some creationist use of the word *chaos* who seek to find in Genesis 1:2 an immense time gap to permit rationale for comprehending the vast age of the universe, thus reconciling the apparent contradiction of a six-day creation.

6. Alexander writes with regard to Babel: "The Babel-Babylon episode highlights two contrasting aspects of human existence: the capacity of people to achieve great things and the hubris of humans who have rejected God's sovereignty over them" (*From Paradise*, p. 128). Coming out of the post Flood era, spawned in Babel, is a like thematic thread (Dempster, p. 74). Sailhamer discerns this narrative importance, seeing Babel as a "land to the east." Thus "when people go 'east,' they leave the land of blessing." In effect, they are separating themselves from God's blessings (p. 134).

7. Lewis, *Chronicles*, Chapter 15.

8. Various Bible translations differ as to the spelling of this word. The RSV uses "Eli" in Matthew's account but "Elo-i" in Mark's.

9. Wright, *How*, p. 5-10.

Chapter 10

1. The story retell of Isaac uses the Jewish term *binding*. See footnote #3 below.

2. A footnote to Gen. 12:1, in some editions of the RSV records: "God's call of Abraham is sketched against the background of divided mankind." In a literal sense, Abraham's separation is from the gods of Sumer. Of its people, Thomas Nobel writes: "In religion, people were polytheists and syncretistic," referring to Mesopotamia (Noble, p. 8).

3. Bruce Feiler's work *Abraham* provides an interesting insight into how this event is classified. "God demands only that Abraham

take Isaac to a mountain and *offer* him as a burnt offering. Abraham is never explicitly given the order to slay his son. Early Jews, mindful of this nuance, referred to the event as an *offering*, not a *binding* and not a *sacrifice*." Previously Feiler wrote: "Even more, [God] *never asks Abraham to kill his son*" (p. 87). This nuance is not picked up by all Bible translations. The NASB, the RSV, and the KJV all render Genesis 22:2 by stating *offer* twice, such as seen in the NASB: "and *offer* him there as a burnt *offering*." By comparison, more modern and/or literary translations use the word *sacrifice* in conjunction with *offer*, as is the case of the quoted NIV. The REB and the Immerse edition also handle this phrasing.

4. The two servants are placed in the story as representatives of a future "twosome." But whom do they represent? One consideration is, as members of Abraham's family, they are those God intends to bless (see Gen. 12:2–4). In this way the future Hebrew nation, and the more distant but in-grafted Gentile world, are in view. However, in the story, they sit impotently apart from the place of sacrifice, symbolizing Jesus' forsakenness as mankind turns its back on God's Sent One.

5. While the subject of Christ's divinity may be debated, when a biblical **hermeneutic** is applied (i.e., in this case, Scripture acting as its own interpreter), the clarity of that voice leads to the conclusion that Jesus is the Divine-Man.

6. This odyssey is a figural echo of Abraham's call and Israel's national exodus as the young family comes to live once again in the land of promise. In this context Herod, who is king of Israel, ironically comes to represent Pharaoh, Egypt's king (see Ex. 1:22). The text anticipates Christ's liberation journey "out of Egypt." Further, it is a scathing indictment of Jewish leadership's unfaithful role as Yahweh's people. See Hosea and the unfaithful wife. Also Micah 3:5–12.

7. I am indebted to Thomas Rausch for this affirming conclusion on baptism and Jesus as the Son of God. See Rausch in *Son of God Christologies*, pp. 131–137, with emphasis on the baptism account in Mark's Gospel, p. 132.

8. Rausch, p. 132.

9. On the question of Christ's dual nature and modern man's view, Rausch remarks: "Popular Christianity today tends to focus on the divinity of Jesus, often at the cost of his humanity" (p. 2).

10. Persistence on the devil's part ("If you are the son of God") is aimed at this strategy: If he can get Jesus to abandon the idea of being God's son, then the serpent of old will have won. This is an enormous gambit, one that echoes throughout the life of Christ.

11. Rausch, p. 132.

12. This passage in Isaiah is symbolically embedded with reference to sheep. See 53:6–7. The passage is acclaimed for its messianic portrait of the Suffering Servant.

13. Rausch, p. 107.

14. Along with the RSV, the NASB and REB also use the word *acceptable* in verse 13.

15. William H. Willimon writes, "In the Bible, to 'thirst' is usually for more than water. To thirst in Scripture is to yearn, to long for, to be desperate with desire" (p. 54). He connects this metaphorical understanding to Psalm 42:2. Adam Hamilton also leans this way, writing, "Perhaps when Jesus said, 'I thirst,' he was speaking of his own inner thirst—his longing for God" (p. 96).

16. In *Saved From Sacrifice*, S. Mark Heim presents the defeat of the devil by means of the serpent's own modus operendi, which is deception. Heim offers support for this view, asserting early Christian thinkers espoused this idea (p. 160–164).

17. The idea that Christ's victory over the devil is bound to God's wisdom (truth over deception) is sponsored by a number of writers.

For example, Gregory Boyd, writing from a Christus Victor view of atonement, identifies five aspects to explain how Christ brings down the reign of the devil. His points are contextualized by the entire life of Christ—his birth, ministry, death, and resurrection (pp. 36–37).

18. Rausch finds, within the sayings of Jesus, existence of a *reversal* thread. It is heard, for example, in the phrase "the last shall be first." Thematically, this portends an eschatological view. See Rausch, p. 79.

Chapter 11

1. The enormity of what Christ accomplishes on the cross and through the resurrection far exceeds the focus of his last words. From a broad view of the Bible, the overall efficacy of the cross work may be seen as falling into three theological frameworks: forgiveness, restoration, and atonement. Of these, the first two form content for this book. Of the latter, atonement is a theological minefield that would take this manuscript far afield and embroil it in unnecessary controversy. Yet much can be gained by such an exploration. While the cross words themselves do not lend well to this esoteric subject, nevertheless a logical jumping off point would begin with John's iconic descriptor of Jesus as "the Lamb of God, who takes away the sin of the world" (1:29). Immediately this leads to controversy in the debate over expiation and propitiation, suggested by "takes away the sin of the world." In this biblical dot is a bread-crumb trail where expiation may be more strongly involved in atonement than current models (i.e., penal substitution) would suggest. Certainly, this keyword phrase alludes to Passover and the application of blood to the household thresholds (possibly a precursor to cultic blood rites described in the book of Leviticus). Further, this image is picked up in Leviticus's day-of-atonement description with its dual emphasis on the

two goats. For readers desiring to explore atonement, an excellent overview is Beilby and Eddy's work expressing four broad views. An intriguing small book on atonement images is Christian A. Eberhart's *The Sacrifice of Jesus*. Perhaps the closest I came in this manuscript to atonement is proximity to the classical view of Christus Victor. This close tie is nearly inescapable with the biblical meta-story's emphasis on the restoration of God's kingdom and the victorious rise of Jesus as king.

2. Hauerwas, p. 83.

3. My intention is not to ignore or minimize salvation; rather it is to contextualize it as something far larger in scope than is normally presented in traditional "altar calls" common to evangelical circles. This is the point of Adam Hamilton's subsection entitled *"Finished!"* (pp. 103–108).

4. It is unusual for all four gospels to recount the same story (Mt. 26:50–54; Mk. 14:43–47; Lk. 22:47–51; Jn. 18:10–11). For this reason the importance of this segment on violence calls careful readers of Scripture to reflection.

5. There is no unanimous agreement on the numbering of the Ten Commandments. Of the so-called thou shalt nots aimed at social justice, the first is prohibition against taking life.

6. The Christian tradition most often looks to answer Cain's "brother's keeper" question through acts of social justice and mercy. However, the immediate understanding is found in Cain's violation of the sacredness of life. At its core level, the answer to Cain's question is that mankind is required to be keepers of life, not takers.

7. Tenney, p. 314.

8. Rausch reports a triple taxation system that was widening the divide between affluent and poor: "a tribute to Rome, a tax to support the king, and a tithing paid to the Temple" (p. 57).

9. Heim, p. 125.

10. Heim writes: "And, finally, even here we are concerned almost entirely with the way the cross might bear on one crucial and specific type of social evil, sacrificial scapegoating." Scapegoating is "one aspect of the whole work of Christ" (p. 9).

11. Heim, p. 329.

12. *Seattle Times*, Sept. 7, 2016, p. A2.

13. By the end of 2016, the number of homicides in Chicago had risen to 762, compared to the previous year's total of 485. "Chicago ends 2016 with 762 homicides," *Seattle Times*, Jan. 2, 2017, p. A7.

14. Heim, p. 159.

15. Sailhamer, p. 345.

16. Ibid.

Chapter 12

1. Bright, p. 190.

2. Ferguson's topic from which this quote is drawn is based on the Spirit's work of transforming one's heart from law to the reality of the indwelling Spirit with its resultant product of "holy law." Though Ferguson's content is different than mine, he nevertheless places it within a two-age scenario (p. 166).

3. Treat, p. 137.

4. I have only lightly pursued how biblical numbers comport meaning to the biblical text. But I have associated the number six with mankind, destruction, and death. Noting this number's presence in Mark's statement ("at the sixth hour") leads to an interpretation that *age of man (which is represented by the number six)* is strikingly involved in Mark's metaphor.

5. Treat, p. 136.

6. Neuhaus, p. 189.

7. The bread Judas takes is not the bread and wine associated with the Holy Eucharist. Judas' bread is dipped in a dish; no mention of cup or wine is made. See John 13:26.

8. Neuhaus, p. 191.

9. Schreiner, p. 564.

10. Neuhaus, p. 191.

11. Neuhaus (p. 192), concerning the phrase "It is finished," cites Paul's letter to the Romans where he refers to a time when "the full number of the Gentiles come in" (11:25).

12. Schreiner, p. 630.

Chapter 13

1. As a narrative character, the thief's role is that of repentant humanity.

2. The context of Jesus' seventh statement clearly shows a linkage between death and spirit. As Jesus sheds his earthly body of flesh, he commits what is most sacred, his spirit, to God his father. While this is historically accurate, the exact meaning behind his statement, and the implications for humanity are less clear. By examining Scriptures dealing with Jesus' new body, we gain some insight as believing humanity passes from death into life.

3. Ferguson, p. 249.

4. Ibid.

5. Being tarnished does not reduce humanity to something less than being created in God's image. After the fall, mankind is still fully man, created in the image of God. Francis Schaeffer writes, "It is important to note that fallen man still retains something of the image of God. The fall separates man from God, but it does not remove his original differentiation from other things. Fallen man is not less than man" (p. 50).

6. This is not to say this view into heaven is readily open, only to say that it exists. Cf. Ezek. 1:1.

7. See Ferguson, chapter 6, for a more detailed account of the new birth (p. 116 ff).

8. Previously we read that we are ransomed by Christ. The word *ransom*, like so much of Scripture, can be understood literally as well as metaphorically. Yet, when we come to 1 Timothy 2:6, Paul writes informingly of ransom: "who gave himself as a ransom for all men. This has now been witnessed to at the proper time." Here, ransom is a simile, indicated by the preceding word *as*. Paul compares the ransom paid by Christ. What is that ransom? Paul provides a strong reference, writing, "the testimony given in its proper time." *Narratively, that testimony is truth.* This interpretation finds support in Paul's next line, where we find the phrases "telling the truth" as well as "not lying." Further, in the verse directly above is the word *truth*, all of which transports a reader back to the garden where mankind was felled by deception and distortion. Thus the ransom owed by mankind is this return to truth. The debt the race owes God is to reverse its allegiance from deception to truth. Jesus, since he is "the way, the truth, and the life," is the only one of Adam's race capable of payment in this currency. This debt is contextualized by Christ's **First Word**, which ends, "for they know not what they do."

Chapter 14

1. John Walton describes the importance of reading Scripture with a view to how the ancient world would have considered it. "If we are going to understand Genesis as an ancient document, however, we have to read the text first in ancient terms" (p. 128). See also pages 15–23.

2. Wenham, p. 79.

3. Hoffmeier, p. 35.

4. Hays, p. 105, emphasis added.

5. Ibid.

6. Halton, p. 156. Rausch makes much the same point in his concluding chapter, indicating that the text of the New Testament was a "mostly undifferentiated mixture of narrative, metaphor, mythological imagery, and theological construction" (p. 183).

7. An example is Tyndale's newly published Bible, *Immerse*. Purposely designed to promote reading through its literary stress on biblical genres, it calls readers to value Scripture's original format. "This special reader's edition restores the Bible to its natural simplicity and beauty by removing chapter and verse numbers and other historical additions. Letters look like letters, songs look like songs, and the original literary structures are visible in each book" (Quick Start Guide insert).

8. I recognize this variance, but I also affirm, like many, that a kingdom view is the one most worthy of this designation.

BIBLIOGRAPHY

Alexander, T. Desmond. *From Eden to the New Jerusalem: An introduction to Biblical Theology*, Grand Rapids, MI: Kregel Publications, 2008.

———. *From Paradise to the Promised Land, An Introduction to the Pentateuch*, Grand Rapids, MI: Baker Academic, 2012.

Barclay, William. *The Gospel of Matthew*, vol. 1. Philadelphia: Westminster Press, 1975.

———. *The Letter to the Hebrews*. Philadelphia: Westminster Press, 1976.

Benner, Jeff A. "Hebrew Word Definitions," s.v. "Messiah." http://www.ancient-hebrew.org/27_messiah.html

"Biblical hermeneutics." https://en.wikipedia.org/wiki/Biblical_hermeneutics

Boyd, Gregory A. "Christus Victor View," in *The Nature of Atonement*, James Beilby and Paul R. Eddy, eds. Dowers Grove, IL: InterVarsity Press, 2006.

Bright, John. *The Kingdom of God*, Nashville, TN: Abingdon Press, 1953.

Brueggemann, Walter. *The Theology of the Book of Jeremiah*. Cambridge University Press, 2007.

Cole, Graham A. *He Who Gives Life: The Doctrine Of The Holy Spirit*. Wheaton, IL: Crossway, 2007.

"Crucifixion   darkness."   http://en.wikipedia.org/wiki/Crucifixion_
    darkness

Dempster, Stephen G. *Dominion and dynasty: A theology of the Hebrew
    Bible*. Madison, WI: InterVarsity Press, 2003.

Eerdmans' Handbook to the Bible. David Alexander and Pat Alexander,
    eds. Grand Rapids, MI: Eerdmans Publishing, 1973.

Feiler, Bruce. *Abraham, A Journey to the Heart of Three Faiths*. New York:
    Harper Perennial, 2002.

Ferguson, Sinclair B. *The Holy Spirit*, Downers Grove, IL: InterVarsity
    Press, 1966.

Foster, Richard. *Celebration of Discipline: The Path to Spiritual Growth*,
    New York: Harper Collins Publishers, 1978.

Halley, Henry H. *Halley's Bible Handbook*, Grand Rapids, MI: Zonder-
    van, 2000.

Halton, Charles. "We Disagree, What Now?" in *Genesis: History, Fiction,
    or Neither?* Charles Halton, ed. Grand Rapids, MI: Zondervan,
    2015.

Hamilton, Adam. *Final Words From The Cross*, Nashville, TN: Abing-
    don Press, 2011.

Hauerwas, Stanley. *Meditations on the Seven Last Words: Cross-Shattered
    Christ*, Grand Rapids, MI: Brazos Press, 2004.

Hays, Richard B. *Reading Backwards: Figural Christology and the Four-
    fold Gospel Witness*, Waco, TX: Baylor University Press, 2014.

Heim, S. Mark. *Saved From Sacrifice: A Theology of the Cross*, Grand
    Rapids, MI: Eerdmans Publishing, 2006.

Hoffmeier, James K. "Genesis 1-11 As History And Theology," in *Gen-
    esis: History, Fiction, or Neither?* Grand Rapids, MI: Zondervan,
    2015

Immerse, The Reading Bible: Beginnings. Carol Stream, IL: Tyndale, 2017.

Jones, L. Gregory. *Embodying Forgiveness: A Theological Analysis*, Grand Rapids, MI: Eerdmans Publishing, 1995.

Kendall, R. T. *Holy Fire: A Balanced, Biblical Look At The Holy Spirit's Work In Our Lives*, Lake Mary, FL: Charisma House, 2014.

Klink, Edward W., III and Darian R. Lockett, *Understanding Biblical Theology: A Comparison of Theory and Practice*, Grand Rapids, MI: Zondervan, 2012.

Koenig, Sara. "Outdone by the Almighty," *Response*, Autumn Quarter 2015.   http://spu.edu/depts/uc/response/new/2015-autumn/ bible-theology/outdone-by-the-almighty.asp

Lewis, C. S. *Chronicles of Narnia: The Lion, The Witch, and The Wardrobe*, New York: HarperCollins, 2008.

Limbaugh, David. *The Emmaus Code: Finding Jesus in the Old Testament*, Washington, DC: Regnery Publishing, 2015.

Milgrom, Jacob. *Leviticus: A Book of Ritual and Ethics,* Minneapolis, MN: Fortress Press, 2004.

Neuhaus, Richard John. *Death On A Friday Afternoon*, New York: Basic Books, 2000.

Ninow, Friedbert. "Typology," in *Eerdmans Dictionary of the Bible*, D. N. Freedman, A. C. Myers, and A. B. Beck, eds., Grand Rapids, MI: Eerdmans Publishing, 2000.

Noble, Thomas F. X. *The Foundations of Western Civilization*, Chantilly, VA: Teaching Company, 2002.

Rausch, Thomas P. *Who Is Jesus? An Introduction to Christology*, Collegeville, MN: Liturgical Press, 2003.

Rutledge, Fleming. *The Seven Last Words from the Cross*, Grand Rapids, MI: Eerdmans Publishing, 2005.

Ryrie, Charles C. *The Holy Spirit*, Chicago: Moody Publishers, 1997.

Sailhamer, John. *The Pentateuch As Narrative*, Grand Rapids, MI: Zondervan, 1992.

Schaeffer, Francis A. *Genesis in Space and Time: The Flow of Biblical History*, Downers Grove, IL: InterVarsity Press, 1972.

Schreiner, Thomas R. *The King In His Beauty: A Biblical Theology of the Old and New Testaments*, Grand Rapids, MI: Baker Publishing, 2013.

Shenouda III, H. H. Pope. "The Seven Words of Our Lord on the Cross," 2nd edition, 1991. http://tasbeha.org/content/hh_books/svnwrds/index.html

Spina, Frank A. *The Faith of the Outsider: Exclusion and Inclusion in the Biblical Story*, Grand Rapids, MI: Eerdmans Publishing, 2005.

Strong, James. *Strong's Exhaustive Concordance of the Bible*, New York: Abingdon Press, 1970.

Tenney, Merrill C. *New Testament Survey*, Grand Rapids, MI: Eerdmans Publishing, 1961.

Treat, Jeremy R. *The Crucified King: Atonement and Kingdom In Biblical and Systematic Theology*, Grand Rapid, MI: Zondervan, 2014.

Van Dyke, Michael. *The Story of Dietrich Bonhoeffer: Radical Integrity*, Uhrichsville, OH: Barbour Books, 2001.

Wall, Robert W. and David R. Nienhuis, *A Compact Guide to the Whole Bible: Learning to Read Scripture's Story*, Grand Rapids, MI: Baker Academic, 2015.

Wall, Robert, and Paul T. Walls. "Scripture's Sound and Light Show," *Response*, Summer 2014. http://spu.edu/depts/uc/response/new/2014-summer/bible-theology/sound-and-light-show.asp

Walton, John H. *The Lost World of Adam and Eve*, Downers Grove, IL: IVP Academic, 2015.

Wenham, Gordon J. "Genesis 1-11 As Protohistory" in *Genesis: History, Fiction, or Neither?* Grand Rapids, MI: Zondervan, 2015.

"What is the significance of '14 generations' in Matthew's account of Jesus' genealogy?" https://hermeneutics.stackexchange.com/questions/927/what-is-the-significance-of-14-generations-in-matthew-s-account-of-jesuss-gen

Willimon, William H. *Thank God It's Friday*, Nashville, TN: Abingdon Press, 2006.

Wright, N. T. *How God Became King: The Forgotten Story Of The Gospels*, San Francisco: HarperOne, 2011.

———. *Luke: 26 Studies For Individuals and Groups*, Downers Grove, IL: Intervarsity Press, 2011.

———. *Surprised by Scripture: Engaging Contemporary Issues*, San Francisco: HarperOne, 2014.

Acquire free study discussion materials.
Visit the author's website: **watchmancalls.com**
Select the pull-down menu "Resources"
to locate supplemental materials
to support your group's study of
Last Words of Christ: A Call to Understanding